Energy, Environment and the Economy

Asian Perspectives

Edited by

Paul R. Kleindorfer
The Wharton School, University of Pennsylvania, US

Howard C. Kunreuther
The Wharton School, University of Pennsylvania, US

David S. Hong
Taiwan Institute of Economic Research, Taiwan, ROC

New Horizons in Environmental Economics

Edward Elgar
Cheltenham, UK • Brookfield, US

Published by
Edward Elgar Publishing Limited
8 Lansdown Place
Cheltenham
Glos GL50 2HU
UK

HD 9502 .A782 E536 1996

Edward Elgar Publishing Company
Old Post Road
Brookfield
Vermont 05036
US

British Library Cataloguing in Publication Data
Energy, environment and the economy: Asian perspectives. –
   (New horizons in environmental economics)
   1. Environmental economics – Asia. 2. Asia – Economic
   conditions – 1945–
   I. Kleindorfer, Paul R. (Paul Robert) II. Kunreuther, Howard
   C. III. Hong, David S.
   333.7'095

Library of Congress Cataloguing in Publication Data
Energy, environment, and the economy: Asian perspectives / edited by
   Paul R. Kleindorfer, Howard C. Kunreuther, David S. Hong.
      Selected papers from the international conference held in Taipei,
   Taiwan, R.O.C. from August 22–25, 1994, and organized by the Wharton
   Center for Risk Management and Decision Processes at the University
   of Pennsylvania and by the Taiwan Institute of Economic Research (TIER).
      Includes index.
      1. Energy policy—Asia—Congresses. 2. Energy industries—Asia-
   –Congresses. 3. Energy industries—Environmental aspects—Asia-
   –Congresses. 4. Asia—Economic policy—Congresses.
   I. Kleindorfer, Paul R. II. Kunreuther, Howard. III. Hong, David S., 1939–
   HD9502.A782E536 1996
   333.79'095—dc20   95–40194
                                                                   CIP

ISBN 1 85898 391 6
Printed and bound in Great Britain by
Hartnolls Limited, Bodmin, Cornwall

Contents

Figures

Tables

Contributors

Andrew Chisholm is at the Tasman Institute, Melbourne, Australia

Fulgencio S. Factoran is at the Development Academy of the Philippines, Manila, The Philippines

Chitru S. Fernando is at the A.B. Freeman School of Business, Tulane University, New Orleans, Louisiana, US

Kevin Fitzgerald is at the University of Pennsylvania, Philadelphia, US

Paul Freeman is with the Eric Group Inc., Colorado, US

Manuel S. Gaspay is at the Asian Institute of Management, Makati, The Philippines

Ismid Hadad is with PT Redecon, Djakarta, Indonesia

Chich-Ping Hu is at the Graduate Institute of Building and Planning, National Taiwan University, Taiwan, ROC

Hoi-Seong Jeong is at the Korean Environmental Technology Research Institute, Seoul, Korea

Paul R. Kleindorfer is at the Wharton School, University of Pennsylvania, Philadelphia, US

Howard C. Kunreuther is at the Wharton School, University of Pennsylvania, Philadelphia, US

Maw Lin Lee is at the University of Missouri-Columbia, US

Seong-Uh Lee is at the Korea Institute of Public Administration, Seoul, Korea

Qwanruedee Limvorapitak is at the Thailand Environment Institute, Bangkok, Thailand

Joanne Linnerooth-Bayer is at the International Institute of Applied Systems Analysis, Laxenburg, Austria

Ben-Chieh Liu is at Chicago State University, US

Rolando L. Metin is at the Development Academy of the Philippines, Manila, The Philippines

Alan Moran is at the Tasman Institute, Melbourne, Australia

Mohan P.C. Munasinghe is at The World Bank, Washington, DC, US

Dhira Phantumvanit is at the Thailand Environment Institute, Bangkok, Thailand

Sixto K. Roxas is at the Foundation for Community Organization and Management Technology, The Philippines

Shehzad Sadiq is at the Asian Development Bank, Manila, The Philippines

Daigee Shaw is at the Academica Sinica, Taipei, Taiwan, ROC

Taishi Sugiyama is at the Central Research Institute of Electric Power Industry, Tokyo, Japan

Akihiro Watabe is at Kanagawa University, Yokohama, Japan

Kaoru Yamaguchi is at Kanagawa University, Yokohama, Japan

Kenji Yamaji is at the Central Research Institute of Electric Power Industry, Tokyo, Japan

John Zeitsch is with Swan Consultants, Canberra, Australia

Preface and Acknowledgements

This book contains selected papers from the international conference of the same title held in Taipei, Taiwan, ROC from 22–25 August 1994. The conference was organized by the Wharton Center for Risk Management and Decision Processes at the University of Pennsylvania and by the Taiwan Institute of Economic Research (TIER). In the words of Dr Rong-I Wu, President of TIER and President of the Conference Organizing Committee: 'The conference aimed to bring together experts from Asia, Europe and North America to address one of the most important issues of our times, balancing the conflicting objectives of energy planning, environmental management and economic development'. Finding an equitable and efficient balance is difficult because it requires consent and cooperation among the public and private sectors, policy makers and the affected public. The chapters in this book are concerned primarily with Asian perspectives, but they frequently draw on international comparisons with other regions of the world.

Perhaps the most important characteristic of the conference was its own internal balance among the three E's (Energy, Environment and the Economy) and the three P's (Politics, Policy and the Public) which are the foundations of the current debate about sustainable economic and environmental policies. The structure of this book reflects both the balance and the tension among these elements. Part I discusses the international dimensions, both within Asia and between Asia and the rest of the world, driving current environmental and energy policy. Part II shows how the Asian region and Asian countries reflect their citizens' desire for development in internal decisions related to balancing economic growth and environmental and energy intensity. Part III discusses the growing impact of public opinion and the Green movement in Asia on such decisions as siting of new energy facilities and environmental regulation. Part IV discusses the role of industry in finding the right balance between the three E's and the three P's through risk management and pollution-prevention strategies. Taken together, these chapters present a cross-section of the challenges facing Asian countries in finding a sustainable path of long-term development while simultaneously meeting huge short-term needs for continuing increases in the quality of life of their citizens.

The Energy, Environment and the Economy Conference and this proceedings book were supported by Yin's Education Foundation, China Life Insurance

Company, the Environmental Protection Administration of ROC and the Energy Commission of the Ministry of Economic Affairs, with additional assistance provided by the Taiwan Power Company and the Chinese Petroleum Corporation. The organizers are especially grateful to Messrs P.K. Chiang, Lung-Sheng Chang and Samuel Yin for their personal support of the conference.

The conference could not have taken place without the guidance and support of key individuals who identified the themes represented here and the international scholars and policy makers who participated. We are especially grateful to Edilberto C. de Jesus of the Asian Institute of Management, to Hong-Chang Chang of the National Taiwan University, to Ta-Ho Lin of TIER, and to Mohan P.C. Munasinghe of the World Bank, Washington. The Organizing Committee also recognizes, for important contributions to the planning of the conference and for reviews and critical commentary on the enclosed papers, Lars Bern, Surna T. Djajadiningrat, Brian Emmett, Peter D. Garrucho, Pakit Kiravanich, Ki-Joong Kim, Il Chyun Kwak, Delfin L. Lazaro, Sang-Gon Lee, Dalgon Lee, Vicente Paterno, Jayant Sathaye, Jay Schulkin, Low Kwai Sim, Kazuhiko Takemoto, Haifa Wahyu and Hong-Ting Yih. Many others in Taiwan and elsewhere assisted in making this international undertaking a success. Our special thanks for editorial assistance to Linda S. Brennan of Rutgers University.

This book is dedicated to our families who supported this project throughout and who continue to make our own existence sustainable.

Paul R. Kleindorfer
Howard C. Kunreuther
David S. Hong

PART I

Energy and Environment in
International Perspective

1. Sustainable Energy Development (SED): Issues and Policy[*]

Mohan P.C. Munasinghe

1. ENERGY, ENVIRONMENT AND ECONOMY: THE NEXUS

The state of the environment is a major worldwide concern today. Pollution in particular is perceived as a serious threat in the industrialized countries, where quality of life had hitherto been measured mainly in terms of growth in material output. Meanwhile, environmental degradation has become a serious impediment to economic development and the alleviation of poverty in the developing world. The growing evidence of environmental problems is due to a combination of factors. Over the last three decades the environmental impact of human activities has grown considerably on account of the increase in economic activity, population and per capita consumption.

The environmental effects of energy are: groundwater and air contamination; land degradation and changes in use; marine and coastal pollution; ecosystem destruction and loss of biodiversity; damage to health, manmade structures and natural systems from SO_2 and NO_x and ash particulates which have detrimental air quality implications; and finally, greenhouse gas emissions which may have long-term implications for the global environment.

Despite such problems, however, energy services such as heating, refrigeration, cooking, lighting, communications, motive power and electricity are essential for economic growth and human well-being. Economic growth prior to the 1970s was always accompanied by a corresponding global increase of demand for energy. As a direct consequence of the oil price increases, decoupling between economic growth and energy demand growth was achieved in the mature economies of industrialized countries (ICs) which were able to reduce

*   The author is grateful to Vittal Anantatmula, Asitha Sandanayake and Noreen Beg for assistance in preparing this chapter.

energy wastage relatively easily and also achieve a better energy management through restructuring and energy-efficient technologies. Such decoupling was not observed in developing countries (DCs). As DCs are still in the early stages of economic development and have higher growth rates, there is a much closer linkage between economic growth and energy consumption than in industrialized countries (Munasinghe 1991).

1.1. Current Status

At present developing countries comprise 77 per cent of the world's population but utilize only a quarter of the world's energy. A majority of this population have little or no access to any form of commercial energy. A large proportion of the DC's population live in rural areas and continue to rely heavily on traditional biomass fuels such as wood, crop waste and animal dung. OECD countries, in contrast, consumed over half the world's energy and nearly six times more energy per person than did developing countries and Central and Eastern European countries (CEEs). However, energy demand has been growing rapidly in the developing countries in the past few decades (Table 1.1). In the last decade alone, the rate of growth of DC energy consumption has been about six times that of the OECD countries and twice the average world growth rate.

The rapid growth in energy demand in DCs (driven primarily by economic expansion, population growth, urbanization, the increasing penetration of energy-using products and the transition from traditional energy sources to commercial sources) has surpassed the growth in energy production and power-generation capacities, thus creating shortages in primary fuels and electricity. To meet this rising energy demand, DCs require tremendous financial resources. In addition to the economic burden, environmental degradation associated with an expanding energy sector compound the energy-related problems in DCs.

The crucial dilemma for the developing world is how to reconcile development goals and the elimination of poverty, which will require increased use of energy and raw materials, with responsible stewardship of the environment. This has to be done without overburdening their already weak economies. Hence, the

Table 1.1   Average annual growth rates of energy demand and GDP

Year	Energy Demand				Economic Growth			
	OECD	DCs	CEEs	World	OECD	DCs	CEEs	World
1961–70	5.0	4.1	5.2	4.8	4.7	4.7	5.2	1.7
1971–80	1.8	4.7	3.4	3.0	3.2	4.8	3.4	1.5
1981–90	0.8	4.7	2.2	2.3	2.9	5.6	1.3	3.8

Sources: WEC 1993; Khatib and Munasinghe 1992.

challenge facing DCs today is meeting the rising energy demand in a manner that will not absorb inordinate amounts of investment, which in turn would divert funds from other worthy development goals, such as poverty alleviation and the provision of education and health care.

1.2. Future Economic Growth and Energy Needs

The world economy is expected to continue to grow at a healthy rate over the next few decades. The World Bank estimates the GNP of large ICs to grow at an average rate of 2.7 per cent annually over the 1994–2003 period and that of DCs to grow at 4.8 per cent annually over the same period with above average growth in East and South Asia (7.6 per cent and 5.3 per cent respectively). The prospects for economic growth in DCs prompting a similar increase in energy demand are obvious.

The world's population is expected to grow by 3 billion during the period 1990–2020, with 90 per cent of the increase taking place in DCs. Only eight countries are expected to account for half of global population growth, and a significant portion of global energy demand growth, over the next 30 years: India, China, Pakistan, Bangladesh, Brazil, Indonesia, Mexico and Vietnam (World Bank 1992a; WEC 1993). According to the WEC 'high-growth' case, world primary energy consumption is estimated to double to roughly 17.2 Mtoe (Mega tons of oil equivalent) in the next 30 years, with almost 90 per cent of the demand coming from the DCs. Under this scenario, the share of total energy consumption accounted for by the OECD will have fallen from over 50 per cent in 1990 to under 30 per cent by 2020, while the share of the DCs will almost double to 60 per cent during the same period.

The International Energy Agency (IEA) has forecast that through the year 2010, world energy use will grow at an annual rate of 2.1 per cent, with East Asian countries' energy use growing at more than 4 per cent (International Energy Agency 1994).

2. KEY ROLE OF THE ELECTRICITY SECTOR

Electricity is clean, versatile, easily accessible and simple to distribute. It is also essential to maintain a reasonable quality of life, and for sustainable develop-ment. Because of this, electricity is gaining a larger share of energy in final use and the demand for it is increasing worldwide at almost twice the rate of demand for primary energy. Currently, the worldwide electricity demand is increasing at a rate of over 3.6 per cent annually, which is slightly higher than the world's economic growth rate, twice the population growth rate and more than 1.5 times that of global commercial energy consumption. At present, fuels for electricity

Table 1.2   Electricity demand and its share in total primary energy

	1990 (actual)		2000			2020		
	TWh	per cent of energy	TWh	per cent of energy	growth per cent	TWh	per cent of energy	growth per cent
OECD	6,800	41	8,600	——	2.4	10,900	49	1.2
DCs	2,630	30	5,050	——	6.75	12,000	47.3	4.5
CEEs	2,270	34	2,850	——	2.3	3,700	50	1.2
World	11,700	36	16,500	——	3.2	26,600	48.3	2.4

Source: Khatib and Munasinghe 1992.

production are claiming 36 per cent of total energy demand and in the next 30–40 years more than half the world's primary commercial energy sources would be utilized in electricity production (see Table 1.2).

Electricity has not only transformed the quality of life and work, but also created one of the largest industries, with worldwide revenues estimated at more than $800 billion in 1992 (Flavin and Lenssen 1993). Thus, in addition to its widely recognized role as a catalyst to economic activity in other sectors, the electricity sector itself makes a direct and significant contribution to the economy.

Despite a general recognition of the indispensable nature of electricity, one-third of the world's population is still deprived of access to electricity, mostly in developing countries. The ICs are the most electricity intensive, containing 16 per cent of the world population and consuming almost 60 per cent of the globe's electricity. On average, developing countries use only 500 kWh of electricity per capita per year compared with more than 5,000 kWh in Europe and more than 10,000 kWh in the US (World Bank 1992b).

2.1. Electricity and the Developing World

Of the various forms of energy, electricity is particularly important in the context of the developing world. The provision of electricity greatly enhances the quality of life in DCs particularly for the poor. It improves health standards, and assists in education and in motivating people. Rural electrification (RE) also helps to retard migration from rural areas to cities and enhances opportunities for income generation and employment in rural areas. To the extent that it displaces less efficient and more environmentally damaging fuels, electricity is essential for sustainable development. Hence, given the vital role electricity plays in the development process, the future prospects for economic growth are closely linked to the provision of adequate and reliable electricity supplies. Electricity demand in DCs grew very rapidly over the past three decades with consumption increasing over 13-fold since 1960. During this period electricity consumption

Table 1.3   Growth trends in electricity, energy and economy

Year	Electricity growth per cent OECD	DC	World	Elec/GDP OECD	DC	World	Energy/GDP OECD	DC	World	Elec/Energy OECD	DC	World
61–70	5	4.1	4.8	1.6	2	4.7	1.1	0.9	2.8	1.5	2.3	1.7
71–80	1.8	4.7	3	1.3	2	3.5	0.6	1	0.5	2.4	2	1.8
81–90	0.8	4.7	2.3	0.9	2.2	2.7	0.3	1.3	0.6	3.1	1.8	1.5
91– 2020	0.7	4.2	2.2	0.7	0.9	0.7	0.3	0.8	1.7	2.3	1.2	1.2

Sources: Khatib and Munasinghe 1992; WEC 1993.

has grown at a rate which is almost twice the rate of energy consumption and economic growth (Table 1.3).

A direct relationship between electricity and economic growth cannot be deduced as easily as in the case of total energy. This is mainly because electricity growth depends not only on economic growth, but also on the substitution of electricity for other commercial and non-commercial energy. Such a substitution depends on the cost and productivity of electricity use compared to other commercial fuels, and also on the changes in quality and lifestyle. In the more-developed OECD countries, such substitution decreases as more energy uses are shifted into electricity use, moving the share of electricity in final energy to saturation.

Table 1.3 shows an interesting contrast between the electricity/economy relationship of OECD countries and that of DCs. As a result of the decoupling of economic growth from energy demand in the 1970s, the ratio of electricity growth to economic growth in OECD countries steadily declined. Developing countries which still have a long way to go in satisfying their basic electricity needs showed a very high electricity/economy growth relationship in the past three decades. While it is evident that there is a trend in OECD countries to decouple economic growth from dependence on increased electricity consumption, in developing countries the electricity/economy ratio will remain relatively high. Developing countries will require more electricity in the future and this growth in demand is influenced by the electricity share in their economies and energy demand, as well as by their economic growth. Table 1.4 outlines this relationship. From this table it is clear that the growing share of electricity fuels

Table 1.4   Electricity fuel's share in total primary energy (per cent)

Year	OECD	CandEE	DCs	World
1970	32	27	18	29
1980	38	32	25	34
1990	41	34	31	36

Source: Khatib and Munasinghe 1992.

in total energy is increasing, but at a declining rate. This growth will continue until electricity reaches a point beyond which it cannot fully replace other fuels (Khatib and Munasinghe 1992).

Given the benefits of electricity and its importance to the developing world, the demand for electricity can only grow. In the medium term, assuming no drastic changes in the past trends with respect to demand management and conservation, the World Bank estimates that the demand for electricity in DCs will grow at an average annual rate of 6.7 per cent in the 1990s (Table 1.2). This compares with actual growth rates of 10 per cent and 8 per cent in the 1970s and 1980s respectively. Such rates of growth indicate the need for large additions in capacity. The Asia region's requirements dominate with almost two-thirds of the total, and coal and hydro are the primary sources—both of which have specific environmental problems associated with their use (Munasinghe 1992).

2.2. Power Sector Problems and Investment Needs in DCs

Currently industrial and residential electricity demand in DCs have exceeded their power-generating capacities, resulting in frequent power shortages and blackouts. Power shortages in any country affect it in two ways: they handicap productive activities and delay social development. On the output side, electricity shortages disrupt production. For India the cost of power shortages to the industrial sector has been estimated at 1.5 per cent of GDP and in Pakistan 1.8 per cent (Khatib and Munasinghe 1992). Power shortages also discourage investors by affecting production and requiring more investment for on-site electricity production or standby supplies. This not only requires more investment by entrepreneurs in DCs where capital is already limited, but it also distracts investors from their main productive activity. It would (for small investors) increase the cost of operation, since electricity from small private generation is more expensive than public national supplies (Munasinghe 1990b).

Structural, institutional and financial problems further exacerbate the already inadequate electricity supply in DCs. Poor operating performances, poor maintenance of plants, technical and non-technical transmission and distribution system losses and high fuel consumption have resulted in high energy wastage and economic losses. Poor maintenance practices account for some of the low availability of power-generating capacity, which averages less than 60 per cent for thermal plants in DCs, compared with more than 80 per cent in developed countries (World Bank 1994). In DCs, power plants consume 15–30 per cent more fuel per unit of electricity than that of ICs (WRI 1994). Transmission and Distribution system losses represent a loss to DCs of about $30 billion a year through increased supply costs (Saunders and Gandhi 1994). Inadequate tariffs due to governmental policies and poor revenue collection due to inadequate metering, poor accounting and billing, have led to large financial losses and difficulties in raising investment capital. While institutional building (training of power utility staff, modernization) has continued to progress, conflicts between a government's role as owner and its role as operator of utilities, have affected sector performance. Opaque command and control management of the sector, poorly defined objectives, government interference in daily affairs, and a lack of financial autonomy have affected productive efficiency and institution performance (World Bank 1992b).

To accommodate the projected growth in electricity demand, assuming no major gains in energy efficiency, DCs will require about US$1 trillion (in current terms) to finance future capital investments. In comparison with the total projected annual requirement for DCs of $100 billion for the early 1990s, the present annual rate of electricity-related investment in developing nations is only about $50 billion. Even this present rate is proving difficult to maintain. Developing country debt, which averaged 23 per cent of GNP in 1981, increased dramatically to 42 per cent in 1987 and, although it has since declined to 37 per cent because of improved economic performance and trade conditions, is still significant (World Bank 1992b). Capital-intensive power sector investments have played a major role in this observed increase. Investments required to meet the growth of demand for energy in DCs will rise to an average of $200 billion per annum in the late 1990s, or 4 per cent of GDP. Added to this, private investors are reluctant to re-enter those DCs that continue to experience difficulties in servicing their foreign debt (Saunders and Gandhi 1994).

The future expansion of the power sector in DCs to meet the growing demand, also has serious environmental impacts. WDR estimates indicate that, under the worst scenario, emissions of pollutants from electric power will rise tenfold by 2030. In addition to the basic investments mentioned above, the World Bank, in the 1992 WDR, estimates incremental investment for energy-related environmental management programmes in DCs in 2000 as follows:

- $2 billion for controlling particulate matter emissions from coal-fired power stations;
- $5 billion for reducing acid rain deposition from new coal-fired stations;
- $10 billion for switching to unleaded fuels, and for implementing controls on the main pollutants from vehicles;
- $10–15 billion for reducing emissions, effluents and wastes from industry;
- $3–4 billion per year by the end of the century would enable a major programme of research, development and demonstration projects for renewable energy to be undertaken.

Controlling emissions of particulates will raise investment costs by about 1 per cent, or 0.04 per cent of GDP. In areas where controls on sulphur dioxide and nitrogen oxides are necessary, a further 5–15 per cent of capital costs (or 0.5 per cent of the regions' GDPs) would be incurred if low-sulphur coal or natural gas were not available. With these investments, DCs will be able, in 2030, to produce ten times as much electric power as today, with lower emissions of particulates and acid rain-causing pollutants.

Taking account of the impact of energy efficiency and environmental considerations, the WEC (1993) estimates a broad order of magnitude figure for the cumulative investment requirements (at 1992 prices) of the world's energy industry over the next 25–30 years at about $30 trillion. By comparison world GDP in 1989 was approximately $20 trillion. The WEC estimates that the DCs could be investing in excess of $2 trillion (at 1992 prices) annually by the year 2020, over 50 per cent of world annual energy investments. About $1.2 trillion annually will be needed to raise energy efficiency and environmental standards in the former USSR to the average level of the OECD.

2.3. Electricity, Environment and Regional Concerns

Although electricity is relatively benign in use, the generation of electricity is one of the world's major environmentally damaging activities. While the energy sector contributes 49 per cent of greenhouse gases, electricity generation alone produces more than 25 per cent of energy-related carbon dioxide emissions. During the past 20 years, half of all increases in energy-related carbon dioxide emissions were from electricity (Lawrence Berkeley Laboratory, Energy Analysis Program 1991). Most of the growth in world carbon dioxide emissions from 1971 to 1990 is due to the CEE and developing countries (Table 1.5).

Despite alternative energy sources such as wind, solar and biomass, the largest segment of new electricity in the world is projected to come from coal firing in the next several decades, and this will bring related environmental problems along with it (US Industrial Outlook 1994).

The expected growth of electricity generation in DCs described previously, confronts them with a variety of technological, economic and environmental problems. Although the electric power sectors in industrialized nations are concerned with environmental problems related mainly to generation, in many DCs, environmental issues are not considered such a high priority. The problems of the electricity sectors in the developing world differ among regions and countries (Winje 1991a,b).

Table 1.5 CO_2 emissions from energy use

Year	Million Tons Of Carbon				Coal %
	World	OECD	CEE	DCs	
1971	4,380	2,427			
1980	5,500	2,750	1,570	1,180	37%
1985	5,800	2,640	1,700	1,460	
1990	6,550	2,900	1,700	1,950	39%

Source: Khatib and Munasinghe 1992.

Africa

Many African nations import oil, and indigenous commercial energy resources play a small role in domestic electric power generation. This practice has worsened the debt situation in these countries. In much of Africa, existing electricity systems are isolated, and consist of small generation units that have low efficiency and reliability. Therefore, the demand for electricity usually exceeds supply. Confronted with these basic problems, many African governments are concentrating mainly on improving and expanding existing systems, and believe that environmental issues in the power sector are relatively unimportant. Therefore, in this region, there is an urgent need for the development of national and regional electricity master plans, with assistance from industrialized nations (Winje 1991b). In many parts of Africa there is substantial hydroelectric potential, but its exploitation has been subject to many environmental and social problems (Akosombo Dam in Ghana, Aswan Dam in Egypt).

Asia

The consumption of commercial energy in developing countries in the Asian region has grown rapidly in the last two decades. Between 1980 and 1992 energy consumption grew at an annual rate of 5.6 per cent in East Asia and the Pacific and 6.8 per cent in South Asia. While the dependence of oil has decreased in many countries, the use of coal, an abundant resource in the region, has increased especially in China and India. China is currently the world's largest coal producer, with an output of 1,082 Mt, followed by India. The consumption of coal is expected to increase rapidly in the next two decades. While the percentages of electricity generated from coal are 92 per cent for China and 70 per cent for India, current electricity generation is inadequate to meet the needs of their growing economies and the improvements in people's living standards. China and India, which have almost 37 per cent of the world's population (mostly rural and poor), are currently following a path of economic reform and will continue to depend on coal for electricity generation in the next two decades. Therefore, these nations will continue to be the largest regional sources of transnational and global environmental problems in the future. With an increasing awareness of regional and global environmental impacts of coal combustion, both China and India are increasingly searching for ways to minimize environmental impacts of power generation while focusing on problems such as inadequate supplies of electricity for economic growth, and to improve living standards of poor rural populations.

Another major problem facing countries in this region is the loss of power in transmission and distribution. When compared to the typical rates of 6–8 per cent in the industrialized countries, these are enormous: China, 16 per cent; India, 22 per cent; Pakistan, 28 per cent; Bangladesh, 31 per cent; South Korea, 12 per cent; Sri Lanka, 18 per cent; and Thailand and the Philippines, 22 per cent each. In contrast, the United States and Japan had corresponding values of 8 per cent and 7 per cent respectively (Munasinghe 1991).

Apart from the above problems, nations in the region suffer from inefficiencies resulting from inadequate pricing and excessive governmental interference.

Latin America and the Caribbean (LAC)

Electricity generation in the LAC region is distributed evenly between hydro-electric and thermo-electric plants. The development of the power sector in many nations has been overshadowed by the general debt problem in Latin America. In spite of this, the environmental impact of electricity supply has been given increasing attention in the last ten years. Many countries have begun to consider the environmental impacts of mining fossil fuels and constructing large hydro-power and thermal power plants. In some cases re-forestation projects are now required by law. Concerted international action in Latin America will ensure the development of an efficient electricity system in a sound environment (Winje 1991a).

Eastern Europe (EE) and Former Soviet Union (FSU)

EE and FSU countries consume a larger amount of primary energy and electricity than industrialized countries in terms of energy intensity. Their electricity intensity is two or three times, and the energy intensity is three or four times, higher than that of developed nations. This is mainly the result of the existence of vast energy resources in the region, which were made available at highly subsidized prices. The inefficiency of energy generation, the poor quality of commonly used energy carriers such as coal and lignite, and the large portion of primary industries, contribute to these high ratios. Many of the above factors have also resulted in the emission of high levels of sulphur dioxide, nitrogen oxides and fly ash. Cooperation with industrialized nations is needed to implement measures such as restructuring the fuel mix in the power sector, and the implementation of stack gas cleaning equipment (Winje 1991a). Technology could be one solution to lower energy-intensity levels. Historically, such technical advances have led to large reductions in the amounts of energy required for any given economic activity—for example, the electricity required to produce a ton of aluminium has declined steadily since the last century.

In Central Asia, another area of high hydroelectric potential, electricity planning is made difficult by conflicts with irrigation, and by the problems faced by the newly independent states in continuing development towards an integrated system.

3. THE NEED FOR SUSTAINABLE DEVELOPMENT

The increasing level of environmental pollution in both industrialized and developing countries as well as resource depletion, have led to a recognition of the need for ICs and DCs to find a less material-intensive development path. In the past, industrial countries that faced a tradeoff between economic growth and environmental preservation invariably gave higher priority to the former. These richer countries have only recently awakened to the environmental consequences of economic progress. This model of economic and social development has been adopted by many third world regions. However, an increasing awareness by both ICs and DCs of the consequences of following such a path have led them to explore the concept of sustainable development. This is an approach that will permit continuing improvements in the present quality of life at a lower intensity of resources use, thereby leaving behind for future generations an undiminished or even enhanced stock of natural resources and other assets.

3.1. Economic, Environmental and Social Approaches

Sustainable development has three key elements—economic, environmental and social. The economic approach to sustainability is based on the Hicks–Lindahl concept of the maximum flow of income that could be generated while at least maintaining the stock of assets (or capital) which yields these benefits (Solow 1986; Maler 1990). There is an underlying concept of optimality and economic efficiency applied to the use of scarce resources. Problems of interpretation arise in identifying the kinds of capital to be maintained (e.g., manufactured, natural and human capital) and their substitutability, as well as in valuing these assets, particularly ecological resources. The issues of uncertainty, irreversibility and catastrophic collapse pose additional difficulties (Pearce and Turner 1990).

The environmental view of sustainable development focuses on the stability of biological and physical systems. Of particular importance is the viability of subsystems that are critical to the global stability of the overall ecosystem. Protection of biological diversity is a key aspect. Furthermore, 'natural' systems may be interpreted to include all aspects of the biosphere, including manmade environments like cities. The emphasis is on preserving the resilience and dynamic ability of such systems to adapt to change, rather than conservation of some 'ideal' static state.

The social concept of sustainability seeks to maintain the stability of social and cultural systems, including the reduction of destructive conflicts (United Nations 1992). Both intragenerational equity (especially elimination of poverty), and intergenerational equity (involving the rights of future generations) are important aspects of this approach. Preservation of cultural diversity across the globe, and the better use of knowledge concerning sustainable practices embedded in less dominant cultures, should be pursued. Modern society would need to encourage pluralism and strengthen empowerment and grass-roots participation into a more effective decision-making framework for socially sustainable development.

Given the foregoing three criteria for sustainable development, the rapidly increasing demand for energy, particularly electricity, in the DCs, and the corresponding increase in investment requirements, the need for a comprehensive and integrated conceptual framework for analysis and decision-making is evident. Sustainable energy options may be identified by using a framework that takes into account multiple actors, multiple criteria, multilevel decision-making, and many impediments and constraints. However, any discussion of a framework within which to define sustainable energy options would be incomplete without a delineation of the environmental and social implications of energy use. They can be broadly categorized into national, transnational and global issues.

3.2. National Issues

National environmental and social issues arising from energy use are related mainly to electricity generation. While electricity has relatively few environmental and health consequences at the point of end use, the same cannot be said for electricity generation. However, the extent and nature of impacts differ among energy sources. Oil- and coal-fired plants not only have national impacts but also regional and global environmental and health effects. Even sources like wind power, geothermal energy and ocean energy, which are perceived to be 'clean', have some negative impacts on the surroundings. The environmental and social consequences of some typical energy sources are described below.

Fossil-fuel-fired plants

In the case of oil- and coal-fired plants, a significant public health risk results from exposure to the large amounts of gaseous and solid wastes discharged in the combustion process. These emissions include sulphur dioxide, carbon monoxide, nitrogen oxides, hydrocarbons, polycyclic organic matter and in the case of coal, additional pollutants include fly ash, trace metals, and radionuclides. The presence of these pollutants leads to an increased incidence of respiratory disease, toxicity and cancer. Disposal of solid waste leads to health risks associated with leachate and groundwater contamination. Natural gas-fired plants pose a public health risk from nitrogen oxides and particulate emissions, but are significantly less hazardous to health in comparison with oil- or coal-fired plants. Coal-mining, transportation and washing also have substantial adverse impacts on the environment.

The contribution of fossil fuels to carbon dioxide emissions depends on the carbon content of the fuel. Fuel oil emits 87.7 per cent as much carbon dioxide as coal, and natural gas only 58 per cent for the same thermal content. Without control or treatment, coal emits more particulate matter (PM), sulphur dioxide and nitrogen oxides, than any other fuel. While PM emissions in the case of oil and gas are negligible, coal emits almost 10 per cent of its oil equivalent in weight as ash and other matters. Sulphur dioxide emissions depend on the sulphur content of the fuels, while emissions of nitrogen oxides are not significantly different between fuels, with gas emitting only two-thirds that of coal.

Nuclear fission reactors, currently producing almost 17 per cent of electricity worldwide, were intended to replace fossil-fuelled capacity in the medium term. Safety concerns, driven by accidents at Three Mile Island and Chernobyl, have contributed to the current status of nuclear energy as neither politically nor economically attractive in many countries. However, in a few countries, such as France and Japan, nuclear reactors are used extensively. Though nuclear energy has the advantage that it emits none of the atmospheric pollutants of concern with fossil-fuel technologies, the fission reaction does generate long-lived highly radioactive wastes, the ultimate disposal of which is extremely controversial. Nuclear power also causes groundwater contamination. It is more capital intensive than fossil-fuel power generation. There is also a great deal of controversy about the true cost of nuclear power.

Studies indicate that occupational health risk, which may have intergenerational consequences, exists from exposure to radiation. Public health risk results from exposure to low-level radiation from power production, waste storage and waste disposal. High exposure to radiation is possible in the event of major accidents, with potential long-term health implications. While actual public risk may be relatively small, public fears of risks from nuclear plants and waste-disposal sites are extremely strong and cannot be dismissed (often based on risk-averse reactions to potentially catastrophic but rare accidents).

Hydroelectricity
Nineteen per cent of worldwide electricity is currently produced by flowing water, mostly in large hydroelectric dams that utilize reservoirs or natural steep drops and waterfalls. Since the capital investment requirements for large hydroelectric schemes are significant, many sites in DCs must compete for scarce capital. Hydroelectric power utilizes a renewable indigenous resource without producing air emissions or radioactive wastes. However, this technology is not entirely environmentally benign. Hydroelectric power generation has primarily local major environmental and social consequences. These consist of the damage caused by dam construction: destruction of habitats and loss of local/national biodiversity, the inundation of productive land and forests, siltation, and possibly the loss of cultural sites and mineral resources. Watershed disturbance sometimes leads to increased flooding, and low flow in the dry season. (On major river systems, this can have transnational consequences causing significant political and social unrest over water rights.)

Such environmental and social impacts of hydropower projects have recently led to public protest against proposed projects in South Asia and South America. Furthermore, still water reservoirs create ecological environments favourable to the spreading of parasitic and waterborne disease. Decades of experience have been developed internationally with mini- and micro-hydro schemes that cascade many small run-of-the-river turbines. These designs are becoming a visibly popular means for providing local power supply and irrigation without the massive environmental and social impacts that have plagued some large hydro schemes. Micro-hydro projects are currently under way in India and Malaysia and other DCs. These projects also have the advantage of providing electricity to rural areas beyond the central grid.

Hydropower plants have many other advantages which include longer service life, lower manpower requirements, operational flexibility, reliability and fast response time to changes in demand.

Solar energy
Direct solar radiation is another vast potential energy source for electricity generation. Advances in solar thermal technologies and direct electricity generation by photovoltaics (PV) have reduced costs significantly over the past decade (Ahmed 1994). While these techniques pose no significant occupational and health risks at the generation stage, some environmental impacts of solar thermal generation may arise from the loss of land use resulting from its high land intensity. Solar energy is constrained by its limited applicability.

Geothermal energy
Geothermal energy is harnessed in several countries (e.g., the United States and the Philippines) by using geothermal steam to drive steam turbines. Cost-competitive exploitation of geothermal energy with current technology is largely limited to the volcanically active Pacific 'Ring of Fire' and the Mediterranean, where suitable steam reservoirs are located within one mile of the surface. Geothermal steam carries with it a number of atmospheric pollutants including carbon dioxide, mercury and radon. Under current technologies, the toxins are commonly reinjected into the reservoir. With commercialization of designs expected late in the 1990s, hot dry rock technology is expected to be competitive with conventional geothermal technology and fossil-fuelled plants.

Biomass
A wide range of options exist for converting biomass into electric power. Dendrothermal power plants burn wood from fast-growing species (grown on a dedicated plantation), in boilers, to generate electricity through a conventional steam cycle. Most potential applications are for remote power supply in DCs. Concerns about the effects of dedicated fuelwood plantations, on the local environment and competing land uses, impose major constraints on the widespread adoption of dendrothermal power supply schemes.

It is economical to use biomass for energy purposes only where it is available as a byproduct of other processes. Crop residues, agricultural waste and animal dung produced in DCs are currently used as fuels—mainly by the poor.

Another source of biomass for power generation is municipal solid waste. High temperature incinerators for municipal solid waste have been developed in Germany and the United States. The public has voiced opposition to incineration in both countries because of concerns over emissions of dioxin, furans and other toxins that are released when plastics are burned. Virtual elimination of toxic effluents is achieved in some of the new high temperature designs that utilize a slanted bed to ensure total combustion, and wet scrubbers. A 25 MW incinerator can consume about 400,000 tons of municipal solid waste each year, thereby reducing the volume of waste ash for disposal. In addition to energy recovered, and reducing urban waste disposal problems, leading-edge technologies for waste incineration do not emit more atmospheric greenhouse gases than if the wastes were allowed to decay. In addition to the option of direct incineration, small power plants that burn landfill gases (mostly methane) have been employed for decades around the world. The ultimate potential of municipal solid waste incineration and landfill gas plants as an energy source, is limited both by public concern over emissions and concentrated sources of solid waste. In tropical areas, the water content of municipal solid wastes reduces its attractiveness as a fuel.

Wind power

Large grid-connected wind generators (75kW–450kW), configured in multi-turbine 'wind farms', now supplement fossil-fuel capacity in a number of countries. Research is currently under way in the United States on combined wind and gas turbine power supply schemes that would provide reliable power on demand, at minimal cost. Although wind generators do not produce air or water emissions, planners often face public opposition since the larger turbines do present a visual impact on the landscape, emit acoustic noise, generate electromagnetic interference and present a hazard to birds.

Ocean energy

Pilot plant experience has indicated that temperature differences of 20 degrees centigrade between surface waters and waters about 1000 metres below are sufficient for economic power generation. As a large proportion of the tropical oceans contain such thermals, a vast potential resource is available. Because of significant capital requirements and risks inherent in an unproven technology, no commercial plants have been built to date. In addition, this technology poses some environmental concerns about effects on sea life and atmospheric release of carbon dioxide stored in deep ocean waters.

3.3. Transnational Issues

Acid deposition is perhaps the most serious of the transnational issues faced today. Acid deposition is a result of oxides of sulphur and nitrogen that originate from fossil-fuel combustion, falling to the ground as particulates and acid rain. Coal- and oil-fired power stations emit significant amounts of sulphur dioxide and nitrogen oxides to the atmosphere. The transport of sulphur dioxide occurs over long distances (greater than 1000 km), causing the deposition of emission products over national boundaries. This may result in sensitive ecosystems receiving depositions of sulphur well above their carrying capacity. Acid deposition caused by sulphur and nitrogen oxides results in damage to trees and crops, and sometimes extends to acidification of streams and lakes, resulting in destruction of aquatic ecosystems. It also leads to the corrosion, erosion and discolouration of buildings, monuments and bridges. Indirect health effects are caused by the mobilization of heavy metals in acidified water and soil (IAEA 1991).

Other important transnational issues include environmental and health impacts of radiation caused by severe nuclear accidents (Chernobyl), oceanic and coastal pollution caused by oil spills (Amico Cadez, Exxon Valdez and Braer), downstream siltation of river water in one nation caused by deforestation of water sheds and soil erosion in a neighbouring country, and changes in hydrological flow and water conditions caused by dams.

3.4. Global Issues

The increase in atmospheric concentrations of CO_2 and other radiatively active trace gasses (N_2O, CH_4 and chlorofluorocarbons, or CFCs) has led to an increase in global mean temperatures, or global warming. According to a study conducted by the intergovernmental panel on climate change (IPCC), increases in greenhouse gas concentrations from anthropogenic activities are believed to have resulted in mean surface temperature increases of 0.3–0.6 degrees centigrade over the last century. While the study does not suggest that the case for global warming is fully established, several important issues remain unsolved. The year 1990 was ranked as the Earth's warmest year since measurements of surface temperatures were initiated. Six of the seven warmest years since 1850 have all occurred since 1980. Changes in recent rainfall patterns, and frequency of storms, may also be attributable to the phenomenon. Over the last one hundred years global sea level has increased by 10–20 cm (IAEA 1991). These climatic changes may have contributed to natural disasters, such as the floods in Bangladesh and serious drought conditions in Africa, which resulted in extremely high social costs—high mortality, the spread of diseases such as typhus and cholera, widespread starvation/malnutrition and significant population displacement.

The relative contribution of electricity generation to overall global warming (mainly in the form of CO_2 emissions) has been estimated at about 25 per cent compared to about 14 per cent caused by deforestation. Of this amount, coal and oil each contribute about 40 per cent of anthropogenic carbon dioxide emissions, and gas about 15 per cent. OECD and other European countries account for about 75 per cent of global fossil fuel CO_2 emissions, at present. Energy consumption as a whole is the single largest contributor to greenhouse gas emissions in developing countries. While the use of traditional fuels is declining as a share of energy supply in many developing countries as a result of growing prosperity, India and China will be forced to increase coal-fired generation through domestic energy sources to meet the growing energy needs of their citizens.

Given the considerable problems faced by the power sector in DCs, the growing additional concerns about the environmental consequences of energy use considerably complicate the policy dilemma facing the DCs. Developing countries share the deep worldwide concerns about environmental degradation, and some have already taken steps to improve their own natural resource management as an essential prerequisite for sustained economic development. However, they also face other urgent issues like poverty, hunger and disease, as well as rapid population growth and high expectations. This paucity of resources constrains the ability of DCs to undertake costly measures to protect the global commons.

The challenge facing the developing world is how to harmonize development goals and the elimination of poverty (which will require increased use of energy), with environmental goals without worsening their weak economies. In 1992 per capita income in low-income developing nations was almost one-sixtieth of that in the high-income nations ($390 in low-income countries versus $22,600 in high-income countries). Correspondingly, per capita energy consumption in low-income countries was 338 kg of oil equivalent as compared to 5,101 kg of oil equivalent in high-income countries (World Bank 1994b).

The disparity in both per capita income and energy use among different countries also raises additional issues in the context of current global environmental concerns. Fossil-fuel-related carbon dioxide accumulation in the atmosphere is a relevant example. The developed countries accounted for over 80 per cent of such cumulative worldwide emissions during 1950–86—North America contributed over 40 billion tons of carbon, Western and Eastern Europe emitted 25 and 32 billion tons respectively, while the DCs share was only about 24 billion tons. On a per capita basis the contrasts are even more stark, with North America emitting over 20 times more and the developed countries as a whole being responsible for over eleven times as much total cumulative carbon dioxide emissions as the DCs. The DC share would be even smaller if emissions prior to 1950 were included. Clearly, any reasonable growth scenario for developing nations that followed the same material-intensive path as the industrialized world, would result in unacceptably high levels of future greenhouse gas accumulation as well as more general depletion of natural resources.

Up to now, scientific analysis has provided only broad and rather uncertain predictions about the degree and timing of potential global warming. However, it would be prudent for mankind to buy an 'insurance policy' in the form of mitigatory actions to reduce greenhouse gas emissions. Ironically, both local and global environmental degradation might affect developing nations more severely, since they are more dependent on natural resources while lacking the economic strength to prevent or respond quickly to increases in the frequency, severity and persistence of flooding, drought, storms, and so on. Thus, from the DC viewpoint, an attractive low-cost insurance premium would be a set of inexpensive measures that could address a range of national and global environmental issues without hampering development efforts.

The report of the Brundtland Commission (WCED 1987), which has been widely circulated and accepted, has presented arguments along the theme of sustainable development, which consists of the interaction of two components: needs, especially those of the poor segments of the world's population, and limitations, which are imposed by the ability of the environment to meet those needs. The development of the presently industrialized countries took place in a setting which emphasized needs and de-emphasized limitations. The development of these societies has effectively exhausted a disproportionately large share of global resources—broadly defined to include both the resources that are consumed in productive activity (such as oil, gas and minerals), as well as environmental assets that absorb the waste products of economic activity and those that provide irreplaceable life-support functions (like the high altitude ozone layer). Indeed, some analysts argue that this development path has significantly indebted the ICs to the larger global community.

The division of responsibility in this global effort is clear from the above arguments. The unbalanced use of common resources in the past should be one important basis on which the developed and developing countries can work together to share and preserve what remains. The ICs have already attained most reasonable goals of development and can afford to substitute environmental protection for further growth of material output. On the other hand, the DCs can be expected to participate in the global effort only to the extent that this participation is fully consistent with and complementary to their immediate economic and social development objectives.

4. A FRAMEWORK FOR SUSTAINABLE ENERGY DEVELOPMENT

The broad rationale underlying all national level planning and policy-making is the need to ensure the best use of scarce resources, in order to further socioeconomic development efforts and improve the quality of life of citizens. Power and energy planning must also be part of and closely integrated with overall economic planning and policy analysis, to meet many specific, interrelated and frequently conflicting national objectives. Specific goals might include: (a) ensuring economic efficiency in the supply and use of all forms of energy, to maximize growth—other energy efficiency-related objectives are energy conservation and elimination of wasteful consumption, and saving scarce foreign exchange; (b) raising sufficient revenues from energy sales, to finance sector development; (c) meeting the basic energy needs of the poor, and income redistribution; (d) diversifying supply, reducing dependence on foreign sources, and meeting national security requirements; (e) contributing to the development of special regions (particularly rural or remote areas), and priority sectors of the economy; (f) price stability; (g) preserving the environment; and so on.

4.1. Integrated Approach

Successful planning and implementation of national energy programmes must explicitly take account of the role of the energy sector in economic development *vis-à-vis* those of the other parts of the economy. This will require an integrated approach that will help decision makers in formulating policies and providing market signals and information to economic agents that encourage more efficient energy production and use. Summarized in Figure 1.1 is such an approach to decision-making which emphasizes a hierarchical conceptual framework for sustainable energy development (SED) that can be implemented through a set of energy supply and demand management policies.

The core of the SED framework is the integrated multilevel analysis shown in the middle column. Although SED is primarily country-focused, at the global level it is recognized that there are transnational energy–environmental issues. Thus individual countries are embedded in an international matrix, and economic and environmental conditions at this global level will impose exogenous inputs or constraints on decision makers within countries. The next hierarchical level in the figure focuses on the multisectoral national economy, of which the energy sector is a part. This suggests that energy planning requires analysis of the links between the energy sector and the rest of the economy. Such links include the energy needs of user sectors (e.g., industry, transport and agriculture), input requirements of the energy sector, and impact on the economy of policies concerning energy prices and availability. The intermediate level of SED treats the energy sector as a separate entity composed of subsectors such as electricity, petroleum products and so on. This permits detailed analysis, with special emphasis on interactions among the different energy subsectors, substitution possibilities and the resolution of any resulting policy conflicts. The most disaggregate and lowest hierarchical level pertains to energy analysis within each of the energy subsectors. At this level most of the detailed energy resource

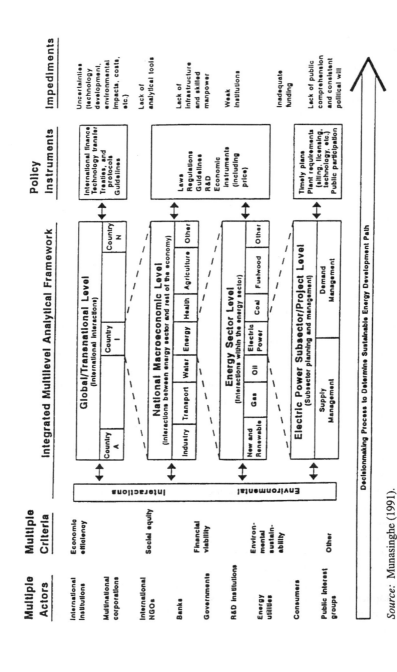

Source: Munasinghe (1991).

Figure 1.1 Comprehensive framework for sustainable energy development

22

evaluation, planning and implementation of projects is carried out by line institutions (both public and private).

In practice, the various levels of SED merge and overlap considerably, requiring that (inter-) sectoral linkages should be carefully examined. Energy–environmental interactions (represented by the vertical bar) tend to cut across all levels and need to be incorporated into the analysis as far as possible. Such interactions also provide important paths for incorporating environmental considerations into national energy policies.

SED facilitates policy-making and does not imply rigid centralized planning. Thus, such a process should result in the development of a flexible and constantly updated energy strategy designed to meet national goals. This national energy strategy (of which the investment programme and pricing policy are important elements), may be implemented through energy supply and demand-management policies and programmes that make effective use of decentralized market forces and incentives.

Consequently, SED implies improvements in overall economic efficiency through better energy management. As shown in Figure 1.1, a variety of policy instruments are available for decision makers for instituting sound energy management. While formulating policy, it is desirable also to consider the interests of multiple actors (shown in the figure), ranging from international institutions to local energy users. This figure also indicates the most important impediments that limit effective policy formulation and implementation.

New investments offer a good opportunity to pursue sustainable energy development. In ten years, new plants will account for more than half of the industrial output of developing countries and in twenty years, for practically all of it. As a result, it will be possible to have a major impact by putting in place policies, legislation, mechanisms, systems and incentives that facilitate sustainable energy development.

4.2. Identifying Sustainable Energy Options: 'Win–Win' Options Versus Tradeoffs

The primary objective of sustainable energy development (SED) is to maximize welfare, while maintaining or increasing the stock of economic, ecological and sociocultural assets over time (to ensure the sustainability of income and intragenerational equity) and providing a safety net to meet the basic needs and protect the poor (thereby advancing intergenerational equity). In considering sustainable energy options, policy makers must therefore take into account all three aspects of sustainable development (i.e., economic, social and environmental). Options that lead to improvements in all three indices are referred to as 'win–win' options. Once 'win–win' options are realized, policy makers are able to make tradeoffs among other available options.

The incorporation of environmental externalities into decision-making is particularly important in the power sector, where environmental concerns (ranging from greenhouse gas emissions of fossil-fuelled plants to the impacts of inundation at hydro plants) have posed increasingly difficult constraints to project implementation. It is also clear that in order for environmental concerns to play a real role in power-sector decision-making, one must address these issues early—at the sectoral and regional planning stages, rather than only at the stage of project environmental assessment.

Unfortunately, as soon as one is dealing with power-sector issues at this aggregate planning level, the application of many project-level valuation techniques becomes extremely difficult, for two main reasons. The first is the nature of the impacts themselves—the health effects of pollutants from coal-fired generating stations, the potential loss of biodiversity associated with large-scale hydro reservoirs, and the impacts of greenhouse gas emissions are all exceptionally difficult to value. Indeed, attempts to do so would very likely focus attention on the validity of the valuation techniques themselves, rather than the policy tradeoffs that must be made. The second reason concerns the scale of analysis. Many techniques used are most appropriate at the micro-level: the use of the contingent valuation approach is much more valid where respondents can be asked specific questions about impacts of a particular project to which they can relate. However, this may be very difficult to apply in situations where one is dealing with a potentially large number of technology, site and mitigation options.

It is in these kinds of situations that the techniques of multi-criteria analysis (MCA) may be applied. Such techniques first gained prominence as practical

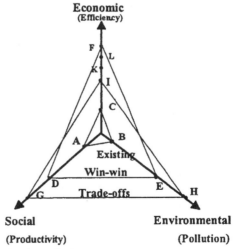

Figure 1.2   Multi-criteria analysis

evaluation tools in the 1970s, when the intangible environmental externalities lying outside conventional cost–benefit analysis (CBA) methodologies were increasingly recognized. It also met one objective of modern decision makers, who preferred to be presented with a range of feasible alternatives as opposed to one 'best' solution. MCA allows for the appraisal of alternatives with differing objectives and varied costs and benefits, which are often assessed in differing units of measurement.

Multi-criteria analysis offers policy makers an alternative when progress towards multiple objectives cannot be measured in terms of a single criterion (i.e., monetary values). Take the case of an efficient fuelwood stove—an end-use option for sustainable energy development (see SED matrix, Table 1.6). While the economic value of an efficient fuelwood stove is measurable, its contribution to social and environmental goals is not easily valued monetarily. As shown in Figure 1.2, outward movements along the axes trace improvements in three indicators: economic efficiency (net monetary benefits), social equity (improved health), and environmental pollution (reduced deforestation).

We may assess the policy options as follows. First, triangle ABC describes the existing fuelwood stove where economic efficiency is moderate, social equity is low, and overall environmental impact is worst. Next, triangle DEF indicates a 'win–win' future option in which all three indices improve, as could occur with an improved fuelwood stove that provided efficient energy and health benefits to the poor. The economic gains would include monetary savings from reduced fuelwood use and increased productivity from reductions in acute respiratory infections, lung disease and cancer caused by pollutants in biomass smoke. Social gains would accrue from the fact that the rural poor benefit the most from this innovation—for example, because of the reduced time spent on collecting fuelwood, thereby increasing time spent on other productive activities, and the lightened health and labour burden on women and children. The environment benefits because a lower demand for fuelwood will reduce deforestation and reduce greenhouse gas emissions resulting from inefficient combustion.

After realizing such 'win–win' gains, other available options would require tradeoffs. In triangle GIH, further environmental and social gains are attainable only at the expense of sharply increasing costs. For example, shifting from fuelwood and LPG or kerosene as a fuel may increase economic costs, while yielding further environmental and social benefits. In sharp contrast to the move from ABC to DEF, which is unambiguously desirable, a policy maker may not wish to make a further shift from DEF to GIH without knowing the relative weights that society places on the three indices. Such preferences are often difficult to determine explicitly, but it is possible to narrow the options. Suppose a small economic cost, FL, yields the full social gain DG, while a large economic cost, LI, is required to realize the environmental benefit EH. Here, the social gain may better justify the economic sacrifice. Further, if purely budgetary constraints limit costs to less than FK, then sufficient funds exist only to pay for the social benefits, and the environmental improvements will have to be deferred.

A recent World Bank study of power system planning in Sri Lanka demonstrated the versatility of the MCA approach (see Meier and Munasinghe 1994). The objective was to demonstrate how environmental externalities could be incorporated into power-system planning in a systematic and efficient manner. Sri Lanka presently depends largely on hydro power for electricity generation, but over the next decade there seems little choice other than to begin building large coal- or oil-fired stations, or to build hydro plants whose economic returns and environmental impacts are increasingly unfavourable. In addition, there are a wide range of other options (such as wind power, increasing use of demand-side management, and system-efficiency improvements), that make decision-making quite difficult—even in the absence of the environmental concerns. The study is relatively unique in its focus on these kinds of planning issues, as opposed to the more usual policy of assessing environmental concerns only at the project level after the strategic sectoral development decisions have already been made.

In this case, end-use energy efficiency measures provided 'win–win' options (i.e., they were superior to all other alternatives on the basis of air quality, biodiversity loss and economic costs). Conversely, several prominent hydro-power projects could be excluded because they performed poorly in terms of both biodiversity loss and economic costs.

In many countries, especially those in the developing world, inappropriate policies have encouraged wasteful and unproductive uses of some forms of energy. In such cases, better energy management could lead to improvements in economic efficiency (higher value of net output produced), energy efficiency (higher value of net output per unit of energy used), energy conservation (reduced absolute amount of energy used), and environmental protection (reduced energy-related environmental costs).

However, it may not always be possible to satisfy all of the above goals simultaneously. For example, in some DCs where the existing levels of per capita energy consumption are very low and certain types of energy use are uneconomically constrained, it may become necessary to promote more energy consumption in order to raise net output (thereby increasing economic efficiency). In spite of this particular case, there are many instances where it may be possible to increase energy efficiency while decreasing energy consumption.

The economic efficiency criterion which helps us maximize the value of net output from all available scarce resources in the economy (including energy), should effectively subsume purely energy-oriented objectives such as energy efficiency and energy conservation. Furthermore, the costs arising from energy-related adverse environmental impacts may be included (to the extent possible) in the energy economics analytical framework, to determine how much energy use and net output society should be willing to forgo, in order to abate or mitigate environmental damage.

Energy use and generation in the developing world can be improved in two main ways to make them more sustainable. First, energy efficiency can be increased by supply- and demand-side improvements. Along with this, environmentally more benign technologies can be introduced. Fuel switching and renewables are relevant in the latter case. In addition, options such as price reform and institutional and regulatory reform can be further implemented in order to achieve the required objectives of SED.

4.3. Improving Energy Efficiency

'Energy efficiency', or the efficiency with which energy is produced and used, is one of the most widely advocated methods of reducing pollution. During the past two centuries, the efficiency of energy producing and using activities, as measured by the amount of energy needed to provide a given output or service, has improved by factors ranging between 50 and 100, sometimes more (Anderson 1993). However, the demand stimulated by subsequent reduction of the cost of energy, the expanding areas of energy utilization, and the growth of population and industry, has dramatically expanded energy use. During the present century, during which energy efficiency grew by factors of more than 10 in key sectors such as electricity, world commercial energy consumption has increased tenfold—an average growth rate of 2.5 per cent a year (Anderson 1993).

The carbon intensity of world economic product dropped by more than 20 per cent during the period 1970–86, and 75 per cent of this was achieved due to energy efficiency measures. In the future, DCs offer even greater potential to improve energy efficiency and a corresponding decline in carbon emissions. In 1990, OECD countries were able to produce a unit of economic output using little more than half the energy required by the DCs and CEE countries.

There is a spectrum of technological options which the DCs could potentially utilize in order to improve energy efficiency. Among these, improvements in both the supply, and the end use of energy, should be considered.

Supply-side improvements
Among the short-term technological options for the DC power sector, reducing transmission and distribution losses, and improving generation plant efficiencies appear to be the most attractive. Recent studies show that up to a certain point, these supply efficiency-enhancing measures yield net economic savings or benefits that are several times the corresponding costs incurred (Munasinghe 1990b). Total energy losses in DC power systems are estimated to average in the 16 to 18 per cent range. The average system losses in South Asia have been estimated at 17 per cent and in East Asia at 13 per cent (Munasinghe 1991). A comparison with OECD countries presents a grimmer situation. It has been

estimated that older power plants in many developing countries consume 18–44 per cent more fuel per kWh produced than is the norm in OECD countries and utilities suffer transmission and distribution losses 2 to 4 times higher (Levine et al. 1991).

The consequences of reducing these losses can be quite important. On the basis of previous estimates of capacity requirements, a one percentage point reduction in losses per year would reduce required capacity by about 5 GW annually in the DCs. The estimated saving in capital investment would be about 10 billion dollars per year. Meanwhile, the Agency for International Development (USAID 1988) has estimated that the average heat rate of DC power plants is about 13,000 Btu/kWh, compared to 9,000–11,000 Btu/kWh if these plants were operated efficiently. The energy savings and positive environmental consequences of efficient plant operation are quite significant.

The use of modern electricity generation with high technical efficiencies, such as combined-cycle power stations, is beneficial to the environment and resource conservation, but these techniques require high investment and technical expertise. Therefore, they may not be feasible for use in financially troubled developing nations. There is an acute need for increased research in cost-effective, efficient, energy-supply techniques.

Demand-side improvements
Significant gains in energy efficiency can also be achieved by conservation on the demand side. Johansson et al. (1992) provides an insightful review of the developments that have been taking place in end-use technologies which can have a major impact on energy efficiency. These technologies, which were developed in the industrialized countries as a response to the oil price escalation in the seventies, can be easily applied to achieve more efficient lighting, heating, refrigeration and air conditioning, around the developing world.

Since major demand growth in DCs is expected over the next few decades, and technologies and appliances are generally based on 1970s' designs, a number of authors have concentrated on the gains in overall electricity system efficiency that are possible from end-use efficiency improvement programmes in DCs. The National Energy Conservation Programme in Brazil (PROCEL) is a case in point. This programme advanced the development and commercialization of a number of energy-efficient lamps, reflectors for fluorescent fixtures, and building control systems. These technologies are now manufactured and sold in Brazil, and their adoption has provided an estimated 1.1 TWh of electricity savings in 1989. For the residential sector, most of the potential cost-effective savings come from the adoption of efficient refrigerators, air conditioners and compact fluorescent lamps (CFLs). The cost of conserved energy (CCE), which is a measure of annualized increased capital costs divided by kWh saved over the life of the device, can be evaluated for each improved technology. Under moderate economic assumptions, the CCE of improved air conditioners, improved refrigerators, standard fluorescent lamps and CFLs, relative to incandescent bulbs in Brazil, are 3.2c/kWh, 3.0c/kWh 6.1c/kWh and 3.1c/kWh, respectively; all well below the marginal cost of residential electricity supply of 12c/kWh. Analysis of a proposed programme to induce the adoption of efficient appliances in seven categories could reduce residential demand in Brazil by the year 2010 by 33 TWh/year, or 31 per cent of projected residential demand, at an average annual cost (CCE) of 3.1c/kWh (Khatib and Munasinghe 1992).

One major reason DCs hesitate to adopt these technologies, is their belief that this will increase costs dramatically. However, the OTA study shows that when all the system-wide financial costs are accounted for, energy-efficient equipment usually can provide the same energy services at a lower installed capital cost than less efficient equipment (OTA 1991). Unfortunately, consumers who purchase end-use equipment see the increase in capital costs of more efficient designs, but not the decrease in capital costs as fewer power plants have to be built to provide a given level of energy service.

In DCs, an important barrier to demand-side energy improvement is lack of information about the availability and reliability of new energy-efficient equipment. Other reasons such as subsidized and low energy prices, absence of competitive end-use markets, and government-regulated weak energy supply sources, are also impediments to efficient use of energy on the demand side. Few energy supply enterprises in DCs have the necessary customer information base to predict results of end-use efficiency improvements. However, the potential for demand-side improvements is attractive. Technically proven cost-effective end-use conservation techniques can save DCs 10–30 per cent of industrial sector energy consumption and 10–25 per cent of power sector energy consumption (Saunders and Gandhi 1994).

Construction for both residential and commercial buildings has special importance, because of the large amount of energy consumed within interior work spaces. For example, over one-third of the total energy consumed in the US is used to heat, cool and light buildings or to operate equipment, such as computers, used by the occupants of buildings (Glicksman 1991). Although DCs in colder regions may have similar energy requirements, those countries which are closer to the tropics will require much less energy for heating purposes. Some of the energy consumption for cooling purposes may be relevant in these cases.

Although new technologies, such as 'smart windows', which control the solar energy entering a building, are being developed, much of the improvement in the energy efficiency of buildings has been achieved by applying technologies already at hand.

A number of market-based incentives have been proposed to improve building standards. These include efficiency standards and labelling for buildings, appliances and lighting; utility fees, offsets and rebates; and urban infrastructure improvements to battle summer heat islands and greenhouse gases

(Rosenfield 1991).

Making these efficient electricity end-use technologies widely available in DCs could contribute in important ways to a global effort to increase electricity end-use efficiency, thus reducing growth in electricity supply, local environmental and social impacts, and in greenhouse gas emissions (Lawrence Berkeley Laboratory 1991).

Cost savings

Increasing efficiency in energy production and use in DCs will result in large savings in the public and private sectors as pointed out by Dennis Anderson (1993). He concludes that the approximately $125 billion per year of cost savings estimated for electricity production in DCs, for instance, amounts to several times the financial requirements of accelerated programmes in each of several other sectors such as education, water and sanitation, health, soil erosion control, agricultural research and extension, and family planning. Price and institutional inefficiencies in energy supply are not only damaging to the (environmentally responsible) growth of the energy industry itself in DCs, but are also a huge burden to the rest of the economy (Anderson 1993).

Figure 1.3 emphasizes the importance of energy efficiency. The reduction of pollution emissions this method alone can achieve is significant, even in the absence of other measures. The figure also illustrates the dramatic reduction of pollution when low-polluting technologies are introduced simultaneously.

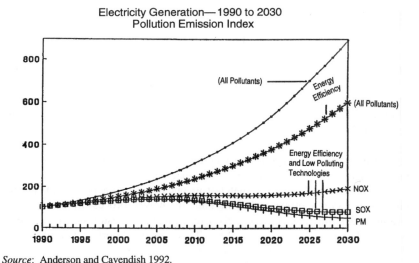

Electricity Generation—1990 to 2030
Pollution Emission Index

Source: Anderson and Cavendish 1992.

*Figure 1.3   Three scenarios of emissions from electricity generation in
developing countries, 1990–2030 (index: 1990 = 100)*

4.4. Implementing Environmentally More Benign Technologies

In the longer term, DCs will need to rely on more advanced technological options which are currently being developed in industrialized countries. As discussed earlier, power generation capacity in DCs is expected to nearly double by the turn of the century, and will increase further thereafter. This provides many opportunities for developing nations to add state-of-the-art technologies which have been designed with consideration of economic and environmental criteria. Clean coal technologies, cogeneration, gas turbine combined cycles, and steam-injected gas turbines, are part of this menu of technologies which have important potential in developing nations. Similar applications will become available for emission-control technologies. However, the DCs will look to the industrialized nations to provide leadership in refining and testing these technologies before they are implemented in the developing world.

Fuel switching, and the use of renewable energy sources, are two important technology changes which should be implemented in the developing world.

Fuel switching

The substitution of primary energy sources in power generation is an important potential means of achieving dual benefits which are evident in the case of substituting natural gas for coal or oil. The economic benefit of natural gas substitution comes from either import substitution for petroleum products or releasing these products for export. As a second benefit, natural gas firing typically achieves a 30–50 per cent reduction in carbon emissions. Many Asian countries are endowed with significant resources of natural gas, including Malaysia, Indonesia and Thailand.

The fuel used for electricity generation often has high sulphur content, thus causing a high level of atmospheric pollution. A considerable reduction of these emissions can be achieved by substituting quality coal or other fuels for low-grade coal. Investing in gas-fired and oil-fired power plants would also reduce carbon dioxide emissions. However, this should be considered more carefully, because it would mean increased dependence on imported oil or gas for most DCs (Winje 1991a).

Finally, when considering fuel switching, the relevant time frames should be taken into account. Historical experience suggests that even under strong incentives, it takes about 15 years to switch from one fundamental production process (e.g. basic oxygen process steel-making) to newer processes, throughout a national industrial sector. Major fuel switches in energy systems have taken even longer—about 25 years (Clark 1991). This has an important bearing on the efficacy and feasibility of proposals for fuel substitution.

Renewable energy sources

The World Energy Council (WEC) estimates that, under an ecologically driven scenario, the contribution of new renewable energy sources (defined as total renewable energy sources minus traditional biomass and large hydro) will reach 13–14 per cent of total energy use by 2020. Total renewable energy use is expected to reach 30 per cent, nearly a tenfold increase over 1990 figures (Darnell et al. 1992). This would allow for a reduction of 30 per cent in annual global energy-related carbon dioxide emissions. It is important to emphasize that this ecologically driven scenario assumes almost immediate radical changes in energy policy and consumer behaviour, leading to a decline in global energy intensity over the next 30 years. These changes would have to occur at a rate three times faster than average annual rates achieved over the past 15 years (Jefferson 1992). Jefferson provides a more conservative estimate, predicting that new renewables would account for not more than 8.5 per cent of total primary energy supply by 2020, with fossil fuels still accounting for up to 70 per cent of total primary energy supply.

In one recent scenario, Johansson et al. (1992) estimate that, given the appropriate technological and financial support, renewable sources of energy could meet three-fifths of the world's energy market (with contributions from hydro power, wind and solar power, and biomass) and two-fifths of the market for fuels (mostly biomass-derived) used directly by 2050.[1] Provided that energy efficiency and renewable energy promotion measures are aggressively implemented, the authors estimate that global carbon dioxide levels could be reduced to 75 per cent of 1985 levels by 2050.

The range of estimates clearly indicates the level of uncertainty regarding the potential of renewable energy to meet global energy demand within the next thirty years. However, while statistics vary, it is evident that non-conventional sources of energy have a key role to play in meeting energy needs in an efficient and cost-effective manner, particularly in DCs where most of the growth in demand will occur.

4.5. Price Reform

Economically efficient pricing policies serve a dual role in the electric power sector, and are especially important in the context of the developing world. Prices that reflect the true value of the resources employed in the supply of electric power, ensure that consumers are given the correct economic signals to use electricity in the most efficient manner. Efficient prices also indicate consumer demand to the power utility, which can accordingly augment supply capacity. Finally, correctly set prices ensure that the power sector is able to internally generate the financial resources required to maintain the requisite investment levels, and thus operate the sector efficiently.

In the past, electric power pricing policy in most countries was determined mainly on the basis of financial or accounting criteria. The practice of raising sufficient sales revenues to meet operating expenses and debt-service requirements, while providing a reasonable contribution towards capital needed for future power system expansion, is an example. However, there has recently been increasing emphasis on the use of economic principles to produce and consume electric power efficiently, while conserving scarce resources. This is especially relevant in the DCs where a great deal of attention has been paid to the use of marginal cost pricing policies.

A comprehensive approach to power pricing recognizes the existence of several objectives or criteria, not all of which are mutually consistent. First, national economic resources must be allocated efficiently not only among different sectors of the economy, but within the electric power sector itself. Second, certain principles relating to fairness and equity must be satisfied. These include (a) fair allocation of costs among consumers according to the burdens they impose on the system, (b) assurance of a reasonable degree of price stability, and (c) provision of a minimum level of service to low-income consumers. Third, power prices should help raise sufficient revenues to meet the financial require-ments of the sector. Fourth, the power tariff structure must be simple enough to facilitate metering and billing customers. Finally, other economic and political requirements, such as incentive and penalty pricing schemes, and subsidized electricity supply to certain sectors or geographic areas, also exist.

Since the above criteria are often in conflict with one another, it is necessary to accept certain tradeoffs among them. The marginal cost approach to price-setting has both the analytical rigour and inherent flexibility to provide a tariff structure that is responsive to these basic objectives. In the first stage of calculating marginal costs, the economic (first-best) efficiency objectives of tariff-setting are satisfied because the method of calculation is based on future economic resource costs (rather than sunk costs) and also incorporates economic considerations such as shadow prices and externalities. The structuring of marginal costs permits an efficient and fair allocation of the tariff burden on consumers. In the second stage of developing marginal cost-based tariffs, deviations from strict marginal costs are considered in order to meet important financial and other social, economic (second-best) and political criteria. This second stage of adjusting strict marginal costs is generally as important as the first-stage calculation, especially in the DC context.

Any marginal cost-based tariff is a compromise among many different objectives. Therefore, there is no 'ideal' tariff. By using the marginal cost approach, it is possible to revise and improve the tariff on a consistent and ongoing basis and thereby approach the optimal price over a period of several years, without subjecting long-standing consumers to 'unfair' shocks in the form of large abrupt price changes.

A study of the electric power sector in DCs indicated that electricity tariffs have not kept up with cost escalation. Based on a survey of 60 developing countries, electricity tariffs on average declined between 1979 and 1988 from 5.21 cents/kWh to 3.79 cents/kWh in 1986 US constant dollars (Besant-Jones et al. 1990). The operating ratio (defined as the ratio of operating costs before debt service, depreciation and other financing charges, to operating revenue) for the almost 400 power utilities studied, deteriorated from 0.68 in the 1966 to 1973 period to 0.8 between 1980 and 1985. In some countries these deviations are significantly greater (Munasinghe 1991).

World Development Report 1992 (World Bank 1992a) emphasizes using taxes and regulations as an incentive for the energy industry and its consumers to adopt cleaner fuels and clean fuel technologies.

Recent advances in low-cost metering and switching equipment have made it possible to consider (where appropriate), more sophisticated approaches to supply–demand balancing such as spot pricing and load control. In spite of the added costs of implementation of these schemes, potential savings to both the power producer and the consumer are often significant. Producers benefit by achieving some of their demand management objectives such as peak shaving and load shifting. Consumers benefit by being able to select service levels according to their individual needs and by a reduction in total cost.

4.6. Institutional and Regulatory Reform

Excessive government interference in organizational and operational matters has been a major problem in many parts of the developing world. This has adversely affected least-cost procurement and investment decisions, hampered attempts to raise prices to efficient levels, mandated low salaries tied to civil service levels, and promoted excessive staffing. This in turn has resulted in inadequate management, the loss of experienced staff due to uncompetitive employment conditions and poor job satisfaction, weak planning and demand forecasting, inefficient operation and maintenance, high losses and poor financial monitoring, controls and revenue collection. Incentives for utility managers to pursue technical efficiency and financial discipline, to consistently minimize production costs and to provide reliable services, are lacking in DCs. Lack of internal funding, together with poor planning, operation, and maintenance practices has resulted in a widespread maintenance backlog and poor availability of generation capacity in DCs, thereby increasing the pressure for new generation. At the same time the cost of maintaining existing plant is far less than the expense of building new capacity.

Therefore, political decision makers, senior government officials and ministry-level staff, should focus on critical macroeconomic and energy sector strategy and policy. The senior management of a power company, appropriately guided and buffered by an independent board of directors, would then conduct their daily operations free from government interference to meet the overall national policy objectives and targets within regulatory guidelines. As far as possible, the utility management should be assured of continuity at the top, even in the face of political changes. While the enterprise is provided wider autonomy, it would now become more accountable in terms of performance measured against an agreed set of specific objectives and monitored indicators.

Although delegation of authority to lower managerial levels can be extremely beneficial, staff training and education at all levels and stages of the career structure would play a critical role in ensuring the success of such an approach.

The natural monopoly characteristics of some power enterprise functions, and necessity to manipulate these enterprises for general policy purposes, have been cited as reasons for maintaining large centralized public sector organizations. Nevertheless, given the observed problems inherent in stimulating management of these enterprises to be cost conscious, innovative and responsive to consumer needs, there may be a need for more fundamental change. It could be worthwhile to trade off some of the perceived economies of scale in energy enterprises for other organizational structures which provide greater built-in incentives for management efficiency and responsiveness to consumers.

In particular, there appears to be considerable interest in the scope for more decentralization and greater private participation. DC power sector officials have been very active in studying such options, and some countries have already prepared the necessary legislative and institutional groundwork for this transition. India plans to install as much as 5,000 MW of private power capacity over the 1990–95 period, and similar plans are under way in Indonesia, Malaysia, Thailand and the Philippines. In Pakistan, the 1,292 MW Hub Power Project is now under construction, with a further 2,000 MW of private power in smaller plants currently under consideration. Jamaica is undertaking a BOT (Build–Operate–Transfer) power project. In Sri Lanka, a private company has been distributing power since the early eighties and significant efficiency and service improvements have been observed during this period.

Options for private and cooperative ownership of energy enterprises could include both local and foreign participation as well as joint ventures. As long as a given regulatory framework prevails, it can be argued that the form of ownership (private and public) would not by itself affect operating efficiency. A first step towards decentralization could be for government-owned power enterprises to competitively contract out activities or functions better handled by others. Many companies already subcontract various construction-related activities. Some portions of the billing and collection process, or routine maintenance, can also be subcontracted. Among the advantages of such arrangements are lower costs and greater programming flexibility.

There are also opportunities for decentralization on a spatial basis. For example, larger countries may have independent regional power grids. Power distribution companies could be separate by municipality, with perhaps limited overlap in some fringe franchise areas, and have the right to purchase from various suppliers, when feasible. If private participation were allowed, one advantage might be that at least the large power consumers could also be legitimate shareholders who would be concerned not only with service efficiency, but also with the financial viability of the company.

Power generation also has potential for efficiency improvements through divestiture. While the bulk power transmission and distribution functions might be regarded as having more natural monopoly common carrier-type characteristics, this is not so with generation. In fact, there is substantial scope for competition in power generation with independent (perhaps foreign-owned enclave) producers selling to a central grid, as in the case of large industrial cogeneration. Free-standing generation companies would put up all or part of the capital and be paid only out of revenues from power sold at guaranteed prices. This would result in the desirable de-emphasis on large lumpy capital-intensive projects.

The case of Africa is an important exception to the above policy of decentralization. The problem in Africa is that electricity generation is too decentralized, and hence inefficient. Some measures to remedy this situation include: (1) modernizing and improving the efficiency of existing power systems; (2) developing and using local and regional primary energy for large-scale generation; (3) developing grid systems and encouraging regional interconnections; (4) recognizing the need for a national and regional master plan for electrification; and (5) putting into place sound energy policies, standards and regulations that improve environmental aspects of energy use (Boutros 1991).

During the Cold War period, the power systems of the Eastern European nations were interconnected. Development plans for the system were coordinated by the Central Dispatching Organization (CDO), located in Prague. Many of the nations had plans to construct nuclear power plants. However, because of the persisting input capacity deficiencies and unreliable equipment, significant efforts are currently being made to enable connection to the 330,000 MWe Western European grid (UCPTE). Advantages to an East–West grid are outlined by Jaszay and Levai: (1) a mutually advantageous energy exchange through improved electricity generation and utilization will be financially beneficial for both East and West. For example, the peak of an 'all European' load can be reduced by 1.5 to 2.5 per cent (or even 5 to 8 per cent) because of the time zone differences between regions. Maximum consumption occurs at a different time in Eastern and Western European countries. Seasonal and daily fluctuations in energy demand may also increase availability of energy resources for both regions; (2) an integrated grid permits savings of 10–15 per cent in spinning reserves, generating capacity, compared with the total reserve required when the two systems operate independently; and (3) it would be easier to provide mutual assistance in emergencies (Jaszay and Levai 1991).

4.7. SED Options Matrix

In summary the Table 1.6 shows the impacts of the various options on the three elements of sustainable development. While efficient supply-side options (i.e.,

Table 1.6   *SED options matrix*

Option	Economic	Environmental	Social
Supply Efficiency	+	+	
End-Use Efficiency	+	+	+
Advanced Technologies	–	+	+
Renewables	–	+	+
Pricing Policy	+	+	+/–
Privatization/Decentralization	+	+/–	+/

reductions in transmission and distribution losses), have clear economic gains in terms of savings in capital investments and environmental benefits from reductions in greenhouse gas emissions that result from increased electricity supply, they do not have obvious social benefits. Efficient end-use options as shown in the case of an efficient fuelwood stove have benefits relating to all three elements. Although advanced technologies such as clean coal combustion technologies are essential for reducing air pollutants such as CO_2 and NO_x which cause respiratory diseases and reduce productivity, many developing countries cannot afford such high-cost technologies. Likewise renewable energy sources also provide environmental and social benefits by reducing a country's dependence on traditional fossil fuels. However, in terms of generating costs renewables are more expensive than fossil fuels.

5. CONCLUSIONS

Increasing levels of energy-related environmental degradation in both industrialized and developing countries have led to a recognition of the need for improved energy options for sustainable development. The primary objective is to maximize net economic welfare of energy development while maintaining the stock of economic, ecological and sociocultural assets for future generations and providing a safety net to meet basic needs and protect the poor. Sustainable energy options may be identified using a comprehensive and integrated framework for analysis and decision-making that takes into account multiple actors, multiple criteria, multilevel decision-making and many impediments and constraints. In the past the principle planning objective of energy development has been to meet the anticipated needs at least economic cost. Now, environmental and social concerns also must be incorporated early at the regional and sectoral planning stages in order to ensure sustainable energy development. However, difficulties in valuing certain environmental and social impacts of energy development and the large number of options, may require techniques of multi-criteria analysis (MCA), rather than conventional cost–benefit analysis (CBA) methods, to provide a range of feasible alternatives as opposed to one best solution. Using MCA, 'win–win' energy options that satisfy all three elements of sustainable development (i.e., economic, environmental and social) may be identified and after having done so, tradeoffs can be made from other available sustainable energy options.

Dealing with energy-related environmental and social issues will require increased cooperation between industrialized countries and developing countries. Developing countries have limited capabilities to address global environmental concerns. Without enhanced flows of incremental technical and financial resources from industrialized countries, positive prospects for energy development that will move the world towards a more sustainable development path will be hampered.

NOTE

1. This renewables-intensive energy scenario assumes an eightfold increase in world economic output by 2050, as projected by the Response Strategies Working Group of the Intergovernmental Plan on Climate Change (IPCC). In this forecast the demand for electricity increases 265 per cent between 1985 and 2050, in spite of a marked increase in energy efficiency.

REFERENCES

Ahmed, Kulsum (1994), *Renewable Energy Technologies: A Review of Status and Costs of Selected Technologies*, The World Bank Technical Paper No. 240, Washington, DC: The World Bank.

Anderson, Dennis (1992), *The Energy Industry and Global Warming: New Roles for International Aid*, London: Overseas Development Institute.

Anderson, Dennis (1993), *Energy Efficiency and the Economics of Pollution Abatement*, Washington, DC: The World Bank.

Anderson, Dennis (1994), *Energy, Environment and Economy: Complementaries and Conflicts in the Search for Sustainable Growth*, Washington DC: The World Bank.

Anderson, Dennis and Kulsum Ahmed (1993), 'Where We Stand with Renewable Energy', *Finance and Development*, June.

Anderson, Dennis and Catherine Bird (1992), 'Carbon Accumulations and Technical Progress—A Simulation Study of Costs', *Oxford Bulletin of Economics and Statistics*, Vol. 54, No. 1, February.

Anderson, Dennis and William Cavendish (1992), *Efficiency and Substitution in Pollution Abatement: Three Case Studies*, World Bank Discussion Paper No.186, Washington, DC: The World Bank.

Asian Development Bank (1994), *Environmental Considerations in Energy Development*, Manila: ADB, May.

Berrie, T.W. (1987), 'Power System Planning Under Electricity Spot Pricing', *IEEE Transactions on Power Systems*, Vol. PWRS-2, No. 3, August.

Besant-Jones, John E. et al. (1990), *Review of Electricity Tariffs in Developing Countries*

During the 1980s, IEN Series Paper No.32, Washington, DC: The World Bank, November.

Boutros, John Gindi (1991), 'Electric Power in Africa—Issues and Responses to Environmental Concerns', in Ferrari et al. (eds), *Energy and the Environment in the 21st Century*, Cambridge, Mass: The MIT Press.

Bronocki, L.Y., B. Doron and M. Lax (1992), 'Geothermal Energy', draft, World Energy Conference Committee on Renewable Energy Resources, April.

Clark, William, C. (1991), 'Energy and the Environment: Strategic Perspectives on Policy Design', in Ferrari et al. (eds), *Energy and the Environment in the 21st Century*, Cambridge, Mass: The MIT Press.

Darnell, J.R. (1992), 'Solar Energy', draft, World Energy Conference Committee on Renewable Resources, April.

Darnell, Jack R. et al. (1992), *Renewable Energy Resources: Opportunities and Constraints 1990–2020*, World Energy Council, 15th Congress, Interim Report, September.

Del Hieffo, Eduardo (1991), 'Policy Making Pertaining to the Environmental Impact of Energy Use in Latin American and Caribbean Countries', in Ferrari et al. (eds), *Energy and the Environment in the 21st Century*, Cambridge, Mass: The MIT Press.

Dormstadter, Joel and Robert W. Fri (1992), 'Interconnections Between Energy and the Environment: Global Challenges', *Energy Environment Annual Review*.

Edens J. J., P.R. Bapat, S. de Salvo Brito and A.A. Eberhard (1992), 'Biomass Energy', draft, World Energy Conference Committee on Renewable Energy Resources, May.

Elliott, Philip and Roger Booth (1990), *Sustainable Biomass Energy*, London: Shell International Petroleum Company Ltd, London: December.

Ferrari, Nancy, Jefferson Tester and David Wood, (eds) (1991), *Energy and the Environment in the 21st Century*, Cambridge, Mass: The MIT Press.

Flavin, C. and N. Lenssen (1993), *Reshaping the Power Industry*, Washington, DC: World Watch Institute, September.

Geller, H.S. et al. (1988), 'Electricity Conservation in Brazil: Potential and Progress', *Energy*, Vol. 13, No. 6.

Glicksman, Leon R. (1991), 'Building Systems', in Ferrari et al. (eds), *Energy and the Environment in the 21st Century*, Cambridge, Mass: The MIT Press.

Global Environment Facility (1992a), *Economic Costs of Carbon Dioxide Reduction Strategies*, Working Paper Series No. III, Washington, DC: World Bank, UNDP, and UNEP, September.

Global Environment Facility (1992b), 'Incremental Costs and the GEF', memo to participants in Workshop on Measuring Incremental Costs for Climate Change, Washington DC: World Bank, November.

Global Environment Facility (1992c), 'Report by the Chairman to the December 1992 Participants' Meeting', Washington, DC.

International Atomic Energy Agency (IAEA) (1991), 'Senior Expert Symposium on Electricity and the Environment', Helsinki: May. (Key Issues papers 3 and 4 and background papers.)

International Energy Agency (1993), *World Energy Outlook: To The Year 2010*, Paris: IEA/OECD.

International Energy Agency (1994), *World Energy Outlook*, Paris: OECD.

Jaszay, T. and A. Levai (1991), 'Present and Future Electric Power Systems in Eastern Europe: The Possibilities of a Broader Cooperation', in Ferrari et al. (eds), *Energy and the Environment in the 21st Century*, Cambridge, Mass: The MIT Press.

Jefferson, Michael (1992), 'The Evolution of Global Energy Demand', 7th International Energy Conference, Royal Institute of International Affairs, The British Institute of Energy Economics and The International Association of Energy Economics, London: December.

Johansson, T., Henry Kelly, Amulya Reddy and Robert Williams (1992), *'Renewables for Fuels and Electricity'*, Island Press.

Johansson, T. et al. (1989), *Electricity*, Lund, Sweden: Lund University Press.

Khatib, H. and M. Munasinghe (1992), 'Electricity, The Environment, and Sustainable World Development', World Energy Council, 15th Congress, Madrid: September.

Lawrence Berkeley Laboratory, Energy Analysis Program (1991), *1991 Annual Report*, Berkeley, CA.

Lenssen, Nicholas (1992), *Empowering Development: The New Energy Equation*, Worldwatch Paper 111, Washington, DC: Worldwatch Institute, November.

Levine, Mark D., Ashok Gadgil, Steven Meyers, Jayant Sathaye, Jack Stafurik and Tom Wilbanks (1991), *Energy Efficiency, Developing Nations and Eastern Europe: A Report to the U.S. Working Group on Global Energy Efficiency*, Washington, DC: International Institute for Energy Conservation, June.

Levine, Mark D. and S. Meyers (1992), 'The Contribution of Energy Efficiency to Sustainable Development', Natural Resources Forum, New York, February.

Maler, K.G. (1990), 'Economic Theory and Environmental Degradation: A Survey of Some Problems', *Revista de Analisis Economico*, Vol. 5, No. 2, pp. 7–17.

Meier, P. and M. Munasinghe (1994), *Incorporating Power Concerns into Power System Planning—A Case Study of Sri Lanka*, Washington, DC: The World Bank.

Moore, E.A. and G. Smith (1994), *Capital Expenditures for Electric Power in the Developing Countries in the 1990s*, Industry and Energy Department Working Paper, Energy Series Paper No. 21, London, February.

Munasinghe, Mohan (1990a), *Energy Analysis and Policy*, London: Butterworths.

Munasinghe, Mohan (1990b), *Electric Power Economics*, London: Butterworths.

Munasinghe, Mohan (1991), 'Electricity and the Environment in Developing Countries with Special Reference to Asia', in Ferrari et al. (eds), *Energy and the Environment in the 21st Century*, Cambridge, Mass: The MIT Press.

Munasinghe, Mohan (1992), 'Efficient Management of the Power Sector in Developing Countries', *Energy Policy*, February.

Munasinghe, Mohan (1993a), *Environmental Economics and Sustainable Development*, The World Bank Environmental Paper No. 3, Washington, DC: The World Bank.

Munasinghe, Mohan (1993b), 'The Economist's Approach to Sustainable Development', *Finance and Development*, December.

Munasinghe, Mohan (1993c), 'South–North Partnership To Meet Energy—Environmental Challenges of The 21st Century', *New Electricity 21: Power Industry and Management Strategies for The Twenty First Century*, Paris: IEA/OECD.

Murray, C.H. and M.R. de Montalambert (1992), 'Wood, Still a Neglected Energy Source', *Energy Policy*, Vol. 20, No. 6, June.

Office of Technology Assessment (OTA) (1991), *Fueling Development*, Washington, DC: Government Printing Office.

OLADE (Latin American Organization for Energy) (1993), *Tables and Statistics*.

Organization for Economic Co-Operation and Development (1989), *Projected Costs of Generating Electricity from Power Stations for Commissioning in the Period 1995–*

2000, Paris: OECD.

Pearce, D.W. and K. Turner (1990), *Economics of Natural Resources and the Environment*, Baltimore: Johns Hopkins University Press.

Pearson, Peter (1993), 'Electricity in The Third World', Surrey University Energy Economics Discussion Paper Series, SEEDS 68, May.

Rosenfield, Arthur H. (1991), 'Energy-Efficient Buildings in a Warming World', in Ferrari et al. (eds), *Energy and the Environment in the 21st Century*, Cambridge, Mass: The MIT Press.

Saunders, Robert J and Sunita Gandhi (1994), *Global Energy Paths: Energy Policy Prescriptions For Sustaining The Environment*, Washington, DC: The World Bank.

Schweppe, F., M. Caramanis, R. Tabors and R. Bohn (1988), *Spot Pricing of Electricity*, New York: Kluwer Publishing.

Solow, R. (1986), 'On the International Allocation of Natural Resources', *Scandinavian Journal of Economics*, Vol. 88, No. 1, pp. 141–9.

Spash, Clive L. and A. Young (1994), 'Sources of Energy and the Environment', Discussion Paper in Ecological Economics, EERG, Dept. of Economics, University of Stirling, March.

Strange, D.L.P. (1991), 'Ocean Energy', draft, World Energy Conference Committee on Renewable Energy Resources, September.

Strange, D.L.P. (1992), 'Small Hydro', draft, World Energy Conference Committee on Renewable Resources, August.

Strong, Maurice F. (1992), 'Energy, Environment and Development', *Energy Policy*, Vol. 20, No. 6, June.

Sullivan, J.B. (1988), 'The A.I.D. Experience with Independent Power Generation', paper presented at the Central American and Caribbean Workshop on Electric Power, San Jose, Costa Rica, August.

United Nations Conference on Environment and Development (1992), 'Protection of the Atmosphere', Preparatory Committee for UNCED, New York, 2 March–3 April.

US Congress Office of Technology Assessment (1992), *Fueling Development: Energy Technologies for Developing Countries*, OTA-E-516, Washington, DC: US Government Printing Office, April.

US Industrial Outlook (1994): *Forecasts for Selected Manufacturing and Service Industries*, Washington, DC: US Department of Commerce, January.

USAID (1988), *Power Shortages in Developing Countries*, Washington, DC, March.

Van Wijk, A.J.M., J.P. Coelingh and W.C. Turkenburg (1992), 'Wind Energy', draft, World Energy Conference Committee on Renewable Resources, July.

White, David (1991), 'Electric Power Systems', in Ferrari et al. (eds), *Energy and the Environment in the 21st Century*, Cambridge, Mass: The MIT Press.

Winje, Dietmar (1991a), 'Electric Power and the Developing Economies', in Ferrari et al. (eds), *Energy and the Environment in the 21st Century*, Cambridge, Mass: The MIT Press.

Winje, Dietmar (1991b), 'Electric Power for Developing Nations', in Ferrari et al. (eds), *Energy and the Environment in the 21st Century*, Cambridge, Mass: The MIT Press.

World Bank (1991a), *The Evolution, Situation, and Prospects of the Electric Power Sector in the LAC Countries*, LACTD Report No. 7, Washington, DC, August.

World Bank (1991b), *Commercial Energy Efficiency and the Environment*, ENVPR Report, Washington, DC, August.

World Bank (1992a), *Development and the Environment: World Development Report*

1992, Washington DC: Oxford University Press for the World Bank.

World Bank (1992b), *The World Bank's Role in the Electric Power Sector—Policies for Effective Institutional, Regulatory and Financial Reform'*, Washington, DC: Industry and Energy Department, The World Bank, March.

World Bank (1994a), *Global Economic Prospects and The Developing Countries*, Washington, DC: The World Bank.

World Bank (1994b), *World Development Report 1994: Infrastructure For Development*, Washington, DC: Oxford University Press for the World Bank.

World Commission on Environment and Development (WCED)(1987), *Our Common Future*, London: Oxford University Press.

World Energy Council (WEC) (1993), *Energy For Tomorrow's World*, New York: St. Martin's Press.

World Resources Institute (1994), *World Resources 1994–95: A Guide To The Global Environment*, New York: Oxford University Press.

2. Trading in Greenhouse Gas Emissions: Implications for ASEAN and Korea

**Andrew Chisholm, Alan Moran
and John Zeitsch**

1. INTRODUCTION

At the United Nations Conference on Environment and Development, held in Rio de Janeiro in June of 1992, 154 countries and the European Community formally signed the Global Framework Climate Change Convention. The stated objective of the Convention was 'stabilisation of greenhouse gas concentrations in the atmosphere at a level which would prevent dangerous anthropogenic interference with the climate system'.

Carbon dioxide is the principal greenhouse gas. According to the 1990 scientific assessment by the Inter-governmental Panel on Climate Change, stabilization of carbon dioxide concentrations in the atmosphere at present-day levels would require reductions in annual emissions from human sources of more than 60 per cent. The less onerous scenario of maintaining atmospheric emissions at 1990 levels would lead to an eventual increase in atmospheric concentrations of about 50 per cent.

Any action to stabilize carbon dioxide concentrations will involve large-scale changes in production processes, consumer behaviour and international trade. Even if annual global emissions are only stabilized at 1990 levels by the year 2000, the potential costs for individual countries are high. Stabilization at 1990 levels in the year 2000 would require a 20 per cent reduction in global carbon dioxide emissions relative to a 'business-as-usual' scenario. The costs of reducing fossil-fuel use would be particularly high for countries in the Asian region because of their resource-dependent economies and rapid growth in fossil-fuel use.

The 1992 Global Framework Convention on Climate Change recognized that developing nations would incur unacceptably high costs if they were obliged to reduce rates of growth in the use of fossil fuels. Consequently the Convention only committed OECD countries to reducing their emissions of greenhouse gases. Even if reductions in emissions were to be limited to OECD countries, there would be spillover effects on the Asian region through reduced demand for fossil fuels and a general decline in worldwide economic activity.

The costs of emissions abatement activity in the OECD, and the spillover effects on the Asian region, could be reduced if the OECD were able to fund greenhouse gas emissions reductions programmes in other countries, as an alternative to undertaking emissions abatement activity themselves. If it could be implemented, a global system of trade in emissions permits has the potential to deliver effective emissions abatement at much lower cost.

In this chapter, a multi-country, multi-industry general equilibrium model called WEDGE is used to assess the potential economic costs of different global emissions reduction arrangements. Effects on the ASEAN countries and Korea are examined in particular. Four policy scenarios are evaluated. In the first two scenarios, carbon taxes are imposed to force individual country emissions abatement targets. The last two scenarios evaluate the effects of introducing a trading regime for emission permits.

2. TRADABLE PERMITS AND EMISSIONS TAXES

2.1. Economic Instruments

All the scenarios evaluated in this chapter use economic instruments, such as carbon taxes and tradable permits, to force reductions in carbon dioxide emissions. Taxing carbon emitters would be an efficient means of reducing a country's level of carbon dioxide emissions, if it were administratively practicable. It would give incentives to emitters to find low-cost ways of abating and would give users of carbon-intensive products and services incentives to find cheaper alternatives.

An alternative policy approach to emissions abatement would involve issuing tradable permits to emit carbon dioxide. International proposals making use of this approach generally revolve around some form of bilateral or multilateral trade between countries in rights to pollute or emissions permits. The Global Framework Climate Change Convention makes express provision for such arrangements by allowing for joint implementation of abatement policies and measures.[1]

Both emissions taxes and tradable permits provide price incentives for emitters to abate without dictating how that abatement is to occur. Emitters within each country are left free to choose the most cost-effective means of reducing emissions. Economy-wide cost savings are obtained, because the burden of abatement action is shifted on to those who have a range of low-cost-abatement options. Generally, market-based price signals provide a more cost-effective means of emissions control than regulation of industry technology, which is of necessity inflexible and detailed.[2]

A carbon dioxide emissions tax would be levied either directly on carbon dioxide emitters or on the inputs that generate carbon dioxide emissions, such as coal, oil and gas. The tax could be seen as representing the additional costs of global warming borne by the world as a whole as a result of energy use in individual countries. It would internalize pollution costs to individual industries and countries; and this cost would then be factored into economic decision-making by private individuals and firms.

Under a system of internationally traded emissions permits, countries would receive a quota of emissions 'permits' entitling firms and industries in each country to emit carbon dioxide. The sum of the emissions allowed under a permit system would be equal to a pre-determined level, for example, 80 per cent of a country's current emissions. The permits would then be traded on the open market both within and across national borders. Countries wishing to increase their emissions beyond their initial permit allocation would need to buy permits from other countries. Those nations with a high cost of emissions abatement would be able to purchase emissions credits from countries with a low cost of abatement, under an agreed set of international protocols.[3]

International trading of emissions permits would most likely result in substantial transfers of wealth between buyers and sellers. Thus, the initial allocation of permits would create winners and losers within a context of an overall efficient outcome.

2.2. Previous Analyses of Global Carbon Dioxide Emissions Taxes and Permits

A number of previous of studies have evaluated the economic costs of carbon taxes and tradable emissions permits in different countries using global economic models. Manne and Richels (1991) estimated the macroeconomic impacts of a tax on fossil fuels designed to curb carbon dioxide emissions in five world regions. They assumed that, through the imposition of the tax, industrialized countries (which include Eastern Europe's former socialist countries) would stabilize carbon dioxide emissions at their 1990 levels by the year 2000, and subsequently reduce them by 20 per cent by the year 2020. They also assumed that developing countries, faced with intense pressure to maintain economic growth, would only limit the growth of emissions to twice their 1990 levels.

According to Manne and Richels, the estimated cost of these actions for the United States is roughly 3.0 per cent of GDP by the year 2030. The former USSR and Eastern European countries experience a greater GDP loss (nearly 5.0 per cent), while China, despite doubling its carbon dioxide emissions, bears the greatest burden (more than 6.0 per cent in 2030 and more than 10.0 per cent by the year 2100). Other OECD losses and Rest of the World losses for the same time period are about 2.0 per cent.

Kverndokk (1993) used the same database but employed different abatement assumptions. He estimated costs and outcomes of a tradable emissions permit scenario where each region was given an initial level of emissions equal to 80 per cent of its 1990 level from the year 2000. Each region's abatement cost functions were used to estimate the tax rates required to bring about its required reductions. By equalizing tax rates across countries for a specific level of global abatement, Kverndokk was able to devise a cost-effective carbon dioxide emissions scenario that had regions with the lowest incremental cost abating the most. This 'tax rate' was also assumed to equal the market value of emissions permits for each tradable permits scenario analysed.[4]

Kverndokk, like Manne and Richels, found that China would be hardest hit by the equal percentage emissions reduction programme. China's estimated losses in GDP relative to a business-as-usual scenario range from 9.9 per cent in the year 2000 to 14.2 per cent in 2050. These are higher cost levels than estimated by Manne and Richels because China is forced to reduce emissions levels by 20 per cent below 1990 levels rather than allow them to grow to twice that of 1990 levels. Kverndokk estimated that the Rest of the World would bear the second-greatest burden (losses ranging from 5.0 per cent to 4.4 per cent). Again, Manne and Richels had much lower costs for the Rest of the World because they assumed this region was allowed to double its emissions levels. Kverndokk's estimates of losses in the United States (2.8 to 3.9 per cent) were similar to those found by Manne and Richels.

Having estimated the cost of equal percentage reductions, Kverndokk calculated the magnitude of income transfers associated with sales of permits under different permit allocation rules. Not surprisingly, an initial allocation of permits based on GDP favoured the United States and other OECD nations, while a population-based allocation rule favoured China and the Rest of the World.

If permits are initially allocated according to GDP, Kverndokk estimated that in the year 2000, China, because of its high level of emissions relative to the number of permits it receives, would be required to purchase permits. The sums involved ($370 billion) are roughly equivalent to China's GDP in 1990! Alternatively, using a population-based allocation rule, Kverndokk estimated the income transfer to China in the year 2000 at $269 billion. The transfer from the developed to the developing nations as a whole would be US$1,360 billion.

3. OVERVIEW OF MODELLING APPROACH EMPLOYED

The model of the world used in this chapter is a computable general equilibrium model called WEDGE. It was developed by the Australian Industry Commission to assess the impact of reducing carbon dioxide emissions on the Australian economy in comparison with other countries and world regions. Its structure is based upon the OECD Walras macroeconomic model (OECD 1990), but incorporates the fuel substitution possibilities contained in the GREEN model developed by the OECD for analysing the economic effects of global greenhouse gas emissions (OECD 1991).

Simply stated, the model brings together the relevant relationships between demand for certain goods, supply factors and income effects. For any given policy change (for example, a new tax), the model predicts subsequent changes that will occur and what the impacts will be on various national economies and on specific product and input sectors in each economy.

The model explicitly allows for trade in different commodities between countries. It also has a household sector in each country purchasing commodities from 32 industries. Base data for each country in the model is taken from input–output data for the latest year at the time the model was built. The databases are updated to reflect a consistent set of 1988 trade flows based on UN data. Money values for each country are converted to 1988 US dollars.

Elasticities capturing the behavioural responses of producers and consumers are taken from surveys of international literature. The model takes into account the ability of producers to substitute one fuel for another in response to relative price movements. In addition, as fuels, labour and capital are all substitutable for one another at the margin, the model depicts the extent of this substitution where relative prices change or demand is modified. Capital and labour substitution for fuel and energy, together with technological change and adaptation, are the primary means of achieving improvements in energy efficiency.

The model estimates the macroeconomic effects of reducing carbon dioxide emissions in nine countries/regions. For each country or region, the model identifies the effects of reductions in carbon dioxide emissions on national income, household income, industrial activity and international trade. Regions, industries and commodity groups contained in the WEDGE model are shown in Table 2.1. The model keeps track of carbon dioxide emissions produced as a result of economic activity. It evaluates the following four energy-related sectors: (1) coal; (2) oil and gas; (3) petroleum and coal products; and (4) electricity, gas and water. The first three sectors represent commodities that actually generate carbon dioxide when they are burned. The fourth sector is not a carbon dioxide emitting commodity *per se*, but rather, generates emissions from combustion of fossil fuels during production. The amount of emissions from this sector depends primarily on the structure of the electricity-generation industry within each country or region.

Industries can minimize the additional costs of any limits on emissions by choosing an appropriate mix of fuel inputs, using more fuel- and energy-efficient production technologies or by reducing output. Consumers, in turn, can adjust their purchases in response to changes in the price of fossil fuels and commodi-

Table 2.1   *Regions, industries and commodity groups contained in the*
                 WEDGE model

Regions

1.	Australia	6.	Korea
2.	New Zealand	7.	European Community
3.	Canada	8.	ASEAN
4.	United States	9.	Rest of the World
5.	Japan		

Industries and Commodity Groups

1. Agriculture
   — Paddy rice
   — Non-grain crops
   — Wheat
   — Other grains
   — Wool
   — Other livestock

2. Food Products
   — Meat products
   — Milk products
   — Other food products
   — Beverages and tobacco

3. Manufacturing Non-Metallic
   — Spinning, dyeing and textiles
   — Wearing apparel
   — Leather, fur and related products
   — Lumber and wood products
   — Pulp, paper and printing
   — Chemicals, rubber and plastic
   — Petroleum and coal products
   — Non-metallic mineral products

4. Other Manufacturing
   — Primary iron and steel
   — Other metals
   — Transport industries
   — Machinery and equipment
   — Other manufacturing

5. Resources
   — Forestry
   — Fishing
   — Coal
   — Oil and gas production
   — Other minerals

6. Services
   — Electricity, gas supply and water
   — Construction
   — Trade and transport
   — Other services (private)
   — Other services(government)
   — Other services (ownership of dwellings)

---

ties using high proportions of fossil fuels in their production. Along with producers, they can choose between commodities from both domestic and imported sources. In this way, the model captures changes in demand for exported and imported goods and effects on international competitiveness for each country or region.

Flows to and from the government sector are separated out in the model. Revenues from taxes (or emission sales) are offset by reductions in income taxes in the country raising the tax or obtaining the sales revenue. Thus, the model captures the partial offset to the costs of an emissions tax or purchase of permits caused by lower efficiency losses from income taxes.

The model is a comparative static, general equilibrium model in which the results represent the economy after a number of years of adjustment when there has been sufficient time for the impacts of the limits on carbon dioxide emissions to have been absorbed. Producers are able to adjust their capital stock, although the national capital stock and the level of aggregate investment is assumed to be fixed. Wage rates vary independently of the consumer price index so as to maintain a fixed employment rate. Nominal exchange rates are assumed to be fixed. The model also assumes that the overall economic structure prevailing for each country in 1988 applies in 2000.

Lastly, because the model shows the effects of a policy change some time after a policy shock is introduced, it does not describe the path of transition or the dynamic effects of the policy on productivity, or economic growth rates in the intervening period. Consequently, the economic costs of emissions abatement are likely to be understated. Chisholm et al. (1994) use the model to estimate the costs of greenhouse gas emissions control. For a more detailed discussion of the model, see Jomini et al. (1991).

4. COSTS AND POLICY IMPLICATIONS OF STABILIZING CARBON DIOXIDE EMISSIONS USING VARIOUS ECONOMIC INSTRUMENTS

The model is used in this chapter to examine the effects of stabilization of carbon dioxide emissions at 1990 levels by the year 2000. This stabilization option, it will be recalled, is one of the less onerous options considered in the IPCC report. A variant of it, stabilization by OECD countries alone, is both a common interpretation of the Framework Convention and a policy goal adopted in principle by several OECD countries.

4.1. Costs of All Countries Reducing Emissions by 20 Per Cent with a Carbon Tax and No Emissions Trade

On a global level, stabilization represents an effective reduction in emissions of 20 per cent. Table 2.2 presents the estimated macroeconomic effects of a uniform 20 per cent reduction in carbon dioxide emissions in every country.[5] Emissions reductions are brought about by imposing a tax on the carbon content of fossil fuels.[6] Overall, there is a loss in world net domestic product of 0.78 per cent.

The tax rate necessary to bring about a 20 per cent reduction in emissions, and thus the incremental cost of abatement, ranges from $17 in the United States to $97 in New Zealand. This range reflects differences among countries with respect to such factors as:

Table 2.2   *Estimated macroeconomic effects of imposing a carbon tax to reduce emissions by 20 per cent in each country and stabilize global emissions at 1990 levels in the year 2000*

	Annual percentage change in real national consumption	Tax per tonne of CO_2 (US$ 1988)	Percentage change in emissions levels
Japan	−0.19	$50	−20
Korea	−1.96	$75	−20
ASEAN	−1.72	$54	−20
Australia	−1.07	$30	−20
New Zealand	−1.65	$97	−20
Canada	−0.35	$34	−20
United States	−0.38	$17	−20
European Union	−0.49	$71	−20
Rest of the World	−1.63	$58	−20

- the ease of inter-fuel substitution;
- the ease of substitutability between fossil fuels and labour and capital;
- the flexibility of demand for energy services in the household sector; and
- the relative share of abatement action required by industry and households.

Living standards, as measured by real national consumption, are projected to decline in all countries and regions as a result of the reduction in carbon dioxide emissions. Korea, ASEAN and New Zealand suffer the largest declines in real national consumption, while Japan is hurt the least (−0.19 per cent). In addition to being affected by the size of the required tax rate in each country, the declines in living standards are influenced by:

- the intensity of use of fossil fuels in the domestic economy;
- the importance of fossil fuels to the export sector.

Korea experiences the largest decline in real national consumption. While Korea is similar to Japan in being largely a fossil-fuel importer, it does not appear to have Japan's ability to achieve low-cost substitution between fuels. Korea's economy also appears to be more highly dependent than that of Japan on fossil fuels, its ratio of carbon to net domestic product being four times Japan's. Nuclear energy supplies a significant proportion of energy consumption (14 per cent), but unlike Japan, natural gas is used very little and the economy is dependent on oil imports and coal. A higher tax rate of $74 per tonne of carbon dioxide is required to force abatement.

The ASEAN countries also experience a large fall in real consumption. This is due to the loss of oil export markets and the countries relatively high dependency on fossil fuels generally. Australia has the second-lowest tax rate, yet it suffers a loss in real national consumption of more than one per cent. This loss is attributable to Australia's large fossil-fuel and metal-processing export sector. Other countries impose direct tax exports of fossil fuels from Australia; and, within Australia, higher-cost energy inputs raise the costs of energy-intensive manufacturing for export. Consequently Australia experiences a decline in its trade competitiveness.

The negative economic effects of reducing emissions are relatively low in the United States. The US has a high usage of fossil fuels in relation to its income, reflecting the country's low rates of fuel taxes. It has, therefore, a wide range of abatement opportunities available at relatively low additional tax rates.

There is a wide range of low-cost abatement opportunities in Rest of the World countries (including developing nations, former centrally planned economies (CPEs), Organization of Petroleum-Exporting Countries (OPEC) countries, China and India). Low-cost abatement possibilities are readily available in the former European CPEs, but costs are much greater for the OPEC countries which would lose considerable export volumes and see their export prices fall. However, with a 20 per cent reduction in emissions, all of these low-cost abatement opportunities are used up and countries in the Rest of the World are forced to undertake high-cost emissions abatement activities which severely impact on real consumption levels.

4.2. Effects on Developing Economies of the OECD Alone Enforcing Emissions Restraints to Stabilize Emissions at 1990 Levels

Recognizing the costs likely to be incurred by developing countries, the 1990 Framework Convention on Climate Change obliges OECD countries only to implement polices to reduce greenhouse gas emissions. If each OECD country were to stabilize its own emissions at 1990 levels in the year 2000, using a carbon tax, the estimated annual global loss in GDP is moderated from 0.79 per cent for a global stabilization target, to 0.11 per cent. However, restricting emissions abatement to the OECD also diminishes global emissions reductions from 20 to 5 per cent of year 2000 levels.

Apart from avoiding the need to reduce emissions in developing countries, restricting emissions abatement activity to the OECD may have some positive spin-offs for the Asian region. As developing countries would face no carbon tax impost, competitive opportunities could open up for lower-cost provision of goods and services formerly provided by OECD countries. However, results from the WEDGE model indicate that even if developing countries remain fully exempt from the global abatement provisions, Asian countries are still likely to face diminished levels of income.

This outcome occurs because the developing nations would face reductions in demand for their products as a result of diminished income levels in OECD markets. Demand for fossil-fuel energy exports would be severely curtailed. In addition, lower overall demand in OECD countries would feed back into reduced

*Table 2.3   Estimated macroeconomic effects of imposing a carbon tax to
stabilize carbon dioxide emissions at 1990 levels in the year
2000 in OECD countries alone*

	Annual percentage change in real national consumption	Tax per tonne of CO_2 (US\$ 1988)	Percentage change in emissions levels
Japan	-0.20	\$53	-22
Korea	-0.12	\$0	0
ASEAN	-0.70	\$0	0
Australia	-1.07	\$32	-21
New Zealand	-0.73	\$42	-12
Canada	0.01	\$7	-6
United States	-0.12	\$6	-11
European Union	-0.06	\$18	-8
Rest of the World	-0.07	\$0	0

trading opportunities for developing countries.

Individual country results for a 1990 stabilization scenario in the OECD are shown in Table 2.3. The high costs that would fall on Asian economies if they were to reduce their emissions by 20 per cent are considerably moderated by confining abatement reductions to the OECD, but these losses are not eliminated. In the case of Korea, a loss of consumption amounting to 1.96 per cent of real national consumption is reduced to a loss of 0.12 per cent. For the ASEAN countries, the loss of 1.72 per cent becomes a loss of 0.70 per cent. For Korea, the heavy decline in exports expected where the country must reduce its own carbon dioxide emissions (3.72 per cent) is cut back to a decline of 0.21 per cent. ASEAN countries actually see their exports rise slightly as they displace OECD production, though the higher cost of OECD imports prevents that rise generating a net increase in real consumption.

4.3. Potential Gains from OECD Countries Trading in Emissions Quotas and Purchasing Emissions Credits from Developing Nations

Improved outcomes for countries in the Asian region can emerge if emissions quotas are traded within the OECD region and the OECD countries can purchase emissions abatement credits from developing nations. Developing countries would benefit from emissions trading because:

- OECD economies are less severely depressed when they have the flexibility to buy and sell emissions quotas—this reduces the spillover costs for developing nations;
- Developing countries can also take advantage of a market for emissions and sell emissions credits in return for undertaking emissions abatement

Table 2.4   *Estimated macroeconomic effects of an emissions trading system where OECD countries stabilize their own emissions or purchase emissions credits from other countries*

	Annual percentage change in real national consumption	Permit price per tonne of CO_2 (US$ 1988)	Percentage change in emissions levels	Sale of Permits (Mt of CO2)
Japan	−0.04	$5	−4	−195
Korea	−0.06	$5	−2	6
ASEAN	−0.13	$5	−3	8
Australia	−0.29	$5	−5	−46
New Zealand	−0.11	$5	−2	−3
Canada	−0.01	$5	−4	−10
United States	−0.11	$5	−10	−96
European Union	−0.04	$5	−2	−145
Rest of the World	0.03	$5	−3	480

activity.

The economic effects of implementing a tradable emission regime within OECD countries and between the OECD and developing countries are illustrated in Table 2.4. The analysis is based on a form of joint implementation foreshadowed in the Framework Convention. OECD countries have initial obligations to reduce emissions to 1990 levels by the year 2000; however, they can also trade emission rights with each other if by doing so they are able to meet this goal more cheaply. OECD countries can also pay for emissions abatement activity in developing nations and in return receive credits towards their own emissions abatement targets. Developing nations would reduce their business-as-usual emissions levels if they have a price advantage to do so. In overall terms such a trading arrangement moderates the estimated global annual loss in GDP to 0.04 per cent compared with 0.11 per cent, where OECD countries stabilize emissions without trading.

The estimated price of emissions (as reflected in the permit price or the carbon tax rate) falls in every OECD country when trade is allowed. Consequently, all OECD countries buy emission permits to help meet their emissions goals at a lower cost. Japan, Australia, New Zealand and the European Union gain the most from emissions trading. For example, Japan sees its loss in real consumption levels cut back from 0.19 per cent to 0.07 per cent. Japan's gains are a result of its relative improved export opportunities and the expanded production that its net purchases of emission quotas facilitates.

Emissions permits are mainly purchased from the Rest of the World region, which includes China, India, Eastern Europe and the former Soviet Union. The most cost-effective opportunities for reducing emissions are available in these nations. For the ASEAN countries and Korea, actual permit sales are very modest. For these countries, the major benefits of emissions trading arise because costs in the OECD are reduced, improving the world economic outlook compared to a no-trade scenario. For Korea, the spillover costs of emissions abatement activity in the OECD are reduced by half. Korea's losses in real national consumption are moderated from 0.12 per cent without trade to 0.06 per cent with trade.

The ASEAN group of countries see their estimated real consumption loss reduced from 0.70 per cent, where there is no trade, to 0.13 per cent. Credits sales by ASEAN are a minor part of this, being worth only about 0.01 per cent of their NDP. The major benefits of emissions trading come from higher sales of fossil-fuel-based energy and an improvement in the terms of trade of the ASEAN group.

4.4. Income Transfers to Developing Countries When Tradable Emissions Permits are Allocated on a Per Capita Basis

Developing countries generally and ASEAN in particular would benefit even more from a system of tradable permits that allocated emissions quotas world-wide on a per capita basis. This would entail most developing countries being awarded quotas far in excess of their needs and would allow them to sell those quotas to other countries. The magnitude of the income transfers entailed, makes it most unlikely that developed countries would agree to such a regime, despite its obvious appeal to the developing world and, perhaps, to principles of equity.

Table 2.5 presents the macroeconomic impacts of a tradable emissions permits system, assuming that permits are initially allocated on a per capita emissions basis. The total amount of permits allocated globally is equal to 80 per cent of year 2000 emissions levels. The table demonstrates that the distri-

Table 2.5   Estimated macroeconomic effects of an emissions trading system where permits are allocated on a per capita basis and global emissions are stabilized at 1990 levels in the year 2000

	Annual percentage change in real national consumption	Permit price per tonne of CO_2 (US$ 1988)	Percentage change in emissions levels	Sale of permits (Mt of CO_2)
Japan	−1.07	$49	−20	−297
Korea	−2.95	$49	−15	−32
ASEAN	31.24	$49	−8	1245
Australia	−5.31	$49	−26	−139
New Zealand	−1.42	$49	−13	−7
Canada	−5.15	$49	−25	−353
United States	−7.92	$49	−33	-4342
European Union	−1.66	$49	−15	−712
Rest of the World	4.52	$49	−14	4637

bution of national income can vary tremendously depending on the initial allocation of permits.

Under a per capita emissions permit allocation rule, highly populated regions with low-income levels, such as ASEAN and the Rest of the World, benefit greatly at the expense of richer countries with high per capita carbon dioxide emissions. The tremendous increase in real national consumption for ASEAN (31 per cent) is almost entirely due to the wealth transfer it receives from selling permits for more than 1,200 megatons of emissions at a permit price close to $50 a megaton.

The countries that need to buy emission permits, particularly the US, Australia and Canada, make major losses in real national consumption (7.92 per cent, 5.31 per cent and 5.14 per cent respectively). Korea is also a major loser because of its relatively heavy dependency on carbon-emitting fuels. It, too, would buy emission permits.

Figure 2.1 shows the value of sales and purchases of emissions as a percentage of net domestic product. The implied wealth transfer to the Rest of the World is a much smaller percentage of net domestic product (5 per cent) than is the case with ASEAN. However, the considerable degree of variability of the Rest of the World category has already been commented upon. Disaggregation of this data indicates that in India, permit sales would be worth 41 per cent of NDP if all permits over and above current emissions were sold. By contrast, Poland would incur a loss of 18 per cent of NDP if permits sufficient to maintain current emissions levels were purchased.

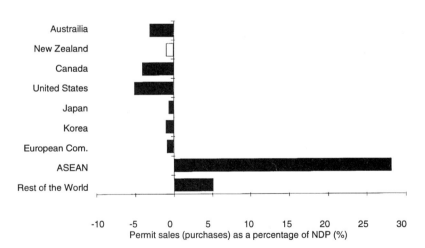

Source: Wedge Model Database.

Figure 2.1   *Permit sales and purchases as a percentage of net domestic product when permits are allocated according to per capita emissions*

5. CONCLUDING COMMENTS

Over the next 20 years, energy use in the Asian region is anticipated to grow by about 5 per cent annually. This is among the highest rates of growth of any world region. Restricting the growth in fossil-fuel use in Asia would severely hamper the region's ability to benefit from the sort of economic growth developed nations have already enjoyed.

The 1992 Global Framework Convention on Climate Change recognized the costs developing nations would incur if they were obliged to reduce rates of growth in the use of fossil fuels Consequently, the Convention only committed OECD countries to reducing their emissions of greenhouse gas. Nevertheless, OECD-wide reductions in emissions will have still have spillover effects into the Asian region through reduced demand for fossil fuels and a general decline in worldwide economic activity.

The costs of emissions abatement activity in the OECD, and the spillover effects on the Asian region, could be reduced if the OECD were able to buy and sell emissions quotas among themselves and fund greenhouse gas emissions reductions programmes in developing nations as an alternative to undertaking domestic emissions abatement activity. Many low-cost emissions abatement opportunities exist in the Asian region, particularly in China and India. These opportunities would range from reducing the flaring of natural gas from oil wells to improving the boiler efficiency of coal-fired power stations.

Unfortunately, not all Asian economies have the potential to gain substantial direct benefits from emissions trading programmes. For example, unless there are large reallocations of emission quotas to developing nations based on per capita emissions, ASEAN will not be a major seller of emissions credits. Nevertheless, emissions trading would have important second-round effects on countries such as ASEAN and Korea by reducing the size of the worldwide economic downturn which stringent emissions limits in the OECD would generate.

NOTES

1. Article 4, Paragraph 2(a) of the Framework Convention on Climate Change states that in adopting policies to mitigate climate change from greenhouse gas emissions, parties to the Convention, 'may implement such policies and measures jointly with other parties and may assist other parties in contributing to the achievement of the convention'.
2. It can be shown algebraically that a competitive market for permits will minimize the cost of reducing emissions to the predetermined target level (Montgomery 1972).
3. In an international context, it is easier to envisage implementing a system of tradable permits rather than a global carbon tax because a permits system need not infringe on the sovereign taxation powers of individual countries.
4. Hinchy et al. (1993) use a similar methodology of estimating abatement cost functions independently for different world regions and using these to analyse tradable permits schemes.

5. Estimates of the required reductions in emissions in this chapter are based on Industry Commission (1992), ABARE (1991) and Ministry of Commerce (New Zealand) (1991).
6. The use of uniform percentage reductions allows ready comparison of the relative costs of abatement in each country if a uniform economic shock is introduced to each country. However, if each country was to reduce emissions by the amount required to return to their own 1990 emission levels, the pattern of gains and losses would be different to those reported here. In particular, countries and regions with high emissions growth rates such as ASEAN, Korea, Japan, Australia and the Rest of the World would have even larger losses, while those with low growth rates, such as the European Community and Canada, would have smaller losses.

REFERENCES

ABARE (1991), *Projections of Energy Demand and Supply, Australia, 1990–91 to 2004–05,* Canberra: Australian Government Publishing Service.

Chisholm, Andrew, Alan Moran, and John Zeitsch (1994), 'The Economic Costs of Stabilising Carbon Dioxide Emissions in New Zealand', *New Zealand Economic Papers,* 28(1):1–24.

Hinchy, Mike, Sally Thorpe and Brian S. Fisher (1993), 'A Tradable Emissions Permit Scheme', *ABARE Research Report 93.5,* Canberra: Australian Bureau of Agricultural and Resource Economics.

Industry Commission (1992), 'Stabilizing Carbon Dioxide Emissions', *Staff Issues Paper No. 6,* Canberra: Commonwealth of Australia.

Jomini, P., J.F. Zeitsch, R. McDougall, A. Welsh, S. Brown, K. Hanslow, J. Hambley and J. Kelly (1991), 'WEDGE—A General Equilibrium Model to Evaluate the Economic Consequences of Controlling Carbon Dioxide Emissions, Model Structure, Database and Parameters', Draft, Canberra: Industry Commission.

Kverndokk, Snorre (1993), 'Global CO_2 Agreements: A Cost Effective Approach', *The Energy Journal,* 14(2):91–112.

Manne, Alan S. and Richard D Richels (1991), 'Global CO_2 Emissions Reductions-the Impacts of Rising Energy Costs', *The Energy Journal,* 12(1):87-107.

Ministry of Commerce (New Zealand) (1991), *Energy Demand Forecasts—Some Initial Results,* A report prepared by the Ministry of Commerce and the NZ Institute of Economic Research, Wellington: Energy and Resource Division, Ministry of Commerce.

Montgomery, D.W. (1972), 'Markets in Licenses and Efficient Pollution Control Programs', *Journal of Economic Theory,* 5:395–418.

(OECD) Organization for Economic Co-operation and Development (1990), 'Walras—a Multi-Sector, Multi-Country Applied General Equilibrium Model for Quantifying the Economy-Wide Effects of Agricultural Policies', in 'Modelling the Effects of Agricultural Policies', *OECD Economic Studies Special Issue No. 13,* Winter 1989–90, pp. 69–102, Department of Economics and Statistics, Paris: OECD.

(OECD) Organization for Economic Co-operation and Development (1991), *The Costs of Policies to Reduce Global Emissions of CO_2: Initial Results With Green,* Note by the Secretariat, Department of Economics and Statistics, Paris: OECD.

3. Economic Instruments to Cope with Global Warming: A Simulation Study on a Tradable Emission Permit Scheme to Reduce Global CO_2 Emissions

Kenji Yamaji and Taishi Sugiyama

1. TRADABLE EMISSION PERMITS

Many countries are now making efforts to stabilize greenhouse gas emissions at the levels realized in 1990. Although it is a significant first step, greenhouse gas emissions must be further reduced in order to stabilize greenhouse gas concentrations in the atmosphere, which is the target set in the Framework Convention on Climate Change (FCCC).

Carbon taxes have been introduced in some countries, and other countries are now considering the possibility. A carbon tax theoretically minimizes the national cost of reducing CO_2 emissions because marginal costs are set equal to the tax rate in all sectors. However, since the marginal cost to achieve each country's reduction target differs from one to another, global efficiency in controlling emissions is generally not maximized by the national carbon taxes.

To improve global efficiency, a system of tradable emission permits has been proposed. In this scheme a country which has a high marginal cost of emission reduction can lower it by purchasing emission permits from another country which has a lower marginal cost. Moreover, if the permits are allocated in an appropriate manner, fair burden-sharing can be realized through money transfer associated with permit trade. Permit trade is theoretically expected to have a potential to be an efficient and equitable institutional scheme for controlling CO_2 emissions.

2. SIMULATION MODELS

Our study consists of three simulation model studies. The first two use the Edmonds–Reilly model (Edmonds and Reilly 1983) with some modifications, and the last one uses a linear programming model developed in CRIEPI.

2.1. Edmonds–Reilly Model

This model solves the supply–demand balance of global energy resources by adjusting their prices. It divides the world into nine regions: (1) United States, (2) OECD Europe, (3) OECD Pacific, (4) Former USSR and East Europe, (5) Centrally Planned Asia, (6) Middle East, (7) Africa, (8) Latin America, and (9) South and East Asia; and it can assess alternative energy strategies until the year 2100 with an interval of 25 years. It computes energy demands for six major primary energy resources: oil, gas, solids, hydroelectric, nuclear and solar energy. In this study we have modified the model to incorporate an international emission permit market and regional CO_2 taxation.

2.2. Linear Programming Model

In this model, total social welfare loss (which is equal to the energy consumer's surplus loss plus energy producer's surplus loss) plus associated transaction costs is minimized by optimizing energy supply systems and the distribution of regional CO_2 emissions, under a constraint of global total CO_2 emission. The shadow price of the CO_2 emission constraint is identified as the emission permit price. The model computes regional energy demands for four types of fuels (oil, gas, solids and nuclear) in the year 2000, and the world is divided into five regions: (1) United States, (2) Other OECD, (3) Former USSR and East Europe, (4) China, (5) Other Developing Countries.

3. PERMIT TRADE WITH A BUDGET RULE[1]

In this section we simulate the global emissions permit trade market by setting a budget rule connecting a regional carbon taxation, permit trade and afforestation as shown in Figure 3.1.

Region A in Figure 3.1, which emits more CO_2 than its initial allocation, imposes a regional carbon tax. The carbon tax is assumed to be levied in proportion to the carbon content of fossil fuels and added to the secondary energy price. The revenue is used for two purposes: purchasing permits and/or afforestation. The amount of CO_2 absorbed by the afforestation is subtracted from the emission. Tax rates are raised until the region's net emissions are equal to the

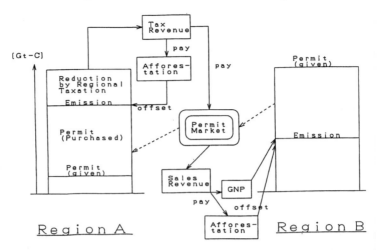

Figure 3.1   The budget rule incorporated in the Edmonds–Reilly model

number of permits.

Region B in Figure 3.1, which emits less than its initial allocation, imposes no carbon tax. It sells the excess permits, including the amount absorbed by afforestation. The costs of afforestation are financed by the permit sales. The global total number of permits is set and ranges from 4 to 6 giga tonne-carbon.

The maximum potential of land available for afforestation is assumed to be equal to the amount of forest destroyed by past human activities, that is, approximately 800 million hectares. We also assume that the limit of the area afforested annually is one per cent of the maximum potential. The afforestation costs, which vary across regions, are assumed to increase as the land available for afforestation is depleted.

Figure 3.2 illustrates one of the results of the simulation study. The permit-importing regions (upper half of the figure) emit a combined total of 4,370Mt-C in the year 2000 in the business-as-usual case (Reference Case). The amount is reduced to 2,528Mt-C in the Permit-Equilibrium Case in which the afforestation option is not included and to 3,900Mt-C in the Afforestation-Option Case. The permit-exporting regions (lower half) emit 2,194, 2,472, and 2,230Mt-C respectively.

As a result of this simulation we find that: (1) the regional CO_2 tax is significantly reduced by the introduction of international permit trading, when compared to the case where each region achieves its CO_2 limit by independently imposing a CO_2 tax; (2) the introduction of CO_2 absorption options further reduces levels of regional CO_2 tax by increasing permit supply in the market.[2]

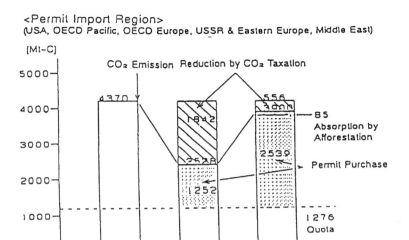

<Permit Import Region>
(USA, OECD Pacific, OECD Europe, USSR & Eastern Europe, Middle East)

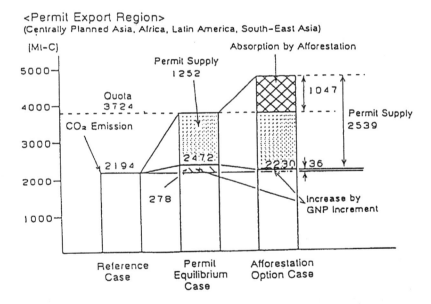

<Permit Export Region>
(Centrally Planned Asia, Africa, Latin America, South-East Asia)

Figure 3.2   A result of the permit trade market with the budget rule

4. PERMIT TRADE WITH MAXIMUM EFFICIENCY[3]

In the previous section we have assumed the budget rule which connects the carbon tax, permit trade and afforestation. Even though the marginal costs of CO_2 control are reduced in the case, the global efficiency is not maximized because regional differences in the marginal costs still exist. In this section we obtain a globally efficient result by assuming that all regional marginal costs are equal to the permit price through permit trading.[4] This assumption can be justified if the transaction costs are negligibly small compared to the regional difference in the marginal costs. Here we simply assume that the transaction costs are sufficiently lowered by careful implementation of the economic instruments. In this scheme the problem of 'equity' is separate from the problem of 'efficiency' because permit price is determined solely by the global total emission target and income transfer is determined solely by the initial distribution of the permit.

The income transfer, which is a reflection of equity, is determined solely by the permit distribution but not by the global total target. The separation enables us to analyse the two problems independently. We will show the results in the following. This equity–efficiency separation is called Coase's theorem.

Before going ahead, we note an interesting implication of the separation. The separation implies that we can have a system practically equivalent to the permit-trade market, with the combination of uniform marginal cost imposition and income transfer. We can further interpret it as follows: we can have a system equivalent to the permit-trade market by the combination of national CO_2 control, joint implementation and income transfer. It gives us a practical strategy to realize the theoretical merit of the permit-trade market. Keeping these ideas in mind, we show the simulation results.

Figure 3.3 illustrates the efficiency improvement by the permit trade. Three cases, (1) no permit trade, (2) permit trade with maximum efficiency, (3) permit trade with a budget rule, are plotted for comparison. In all the three cases the initial allocation is population-based and the global total emission target is 5 giga tonne-carbon. First, the solid curve shows the marginal costs in each world region without permit trade. In developed countries the marginal costs are as high as 300 to 800 dollars per tonne-carbon. Here all dollars are in 1975 value, thus we have to double the values to have the current dollar values. Second, the flat broken curve is the marginal costs in the case of a permit trade with maximum efficiency. The marginal costs are equalized through permit trade to the permit price, that is 55 dollars per tonne-carbon. The marginal costs in developed regions are drastically reduced by the permit trade. Third, the dotted curve shows the result of the permit trade with a budget rule examined in the previous section. Although the high marginal costs of developed regions in the no-permit-trade case are drastically lowered, the curve is not exactly flat and so the global efficiency is not maximized.

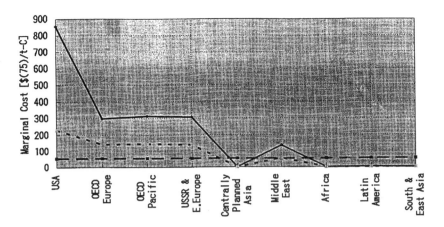

Key
Solid curve: no permit trade.
Broken curve: permit trade with maximum efficiency.
Dotted curve: permit trade with a budget rule.
Initial permit allocation is population based and the global total emission target is five
    giga tonne-carbon.

Figure 3.3   *Marginal CO$_2$ control costs by world regions*

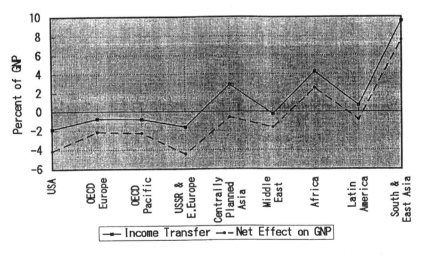

Figure 3.4   *Income transfer and economic impact—population-based
                allocation case*

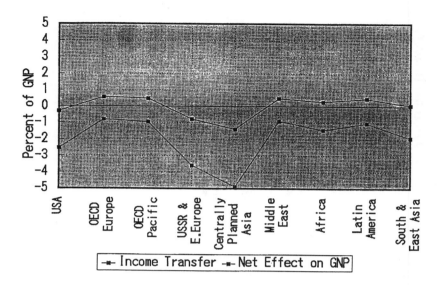

Figure 3.5   Income transfer and economic impact—GNP-based allocation case

So far we have focused on the efficiency aspect of the permit trade. Next we turn to the equity. Figure 3.4 shows the income transfer and economic impacts caused by the permit trade. Again the global emission target is 5 giga tonne-carbon and the allocation is population based. The year is 2000. The vertical axis shows the percent of regional sum of GNP. The solid curve shows the income transfer. The figure shows us, for example, that the United States loses 2 per cent of GNP and Africa gets 4 per cent of GNP by the permit trade. Roughly speaking, several per cent of the developed regions' GNP are transferred to developing countries. The dotted curve shows the net effect on GNP, which is calculated by adding the income transfer curve and the economic damage caused by regional emission reduction.[5] We have to admit that the estimation of the net effect on GNP is preliminary, but developing countries surely have positive net effect on GNP, if the permit allocation is population based.

Figure 3.5 shows the case of GNP-based allocation. The flow of income transfer is totally different from the population-based case. Again, the global target is 5 giga-tonne carbon and the year is 2000. Roughly speaking, the flow of income transfer is from the former communist countries (i.e. former USSR and East Europe, and Centrally Planned Asia) to the developed countries. As a result, the net effects on GNP are negative in all regions. The economic damages of developing countries are not offset by the income transfer. Therefore, from the point of view of equity and responsibility, GNP-based allocation is not acceptable for developing countries. We have also calculated the case in which allocation is emission based (grandfathering), and found that the result is similar to the GNP-based case.

In conclusion, comparing the three types of allocations—population based, GNP based and emission based—we have to choose the population-based allocation if we want to incorporate the equity and the developed countries' responsibility.

5. EFFECTS OF TRANSACTION COSTS[6]

The transaction costs associated with permit trade are investigated using a linear programming model developed at CRIEPI. We assume that the transaction costs are paid by permit-importing regions, in proportion to the number of permits traded. The costs are given exogenously, ranging from zero to one thousand dollars per tonne-carbon. The objective function is the sum of the social welfare loss and the transaction costs.We minimize the objective function under a constraint of global carbon emission.

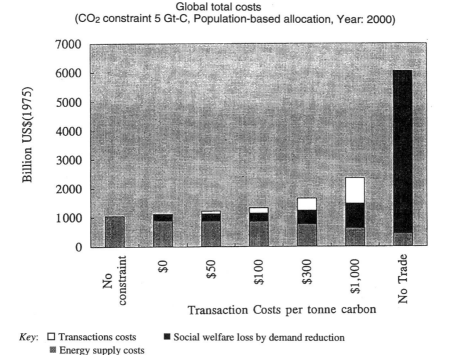

Key: □ Transactions costs   ■ Social welfare loss by demand reduction
      ▓ Energy supply costs

Figure 3.6   The effect of transaction costs

Figure 3.6 shows the case in which global emission target is 5 giga tonne-carbon. Again the allocation is population based and the year is 2000. The vertical axis is the global total costs in billion US dollars, plotted for the various transaction costs. We find that the number of permits traded decreases with the increase in transaction costs. However, even when the transaction costs are high, the total costs of global CO_2 control are significantly reduced compared to the case of no-permit trade.

6. CONCLUSION

The findings from model analysis are as follows:

- the costs of CO_2 emission control are significantly reduced by a global permit trade;
- the costs can be further reduced by afforestation;
- the merits of a global permit trade still exist even when the transaction costs are high.

The findings clearly show the theoretical merit of a permit trade. But it is politically not feasible to have such a worldwide permit-trade market in the near future.

However, following the discussion of equity–efficiency separation, we can have a system equivalent to the permit-trade market with the combination of national CO_2 control, joint implementation and income transfer reflecting equity. As a consequence of these findings, we support the 'joint implementation' mentioned in the Framework Convention on Climate Change, as a method to realize the theoretical merit of the international permit trade.

NOTES

1. See Okada and Yamaji (1993) for details of the model and results.
2. It is interesting to note that the permit sales revenue of developing regions is lowered by the introduction of the afforestation option despite their permit supply increase. It is because a drastic fall in permit price over-offsets the supply increase.
3. See Sugiyama et al. (1994) for details.
4. We incorporate the permit trade scheme in the Edmonds–Reilly model by the following two steps. First, we add the permit price to the secondary energy price. Second, the income transfer associated with the permit trade is calculated as follows:

$$Ai = P(Qi - Ei)$$

   where i is the region number, Ai is the net income transfer to the region i, P is the emission permit price, Qi is the initial permit allocation quota and Ei is the emission.
5. The economic damage caused by regional emission reduction is approximated by the product of the permit price (which is equal to the marginal costs) and the region's emission.

6. See Yamaji et al. (1993) for details.

REFERENCES

Edmonds, J. and J. Reilly (1983) , 'A Long–Term Global Energy–Economic Model of Carbon Dioxide Release from Fossil Fuel Use', *Energy Economics*, Vol. 5, April, pp. 74–88.

Okada, K. and K. Yamaji (1993), 'Simulation Study on Tradable CO_2 Emission Permits', in Y. Kaya, N. Nakicenovic, W.D. Nordhaus and F. L. Toth (eds), '*Costs, Impacts, and Benefits of CO_2 Mitigation*', IIASA CP–93–2, June, pp. 341–54.

Sugiyama, T., K. Yamaji, K. Okada and H. Yamamoto (1994), 'An Analysis of Global Economic Instruments for CO_2 emission reduction—equity and efficiency', CRIEPI Research Report No. Y93015, Tokyo, Japan (in Japanese).

Yamaji, K., K. Okada and H. Yamamoto (1993) , 'Simulation Study on Tradable CO_2 Emissions Permits with a Linear Programming Model', CRIEPI Research Report No. Y93003 Tokyo, Japan (in Japanese).

4. Investing in the Common Good: Financing Global Environmental Initiatives

Chitru S. Fernando, Paul R. Kleindorfer and Mohan P.C. Munasinghe

1. AN ECONOMIC FRAMEWORK FOR MODELLING GLOBAL ENVIRONMENTAL INVESTMENTS

The problem of reducing greenhouse gas (GHG) emissions is greatly complicated by several of its attributes:

- uncertainty in impacts;
- asymmetry in the projected impacts;
- unequal allocation of initial conditions in the use of the global atmosphere as a commons resource;
- unequal ability to shoulder the burden of emissions reductions;
- changes from the status quo (free access) are viewed as losses.

While all nations have a stake in the use of the commons resource, the rights of national sovereignty imply that no international body can impose monitoring or enforcement powers. Therefore participation in any agreement is voluntary and subject to renegotiation. The problem is to design incentives which will be effective in reaching efficient levels of global GHG concentrations resulting from country-specific emissions and sinks.

This framework is built around a group of countries or country groups with heterogeneous preferences and incomes. We first investigate outcomes when countries carry on with 'business-as-usual', (non-cooperatively) maximizing their individual welfare, allocating resources for consumption and GHG-reducing investment accordingly. We compare this non-cooperative outcome with the outcome achieved when countries cooperate in global efforts to mitigate global climate change. Our focus is on analysing the opportunities for efficiency gains through international resource transfers used to leverage the funding of GHG mitigation projects, especially in developing countries where projects could not be undertaken without such support.

The buildup of GHGs in the atmosphere is a dynamic process and should be so modelled. We take the simplest dynamic model, a two-stage model, preceded by a pre-planning bargaining stage. At stage 0 we assume the global community decides on the framework (if any) it will use for coordinating its efforts to reduce GHGs. At stage 1, each country makes investments to either reduce GHG emissions or to set up the possibility of mitigating the effects of these in stage 2. Further investments and mitigation measures are undertaken in stage 2 after uncertainty about the extent and consequences of GHGs on global climate change is resolved. Forward and options contracts may be signed between various countries at stage 0 and the results of these contracts are realized in stage 2.

We use the following notation:

θ = country index, where the set of all countries is denoted Θ
$x(\theta)$ = investment by country θ to reduce GHGs at stage 1
X = $\{x(\theta) \mid \theta \in \Theta\}$, the vector of all country investments
$y(\theta)$ = consumption by country θ at stage 1
Y = $\{y(\theta) \mid \theta \in \Theta\}$, the vector of all country consumptions
$I(\theta)$ = income for country θ in stage 1
ω = uncertain state of the world, realized at stage 2, where we assume

   that $\omega \in \Re^+$

$F(\omega)$ = probability distribution on the states of the world
$s(\theta)$ = monetary transfer payment *to* country θ at stage 1
S = $\{s(\theta) \mid \theta \in \Theta\}$, the vector of all *ex ante* transfers

Let $g(x(\theta), y(\theta); \theta)$ (which may be thought of as the 'GHG impact function' for country θ) denote the total GHGs (measured in units of global climate change potential) generated by country θ in stage 1, and let the total GHGs generated in all countries be denoted by $G(X,Y)$ so that

$$G(X, Y) = \sum_{\theta \in \Theta} g(x(\theta), y(\theta); \theta) . \tag{4.1}$$

We assume throughout that, for each θ, $g(x, y, \theta)$ is increasing in consumption and decreasing in mitigation investments, i.e., $g_x < 0$, $g_y > 0$. We also assume that $g(\bullet, \theta)$ is jointly convex in (x, y), so that investments in x have a declining marginal impact on (reducing) G and consumption has an increasing marginal impact on G. We assume the following aggregate welfare function, denoted $U(\theta)$, for country θ:

$$U(X, Y, \omega; \theta) = V(G(X, Y), y(\theta), \omega; \theta) \qquad (4.2)$$

so that U depends on X only through aggregate GHG emissions G. We assume that V is decreasing in G, increasing in y and jointly concave in G and y. Given these properties of G and V, it is straightforward to show that, for each ω and θ, V is concave in (X, Y), from which it follows that, for each $\theta \in \Theta$, the expected value of V over ω is concave in (X, Y).

We are interested in characterizing the Pareto-efficient outcomes to the collective consumption-investment problem associated with the above country welfare functions $U(\theta)$. For this purpose, we will define a (weighted utilitarian) global welfare function W as

$$W(X, Y) = E_\omega \left\{ \sum_{\theta \in \Theta} \eta(\theta)\, U(X, Y, \omega; \theta) \right\} \qquad (4.3)$$

where $\eta(\theta)$ satisfy:

$$\eta(\theta) \geq 0; \quad \sum_{\theta \in \Theta} \eta(\theta) = 1. \qquad (4.4)$$

Since the expected utility functions $E\{V(\bullet; \theta)\}$ are concave, the Pareto set of allocations from any convex feasible set are given by the argmax W_η as the weights $\{\eta(\theta) \mid \theta \in \Theta\}$ vary over the feasible set defined by (4.4).

U may be thought of as the net economic benefits realized from the country's activities in stages 1 and 2. We assume that investments $x(\theta)$ in GHG reduction and consumption $y(\theta)$ are related by the following budget constraint:

$$I(\theta) = x(\theta) + y(\theta) - s(\theta) \qquad (4.5)$$

Thus, investments in GHG reduction will necessarily reduce consumption $y(\theta)$ unless offset by transfers $s(\theta) > 0$ to θ from other countries. For feasibility, we require the following restrictions on transfers among countries:

$$\sum_{\theta \in \Theta} s(\theta) = 0. \qquad (4.6)$$

1.1. The Non-cooperative Solution

We develop here the benchmark non-cooperative (NC) solution based on uncoordinated actions by individual countries. To characterize this non-cooperative solution, we use the Nash equilibrium concept for the associated game in which each country attempts to maximize (4.2) subject to (4.5), with $s(\theta) =$

0. The problem in this case for country θ will be:

$$\underset{x(\theta),y(\theta)}{Maximize} \ E_\omega\{V(G(X, Y), y(\theta), \omega; \theta)\} \tag{4.7}$$

subject to:

$$I(\theta) = x(\theta) + y(\theta) \tag{4.8}$$

Substituting (4.8) into (4.7), country θ is assumed to solve the following problem, taking other country decisions as given:

$$\underset{x(\theta) \geq 0}{Max} \ E_\omega\{V(G(X, I - X), I(\theta) - x(\theta)), \omega; \theta)\} \tag{4.9}$$

Thus, assuming $x(\theta) > 0$ at optimum, the following first-order conditions characterize the Nash non-cooperative equilibrium:

$$\frac{\partial E \ V(\theta)}{\partial x(\theta)} = 0 = E_\omega\left\{\left[g_x(\theta) - g_y(\theta)\right]V_G(\theta) + V_{y(\theta)}(\theta)\right\} \tag{4.10}$$

1.2. First-Best Framework for Characterizing Cooperative Solutions

By a first-best solution, we mean a Pareto allocation (X, Y, S) for the above country welfare functions and constraints, i.e. a solution which cannot be improved upon for all countries simultaneously. From the above, the Pareto solutions (X, Y) must be solutions to the following problem for some feasible weighting vector $\{\eta(\theta) \mid \theta \in \Theta\}$:

$$\underset{X,Y}{Maximize} \ E_\omega\left\{\sum_{\theta \in \Theta}\eta(\theta)V(G(X, Y), y(\theta), \omega; \theta)\right\} \tag{4.11}$$

subject to (4.5)–(4.6), where E_ω is the expectation at stage 1 with respect to the distribution $F(\omega)$. Thus, the first-best solution is effected by putting all resources in the hands of a central planning authority, which is assumed to solve (4.11) with no transactions costs.

Since (4.5) holds as an equality at the solution to (4.11), we may eliminate $y(\theta)$ by substituting (4.5) into (4.11). The resulting problem of interest is then:

$$\underset{X,S}{Max} \ W(X, S) = \left\{\sum_{\theta \in \Theta}\eta(\theta)V(G(X, I - X + S), I(\theta) - x(\theta) + s(\theta), \omega; \theta)\right\} \tag{4.12}$$

subject to (4.6). From the Lagrangian L^C for this problem we obtain the following first-order conditions:

$$\frac{\partial L^C}{\partial x(\theta)} = 0 = E\left\{ \left[g_x(\theta) - g_y(\theta) \right] \left[\sum_\zeta \eta(\zeta)V_G(\zeta) \right] - \eta(\theta)V_y(\theta) \right\} \quad (4.13)$$

$$\frac{\partial L^C}{\partial s(\theta)} = 0 = E_\omega\left\{ g_y(\theta) \sum_{\zeta \in \Theta} \eta(\zeta)V_G(\zeta) + \eta(\theta)V_{y(\theta)}(\theta) \right\} - \mu \quad (4.14)$$

where μ is the dual variable associated with (4.6). (4.12) implies that the change in global benefits associated with transferring a monetary unit from consumption to investment for GHG reduction in country θ must just equal the marginal cost $E_\omega\{\eta(\theta)V_y(\theta)\}$ in lost consumption.

We can compare (4.10) obtained earlier for the non-cooperative (NC) case with (4.13) above. We see that (4.10) implies a similar benefit–cost equality to that discussed above for (4.13). In the NC case, however, country θ equates the marginal loss in consumption benefits to the benefits *for itself* of transferring a monetary unit in that country from consumption to investment. By contrast, for Pareto efficiency, marginal consumption losses are equated *to global benefits* of increased investment in mitigating GHGs. Proposition 1 below shows that the NC solution is never cost effective in the sense that resources used to mitigate GHGs are never used efficiently in the NC solution, whereas they always are in the cooperative solution. This suggests that the essential focus of institutional design should be in improving efficiency in GHG mitigation efforts by focusing on the best alternatives for GHG mitigation investments globally.

Proposition 1: Let superscripts *C*, respectively *NC*, denote the solutions to the cooperative, first-best problem (4.12) (subject to (4.6)) and the non-cooperative problem (4.9).

i.   The non-cooperative solution is Pareto inefficient in the sense that there are weighting vectors $\{\eta(\theta) \mid \theta \in \Theta\}$ such that the corresponding cooperative solutions $(X(\eta), Y(\eta))$ leave every country better off than under the non-cooperative solution. In particular, unless all countries have identical preferences $V(\theta)$ and identical emission technologies $g(\theta)$, the non-cooperative solution is not efficient in the sense that lower aggregate GHG emissions can be achieved from the total mitigation investments $\sum x^{NC}(\theta)$, i.e.

$$G(X^{NC}, Y^{NC}) > Minimum \left\{ G(X, Y^{NC}) \mid \sum_{\theta \in \Theta} x(\theta) \le \sum_{\theta \in \Theta} x^{NC}(\theta) \right\}$$

ii. The level of aggregate GHG emissions $G(X^C, Y^C)$ achieved under any cooperative solution is efficient in the sense that it is the minimum aggregate emission level achievable from total mitigation investments $\sum x^C(\theta)$. That is, for the cooperative solution:

$$G(X^C, Y^C) = Minimum \left\{ G(X, Y^C) \mid \sum_{\theta \in \Theta} x(\theta) \leq \sum_{\theta \in \Theta} x^C(\theta) \right\}$$

Proof: See Technical Appendix.

2. INSTITUTIONAL MECHANISMS FOR EFFECTIVE GLOBAL RESOURCE TRANSFERS

We briefly consider here the issue of designing institutions for monitoring GHG emissions and for funding GHG mitigation projects and programmes. The nature of the institutions deployed to effect cross-border investments will clearly have a significant impact on the efficacy of the programme and the extent to which the expected benefits are realized. It is an area of formidable complexity given:

- the heterogeneity of sources and sinks;
- information barriers and transactions costs;
- the lack of control or lack of responsiveness to price mechanisms;
- national sovereignty, heterogeneity of interests, and problems of enforcement.

These issues point to difficulties in monitoring results and, given the costs of GHG mitigation, to difficulties in assuring cooperative compliance with commitments made by individual countries who receive resources to undertake mitigation projects. Thus, the key issue for design will be to focus on monitoring, sharing of information and, with this, efficient decentralization of implementation. Decentralization can occur at two levels:

1. between the country/countries financing investments and the recipient country (the global level);
2. within individual countries (the national level).

Our focus here is on institutional mechanisms pertaining to the first of these, the global level. Decentralization at the national level has been extensively analysed and various schemes, most notably tradable permits and taxes, have been developed to achieve target reductions in GHGs in various sectors efficiently. These alternative approaches themselves have yet to be examined fully in an empirical setting, and it seems likely that no single scheme will be optimal for every country (see Wheeler 1992). Thus, decentralization at the national level should be understood in terms of both differing sectoral targets for GHG mitigation, but also differing effectiveness of alternative policy instruments in achieving these sectoral targets in different countries. Thus, the key issue is that each country commits itself to a well-intentioned effort to achieve fair targets for GHG reduction. How they achieve this will be country specific, although sharing of best practices and new technologies across countries should be facilitated (see below).

At the global level, we focus on two polar extremes in the possible set of institutional mechanisms:

- pure multilateral schemes such as the Global Environmental Fund (GEF); and
- pure bilateral schemes such as the joint implementation programmes currently being proposed by the US and some other countries that plan to finance GHG reduction investments in developing countries.

Multilateral schemes are characterized by a central pool of funds contributed by the investing countries which is then disbursed to recipient countries based on specific criteria, such as the incremental costs of the projects funded. Donor countries are not able to identify themselves with individual projects, which places a heavy burden of project monitoring on the central agency. In bilateral schemes, on the other hand, the terms of financing can be agreed by the two sides, and the country putting up the financing can monitor the progress of the projects. In such a bilateral approach, countries making cross-border investments may obtain credit or offsets against their own obligations under the Framework Convention. The benefit accruing to the financing countries, which is the avoided cost differential between the cost of domestic and cross-border investment, is very visible, which makes it politically tenable to put up the financing from public funds. After assessing the advantages and disadvantages of these schemes at some length, we consider the potential for hybrid approaches which combine the better features of multilateral and bilateral schemes. We consider the following criteria in our assessment:

- price per unit of GHG reduced and total cost to investing countries;
- incentives for project nomination and efficient implementation;
- monitoring and informational efficiency;
- transactions costs.

2.1. Cost to Investing Countries

A key issue that arises regarding price per unit of GHG reduced and the cost to investing countries relates to the basis on which transfer payments are made to recipient countries for the 'purchase' of GHG mitigation. In the past, most notably in the case of the Montreal Protocol implementation, the basis for payment has been the incremental cost borne by the country implementing the project. This approach has been criticized for being administratively cumbersome and providing few incentives (if any) for project acceleration by the recipient countries (see Fernando et al. 1993). Recent anecdotal evidence, especially pertaining to the slow pace at which funds have been disbursed for the mitigation of ozone-depleting substances, seems to confirm this view.

Assuming recipient countries agree, incremental cost financing gives the highest 'bang-for-buck' for the investment. If recipient countries are firmly committed to a schedule of investments which is not conditional on the availability of external financing, such an approach may be somewhat realistic, especially if undertaken via a single multilateral agency such as the GEF. On the other hand, if the pace and size of GHG mitigation investment in recipient countries is dependent upon the scale of external financing, which seems to be a plausible scenario especially in the case of larger countries such as India and China, we would argue that payments in excess of incremental costs would be required for effective and speedy implementation of GHG mitigation projects.

Such an outcome is likely in a bilateral scheme where investor countries may be thought of as 'competing' for low-cost GHG mitigation projects especially in the developing world. The likely result of such competition is that investor countries would be willing to pay recipient countries somewhat more than incremental costs to secure offsets through their investment in low-cost projects. In an extreme case, a single global 'market-clearing' price which equals the incremental cost of the last project undertaken will be paid by investor countries for their cross-border GHG mitigation investments. While payments above incremental costs would clearly be more expensive for the investing countries, we argue below that they are likely to be more effective from the standpoint of incentives for implementation of the projects by the recipient countries.

2.2. Incentive Implications

As noted above, the payment mechanism associated with the institutional scheme has a direct impact on the incentives for participation and active cooperation by the recipient countries. Buying GHG reductions at their incremental costs, may be least-cost from the standpoint of the investing countries. However, as pointed out for the analogous case of ozone layer protection in Munasinghe and King (1992), such an arrangement provides no financial surplus to the recipient countries—which is likely to have an adverse effect on their incentives to cooperate by nominating and implementing projects speedily. This may be a less significant factor if the recipient countries are obligated by the Framework Convention to undertake these projects anyway, with or without external financing. However, it is unlikely that the cooperation of many developing countries can be obtained without such financing, and the experience to date shows that this may need to be in excess of the costs that they incur—to provide an additional incentive.

Surplus payments in excess of costs may be viewed as 'lubricants for cooperation'. Since these surplus payments are likely to be highest for the lowest-cost (highest 'bang-for-buck') projects, they create strong incentives for recipient countries to locate and nominate these projects for financing. They also create incentives for accelerated implementation of high 'bang-for-buck' projects, which is very desirable from the standpoint of the objectives of a Framework Convention.

Also as we have noted above, surplus payments are almost inevitable in bilateral schemes if investing countries compete globally for the cheapest projects. However, taking account of the relative strengths and weaknesses of the parties to these bilateral schemes, the considerable barriers to information flow, and the obligations imposed on the parties to the Framework Convention, it is very unlikely that prices will increase all the way to levels associated with full competition for mitigation projects.

Surplus payments may be very desirable in multilateral schemes also, to overcome the incentive problems that were discussed above. One approach to enhance incentives would be to conduct what amounts to a global auction (see Fernando et al. 1993) which is effected by announcing a fixed price (in $/ton) which the multilateral institution would pay for mitigation projects. The effect of such a price offer is to attract all projects that have unit costs of GHG mitigation that are below the offered price, which will be the best projects available globally. Over time, the bid price can be increased progressively to attract higher cost projects, up to the desired aggregate level of GHG mitigation.

2.3. Monitoring and Informational Efficiency

In order for a scheme of cross-border investments to work, the following criteria must be met regardless of the institutional mechanism that is adopted for implementing the scheme of resource transfers:

1. the investing countries should be able to monitor the investments/measure emissions and whether or not the desired results have been achieved;
2. the investing countries should be able to impose (at least moral if not financial) sanctions on non-compliant countries.

A third desirable characteristic of efficient decentralized implementation is that the shadow price of GHG reduction in each country and sector be estimable so that a rough efficiency benchmark (namely, equalized incremental abatement costs) is evident to all participating countries. Using market mechanisms at the national level could enhance significantly the estimation of incremental abatement costs in each country. For example, in the electric power sector if an efficiently functioning emissions trading market were present, the market price for an emissions permit for GHGs would represent the cost of a unit reduction in GHGs in that sector. The challenge is to link sectors such as electric power, which are more easily monitored and controlled, with other sectors, such as agriculture and manufacturing, where the total GHG emissions and the cost of reducing these will be considerably more difficult to estimate on an ongoing basis. In these sectors, from both a national as well as a global perspective, it seems likely that a variety of country-specific instruments and projects will be required to achieve efficient GHG mitigation.

From the standpoint of monitoring and enforcement pertaining to specific projects, there appears to be no obvious advantage to one or other of the two mechanisms we have been considering here. Where it is possible to leverage off existing trade/investment/aid links between two countries, monitoring in a bilateral scheme could be very effectively handled. A multilateral agency, on the other hand, would have the benefit of some scale economies, especially in the use of specialized expertise.

From the standpoint of gathering and disseminating information across countries, on the other hand, a centralized multilateral agency is at a clear advantage. Thus, even with bilateral investment flows, such a multilateral agency established and funded by the investing countries could perform a very valuable role in promoting cooperative activity by each signatory country, including sharing of best practices, publishing information on potential investments and their costs, highlighting priority areas and providing technical assistance.

2.4. Transactions Costs

The transactions costs of project selection, implementation and monitoring are clearly an important consideration in institutional design for GHG mitigation investment. Because of issues of national sovereignty and physical separation between investing and host countries, it is clear at the outset that the magnitude of transactions costs associated with specific projects will depend on the stance taken by the host country institutions towards these projects. Thus, for example, much of the work associated with the project could occur at the local or project level if the host countries were to take an active interest in the project, which would depend in part on their stake in the project. It is clear also that the transactions costs associated with project identification, financing and monitoring are likely to be very much a function of the size and complexity of the project, and also the role and competence of its local partners. If the incentives for local participation can be correctly structured to be consistent with the overall objectives of the project, this would greatly reduce monitoring needs and associated costs.

The level of transactions costs would also depend upon existing institutions.

Many industrialized countries have existing agencies for the purpose of channelling foreign aid on a bilateral basis, which could also be used for the purpose of channelling these investments. On the other hand, there is a long tradition of channelling development aid through multilateral institutions such as the World Bank. Hence, from the standpoint of transactions costs, the success of a new scheme of financing GHG mitigation projects would depend upon the extent to which existing institutional resources can be utilized.

2.5. Hybrid Approaches

It is clear from the foregoing that multilateral and bilateral schemes have their relative advantages and disadvantages. Multilateral approaches are informationally more efficient, since all available information can be centrally aggregated and then disseminated as available. On the other hand, paying out only incremental costs, as is currently the practice of the GEF, greatly reduces the incentives for host countries to take a proactive role in nominating and implementing projects. In the longer term, the cost of this may be considerably higher than the immediate savings in disbursements to the host countries.

A potential hybrid arrangement is where a centralized multilateral institution (e.g. a Global Environmental Coordinator) would undertake information transfers, assisting in project identification and technical assistance, and possibly keeping a scorecard of environmental investments and setoffs by individual countries. Investments themselves can be undertaken bilaterally, or directed through multilateral funds such as the GEF, depending upon the preferences of the countries concerned.

3. CONCLUSIONS

This chapter has focused on two key issues associated with the current debate on a global initiative for reducing greenhouse gases—understanding the benefits of global cooperation through international resource transfers and developing effective institutional arrangements to put such cooperation into practice. The theoretical framework summarized here and elaborated in our other work (e.g. Fernando et al. 1995) clearly shows that cooperative outcomes can dominate business-as-usual non-cooperative outcomes in terms of GHG reduction and welfare improvement for all countries. Unlike in the case of the Montreal Protocol, where resource transfers to developing nations were motivated primarily by equity considerations, the cost effectiveness of a programme to reduce the emission of greenhouse gases hinges critically on the cooperation of developing nations.

Capturing the fruits of cooperation is contingent upon the development of effective institutional arrangements to transfer resources between countries. Given the nature of the investments (not so much the technology itself but the overlay of issues related to the externalities associated with the investments, national sovereignty and spatial dispersion), it is very important to have as many actions as possible undertaken by the host countries themselves in a way that is consistent with the objectives of the investing countries. As we have noted, this can be accomplished by a more equitable sharing of benefits between host and investing countries. Both bilateral and multilateral institutional arrangements can play a valuable role in achieving this end.

TECHNICAL APPENDIX

Proof of Proposition 1

(*ad* i): The fact that the Nash non-cooperative solution characterized by (4.10) is Pareto inefficient follows from the original Kuhn–Tucker approach to vector optimization problems. Let $v \in \Theta$ be any country and consider the following problem:

$$\underset{X,S}{\textit{Maximize}}\ E_\omega \left\{ V(G(X, I - X + S, I(v) - x(v) + s(v), \omega;v) \right\} \quad (4\text{A.1})$$

subject to (4.6) and:

$$E_\omega\{V(\theta)\} \ge E_\omega\{V^{NC}(\theta)\}, \quad \text{for all } \theta \in \Theta \setminus \{v\} \quad (4\text{A.2})$$

where $V^{NC}(\theta)$ represents the payoff for country θ from any non-cooperative solution. A feasible solution to (4A.1–4A.2) is clearly the given Nash non-co-operative solution which satisfies both (4A.2) as well as (4.6) (note that (4.12) implies $s(\theta) = 0$ for all θ). So much verifies that the solution to (4A.1–4A.2) weakly dominates the non-cooperative solution. Actually, by assigning Lagrange multipliers to the constraints (4A.2), it is easily verified that any solution to the necessary and sufficient conditions obtained for (4A.1–4A.2) cannot be a solution to the first-order conditions (4.10) for any weighting vector satisfying (4.4). Thus, the solution to (4A.1–4A.2) strictly dominates the non-cooperative solution, as claimed.

(*ad* ii) The fact that resources are used efficiently in mitigating GHGs under the cooperative solution is evident from the structure of the problem. Assuming the country leads directly to a contradiction, since aggregate welfare is always decreasing in total emissions G and increasing in consumption. Thus, if aggregate emissions can be lowered without affecting consumption (i.e. without using additional mitigation investments) they will be at the cooperative solution. An alternative method of seeing the same result is to note from (4.13) and (4.14) that the marginal emissions $g_x(\theta)$ are equal across countries θ for which $x^C(\theta)$ > 0, which is the necessary and sufficient condition for minimizing total emissions using a fixed investment pool.

To see that the non-cooperative solution is inefficient (when not all countries are identical) requires only an examination of the first-order conditions (4.10). If not all countries have identical preferences and emissions technologies, then (4.10) implies that the just-mentioned condition of equalized marginal emissions will not obtain. Clearly, lower total emissions could be achieved by transferring some mitigation resources from one country to another to equalize marginal emissions.

REFERENCES

Barrett, Scott (1992), 'Acceptable Allocations of Tradeable Carbon Emission Entitlements in a Global Warming Treaty', Chapter VI in *Combating Global Warming: Study on a Global System of Tradeable Carbon Emission Entitlements*, Geneva: UNCTAD.

Fernando, Chitru S., Paul R. Kleindorfer and Mohan Munasinghe (1993), 'Economic Design for Implementing the Montreal Protocol: Country Plans and Global Efficiency', World Bank Environment Department Divisional Working Paper No. 1993–41, Washington, DC.

Fernando, Chitru S., Kevin B. Fitzgerald, Paul R. Kleindorfer and Mohan Munasinghe (1995), 'Financing Global Environmental Programs: Efficient Approaches to Cooperation and Institutional Design', World Bank Environment Department Working Paper, Washington, DC.

Hoel, Michael (1991), 'Efficient International Agreements for Reducing Emissions of CO_2', *The Energy Journal*, 12: 93–107.

Munasinghe, Mohan and Kenneth King (1992), 'Accelerating Ozone Layer Protection in Developing Countries', *World Development*, 20, April: 609–18.

Nordhaus, William D. (1991), 'The Cost of Slowing Climate Change: A Survey', *The Energy Journal*, 12: 35–67.

Wheeler, David (1992), 'Controlling Industrial Pollution', Environmental Division Working Paper, The World Bank, Washington, DC.

PART II

Balancing Economic Development
and Environment

5. Balancing Economic Growth, Energy Development and Environmental Impact

Shehzad Sadiq[*]

1. INTRODUCTION

This chapter reviews the conceptual, policy and development linkages of the above theme for both the developed and the developing countries of the region. It also highlights the interaction of energy issues with other national policy issues of economy, technology, environment, trade, and investment. A brief description of the development banking role of the Asian Development Bank (ADB) as well as certain policy initiatives and thrusts for the future are also outlined. The chapter also focuses on Japan as a 'role-model' with respect to issues such as sustainable development, energy efficiency and productivity.

It is considered axiomatic that energy is a key factor in the policy planning and development of national economies, interacting with a wide spectrum of economic and fiscal issues such as balance of payments, inflation, employment, investment and trade. As an alliteration, energy interacts with other factors of development policies such as: economy, environment, employment, enterprise, education, efficiency, export and equity. This may be called energy and eight E's. Admittedly, because of the disparate endowment pattern of energy resources, planners have evolved successful models of factor substitution amongst the above set of eight E's. Therefore, it is often said that Nature reveals itself to humankind through Energy, and there can be no human activity possible without the underpinning of energy in one form or another.

* The views expressed herein are those of the author and do not necessarily reflect the views of the Asian Development Bank.

2. UNIQUE FEATURES OF THE ASIA AND PACIFIC REGION

I also wish to emphasize that the Asia and Pacific region is unique and extraordinary in many respects. First, with respect to population figures. As we know, it is the home for the majority of the world's population. But, in spite of the envious economic growth of some East Asian countries, the region still carries the burden of about 600 million people living below the poverty line, which is more than the entire EC and US populations. It also has very large sections of younger populations; Indonesia alone has more young people today than in all of the EC. Consequently, urbanization has mushroomed: in 1950, the Asia and Pacific region had only one city with more than five million people, but by the year 2010, it is estimated that there will be 16 Asian mega-polis cities (out of the 35 largest in the world) with more than four million people each. The consequences of such a skewed demographic picture are only too well known in terms of economic and social costs.

Second, there is enormous diversity in Asian cultures, geography, geology (the Himalayas, rivers and the oceans), markets and systems of government. India is the largest democracy and China is the largest economy in transition. Nepal is now the only country in the world with a communist party in parliamentary action.

Third, the Asia and Pacific region is also rendered unique by the fact that the four newly industrialized countries (NICs)—South Korea, Taiwan, Singapore and Hong Kong—as well as Japan have made it to the top leagues in spite of being almost entirely dependent on energy imports. The four NICs as well as Indonesia, Malaysia and Thailand—all seven East Asian economies—have quadrupled their per capita income during the past 25 years. Their success is attributed to pursuit of right policies aimed at low inflation, stable legal framework, competition, undistorted prices, education, disciplined workforce, etc.— all contributing to a sense of participation, security and stability.

Fourth, a word about Japan and other developed economies of the region. The Japanese miracle is premised, *inter alia*, on successful substitution among resources of financial, intellectual and natural origins. There is perhaps no other example with such a remarkable (emulative) track record of improvements in energy intensity, efficiency, labour productivity, investments in (civilian) research and development, pollution control and capital investment, as achieved by Japan during the past three decades.

Fifth, it may be noted that certain developing countries with large populations (notably India and China) are endowed with extremely large coal deposits, thus influencing their policy choices to a single fuel source. Fuel diversification, therefore, comes into sharp focus from the standpoint of security of supplies and environmental redemption.

Finally, the region as a whole is dependent on energy trade from within and from outside sources, thus increasing the degree of vulnerability to its recent economic accomplishments. For example, the region's overall economic growth has been supported by its manufacturing strength and complemented by its consumer market (already greater than the US or the EC). Steel consumption in Asia, excluding Japan, is also greater than the US or EC; and so is semi-conductor demand, container trade and air freight traffic. In fact the Asia and Pacific region market is forecast to grow by about five trillion dollars by the year 2000, which is about the current size of US GNP.

Therefore it is not unlikely that by the end of this decade, the Asia and Pacific region will account for about one-third of entire global growth forecast and the global scene will emerge roughly with equal shares among the four players: North America, the EC, the Asia and Pacific region and the rest of the world.

Against the above unique backdrop of the Asia and Pacific region, it is perhaps now convenient to say a word about another unique institution, namely the Asian Development Bank, founded in 1966. The Bank, an international financial institution, is owned by 53 member countries.[1] It is mandated to assist in the economic and social development of the Asia and Pacific Region. Broadly speaking, the Bank's policies aim at bringing 'minds', 'methods' and 'markets' together and to reduce distance between 'ideas', 'people' and 'products'. As of 30 June 1993, the Bank had approved loans and investments amounting to $44 billion for 1,125 projects in 31 countries. About 25 per cent of this assistance has been in the energy sector, for 258 projects including 163 power projects. The Bank's emphasis on sustainable energy development is illustrated by the fact that since 1991, about a billion dollars of its lending has been for energy–environment related projects in India and China alone.

3. ECONOMY–ENERGY–ENVIRONMENT EQUATION OF THE REGION

The region's economic performance during the past three decades has indeed been impressive. Overall GDP growth rates have steadily increased from about 5 per cent in the 1960s to 6.5 per cent in the 1970s and to 7.3 per cent in the 1980s. Both external and internal factors have contributed to these high rates of growth; the external factors include buoyancy in export markets and transfer of capital and technology to the Asian countries from the industrialized countries. Internal factors include ambitious programmes for education, enterprise (private), efficiency, equitable rules and regulations, macroeconomic stability, and so on.

Direct foreign investment in the developing countries of Asia amounted to $60 billion from 1985 to 1990, i.e., nearly 60 per cent of direct foreign investment in all developing countries. Despite the stretch in current global recession, most of the economies of the Asia and Pacific region have managed high growth rates, in spite of their dependence on energy imports and oil price swings. This momentum is likely to continue in the medium term with about 7 per cent rate of growth. A major assumption for such an optimistic scenario is, of course, continued availability of capital *resources.*

Given the resource constraints currently being faced by multilateral and bilateral sources, there exists an increasing role for the private sector in mobilizing capital for energy sector development. The global and regional capital markets, generally referred to as the 'symbol' economy[2] would be a major source of liquidity for such deployment. Another important factor is continued investment in the region by Japan, with its complementary positive influence on promoting energy efficiency both as a role model and as a source of technology.

From 1981–91, energy consumption in the developing member countries (DMCs) doubled from 700 mtoe to 1,350 mtoe and electricity consumption increased two and a half times from 500 TWh to 1,200 TWh. These DMCs, with 51 per cent of the global population, accounted for about 17 per cent of the energy consumption in the world. The region's per capita energy use, though still relatively modest, is about 500 kgoe. However, driven by GDP, population growth, urbanization and labour productivity,[3] this figure is expected to increase by 20 per cent by the year 2000. In this context, it is relevant to note that the overall energy intensity[4] for 16 of the region's DMCs has marginally declined by about 7 per cent from 857 kgoe in 1980 to 793 kgoe in 1990.[5] Similarly, oil intensity of the region has declined from 360 kg to 222 kg.[6] China continues to have the highest energy intensity, ever reported, of about 1250 kgoe. This compares with India's figure of 670. Given the current emphasis on energy end-use efficiency and energy conservation, a further decline of about 10 per cent may be expected by the year 2000.

Perhaps the best articulation, so far, of the impact of energy efficiency and conservation on primary energy use was made by Lovins in 1976.[7] He had then argued that the US annual primary energy forecast of 163 quadrillion (1015) BTU for the year 2000 could be reduced to about 100 quadrillion BTU by resorting to sustainable energy development through efficient energy conversion and end-use technologies (which he elegantly called soft energy technology paths). Recognizing its vast potential, Japan has embraced the principles enthusiastically and in the process become perhaps the lowest emitter of carbon dioxide, sulphur oxides and nitrogen oxides. This is not surprising, given Japan's exceptional energy intensity record which is compared with that of other OECD countries. It may be added that this impressive emission record has been achieved at considerable cost and dedication; the Japanese power utilities alone spend about $2 billion per year for emission control.

4. ROLE MODEL OF JAPAN: HOW DID JAPAN DO IT?

Japan's economic growth, from 3 per cent of world GNP in 1960 to 16 per cent in 1992, has had a remarkable impact on its many Asian trading partners stretching along the diagonal between Tokyo and Jakarta. These will include about 600 million (dynamic) consumers by the year 2000. Japanese investments have continued throughout this region whereas, for the most part, US and European firms have been somewhat hesitant. As a result, Japanese firms are moving into strategic control of the world's fastest-growing new markets.

Keeping its eye on productivity, efficiency and innovation, Japan has invested about 25.4 per cent of its 1991 GNP in plant and new capital equipment, amounting to a total of $725 billion (the US, in comparison invested $495 billion or 11.2 per cent of GNP). Another factor benefiting the Asia and Pacific region is Japan's massive strategic investment in civilian research and development which, in 1991, amounted to $100 billion or about double that of the US on a per capita basis. Another remarkable feature is Japan's end-use efficiency which is influencing the energy consumption 'culture' in the region. In spite of 84 per cent energy imports, Japan has succeeded in producing two and a quarter times the real output with the same energy input as 15 years ago, and its current energy imports account for approximately 1.5 per cent of its GNP—slightly more than the 1.2 per cent share for the US, which has the advantage of being a major oil producer.

In a constrained energy supply environment, energy efficiency, in fact, can serve as the key to economic development. This is cited in a recent study of the OECD countries (Schipper and Meyers 1993), which analysed the impact of three scenarios of energy efficiency improvement on sectoral energy use to support an average GDP growth of 2.8 per cent per year for the period 1985–2010. The three scenarios identified were: (i) trend—based on current and expected trends; (ii) efficiency—energy efficiency given higher priority by governments and the private sector; and (iii) vigorous—restraining energy use becomes a very high priority in public policy. The study concluded that the average yearly rates of decline in primary energy intensity over the study period for these three scenarios would be 1.0, 2.0 and 3.6 per cent, respectively, and that primary energy use in the OECD countries in 2010 could be 20–25 per cent lower than at present, based on scenario (ii), and even 40–45 per cent lower based on scenario (iii) under very challenging circumstances.

Because of the constraints imposed by economic geography considerations, and their commitment to sustainable development and environmental redemption, the Japanese have recently announced two projects of grand scale and concept. They reflect Japanese concern for the security of energy supplies and environment in the national energy equation. First, is the 1,000 km length of underground high voltage cable to interconnect Osaka with Tokyo. Second, is a 1,000 hectare man-made island to be developed 8–10 km off north-east Tokyo, for the production of 7,000 MW of electrical power based on liquified natural gas (LNG).

5. ROLE OF NATURAL GAS IN ENHANCING ENERGY SECURITY

Recognizing that natural gas is considered a user- and environment-friendly source, and its future prospects being meritorious, the Bank had recently commissioned a Regional Technical Assistance Study on Increased Utilization of Natural Gas. This study has evaluated gas resources in eleven countries and the investment required to appraise and develop them. It has also: formulated gas utilization plans taking into account demand and supply scenarios including regional trade; reviewed existing policies, programmes and institutional frame-work; identified policy constraints for strategic gas development; and assessed the impact on competing fuels. Several DMCs are endowed with substantial gas reserves amounting to 445 tcf, i.e., equivalent to about 8 per cent of world reserves. Nevertheless, natural gas has accounted for only 11 per cent of total commercial primary energy consumption in this region in 1992, compared with 23 per cent for the world.

About 75 per cent of the gas trade is in the pipeline mode. There are possibilities of promoting regional gas trade through pipelines such as the trans-ASEAN gas pipeline system, about 8,000 km in length, to link the East Asian markets with production areas in the ASEAN region. Two other pipeline projects have also being outlined: Sakhalin to Japan and from Yakutsk to Japan through South Korea. Another proposal which Japan has recently decided to support, is from the Central Asian Republics to East Asia, called the Energy Silk route.

In the LNG field, Indonesia, Malaysia, Brunei and Australia have since 1991 dominated regional trade by exporting about 40 million tonnes to Japan, South Korea and Taiwan.[8] Transportation of natural gas over long distances in the LNG form requires large dedicated reserves requiring very high investment costs. However, growth in energy demand and rising concerns over environment have made LNG the fuel of choice for these markets. Their demand for LNG is expected to grow to about 65 million tonnes per year by 2000. Supply expansions to meet this additional demand are therefore being planned by Malaysia, Indonesia and Australia.

Natural gas has also shown resilience not only for providing security of supply for consumers but also for providing security of demand for producers. Producers have shown a strong interest in maintaining a fair balance in the security equation, in order to avert the risk of 'trade or fade'. Therefore, pricing has always been a key element in the energy security equation, requiring most careful review of upstream and downstream costs on the one hand and costs of alternative fuels on the other. Japan, South Korea, Taiwan and Hong Kong, which depend on imported sources for 84, 79, 95 and 100 per cent respectively, of their total primary energy requirements, have demonstrated to the world (perhaps even more so to the Asia and Pacific region) that the absence of indigenous energy resources need not lower the curtain on their economic development.[9] A logical next step in this direction could be the accelerated development of marginal oil and gas fields in several DMCs by consumers such as Taiwan, South Korea and Japan, for their mutual benefit.

6. ROLE OF NATURAL GAS IN THE ELECTRIC POWER SECTOR

Power generation accounts for about 55 per cent of the 13 billion cubic feet per day of gas consumption in the Asia and Pacific region. The share of industry is about 38 per cent and the balance is for domestic and other sectors. Total gas consumption of the region is projected to reach 23 billion cubic feet per day by the year 2000. This implies that industrial growth in the region, which has been the major driving force for its economic development, should continue to enjoy security of supplies, price competitiveness and availability of investment funds.

Given the environmental and efficiency advantages of natural gas and against the backdrop of conventional difficulties associated with nuclear and hydro-power projects, it is quite certain that more and more power utilities will continue to turn to gas-fired combined cycle power plants. Current analysis indicates that a gas-fired combined cycle is indeed competitive with alternative power plant types if unit gas price is about $5 per MMBTU (1992). Japan, for example, expects to add about 20,000 MW of natural gas-fired power plant by the year 2010. The power utilities of the Bank's DMCs have also been turning with confidence to the use of natural gas-fired combined cycle plant during the past 5–7 years. It is estimated that about 100,000 MW of additional natural gas-fired power plant would be added to the power systems of Asia and Pacific region by the year 2010.

7. ENVIRONMENTAL ISSUES FOR THE REGION

Energy conversion technology and thermodynamic constraints are at the heart of most environmental issues. As a result of global awareness and concern, technology now exists to curb harmful emissions resulting from energy conversion plants at local and regional levels. However, adoption of such technologies is conditioned by environmental standards in use, their institutional strength and legislative enforcement mechanisms. Furthermore, the new challenge is to avert climatic changes resulting from carbon dioxide and other greenhouse gas emissions. Hence the importance of integrated resource planning for energy development by systematically factoring in environmental considerations, costs and constraints as well as demand-side management strategies for increased energy-use efficiency in the least-cost planning models adopted in the energy sector (Asian Development Bank 1992).

It is against this backdrop that natural gas has a distinct comparative advantage as it produces only half as much carbon dioxide as coal, and about 25 per cent less than oil and contains only traces of sulphur and heavy metals. In addition, natural gas combustion technology has made impressive gains during the past decade and can now show efficiencies of more than 50 per cent in electricity generation (using combined cycle gas turbine facilities) and about 90 per cent in combined heat and power generation systems. Furthermore, the investment costs, operating cost and completion time for natural gas-fired combined cycle power generation facilities are about a half of those using conventional coal-fired facilities.[10]

8. CAPITAL INVESTMENT IN THE NATURAL GAS SUBSECTOR

As mentioned before, East and Southeast Asian region holds promise for increasing LNG supplies to Japan, South Korea and Taiwan by about 25 million tonnes during this decade. Estimated investment for this purpose is about $150 billion. Augmentation of pipeline-based gas supplies is estimated to cost an additional $150 billion. However, since only about 10 per cent of the above investment requirements can be expected from multilateral and bilateral financing sources, most of them will have to depend on self-financing by the utilities in the region and, of course, on private-sector financing.

Institutional and legislative developments in the Bank's DMCs are indicative of the changes that are emerging with respect to securing self-financing and improvements in the performance of gas enterprises. It is being appreciated that one of the major impediments to private-sector investment is lack of adequate regulatory systems which generally lowers credibility as the 'rules of the game' are not fully defined. Undoubtedly, as both investors and governments gain experience, private-sector participation will increase and policies will have to be evolved so that public policy aspects as well as incentives for efficient management of the subsector can co-exist and flourish.

9. THE BANK'S CURRENT ROLE AND FUTURE DIRECTION

The Bank will continue to play a catalytic role in the development of gas transmission and distribution systems leaving upstream gas investment for the private sector. The Bank may also play a selective role in the production of gas where reservoir conditions so merit. The Bank is keen to enhance end-use efficiency improvements, in close cooperation with the private sector. The Bank endeavours to dilute government control so as to improve operational efficiency, autonomy and accountability of public sector utilities. The Bank also encourages divestment and disinvestment of government shareholdings in gas utilities, replacing them with local and foreign equity. Commercialization and corporatization of sector entities, leading to privatization, is a continuing policy goal of the Bank. Therefore the institutional and policy focus of the Bank is to assist DMC governments to undertake sector reforms to: (i) identify the optimal structure and performance; (ii) create independent, credible and quasijudicial regulatory boards; and (iii) prepare necessary legislative frameworks in coordination and symmetry with other multilateral and bilateral donor agencies.

To cope with envisaged challenges in energy sector development of the DMCs, the Bank will focus ly on energy issues such as conservation and efficiency improvement, increased utilization of indigenous energy resources, and intensified environmental assessment and redemption. Besides its traditional lending portfolio for energy projects, the Bank proposes to diversify its lending instruments to support hydrocarbon sector development so as to achieve improved sector performance over the medium term. The Bank will also increase its energy policy and advisory role for sectoral planning, development and management, through country-specific energy strategies and institutions.

In conclusion, I shall remark on the significant role played by energy in development, especially in view of the recent global and regional changes, in fact sea-changes. For instance, a decade ago, it would have been considered foolhardy to suggest that 'USSR' would be replaced by 'FSU' or that the integration of Eastern Europe and the unification of Germany would come about, or the recent Gulf War or even market buoyancy of China or the energy role-model of Japan would be before us. Chastened, I hope, by the acceleration of events globally and in the region, and their close linkages with the energy industry, one would expect the future to continue to outwit us all, both in scale and substance. That is why it can be said that Energy is a protean substance; it can assume many shapes—even the shape of things to come, for the Asia and Pacific region.

NOTES

1. Thirty-seven developing member countries and 16 OECD countries. Uzbekistan, Kazakhstan and Kyrgyzstan are in the process of becoming member countries.
2. The existence of this 'symbol' economy is indicated by the fact that the annual turnover of the world's major financial markets is at least 25 times of world annual trade in goods and services (see Drucker 1984).
3. Labour productivity for South Korea, for example, has grown at about 11 per cent per year during the recent past. The corresponding figure for Thailand was about 10 per cent per year.
4. Expressed in kilograms of oil equivalent per thousand US dollars of GDP in 1980 constant prices.
5. This compares with 590 kgoe in the US and Canada, and 370 kgoe in Western Europe.
6. Energy Indicators of Developing Member Countries of the Asian Development Bank—July 1992.
7. Lovins 1976.
8. Indonesia accounted for about 55 per cent of the supply and Japan accounted for nearly 90 per cent of the demand.
9. In 1991, Japan, South Korea, Taiwan and Hong Kong imported energy to the value of about $54bn, $11bn, $7bn and $2bn, respectively. The value of Japan's imports was less than 1 per cent of its GDP; this value for the other three countries was about 4 per cent of GDP.
10. Typically, a large combined cycle gas turbine based power plant currently costs about $800 per kW (compared to $1500 per kW for coal-fired plant with flue gas desulphurization), has an efficiency of 52 per cent (compared with 36 per cent for coal) and takes 2–3 years to install.

REFERENCES

Asian Development Bank (1992), 'Integrated Energy–Environment Planning—Towards Developing A Framework', May.

Drucker, Peter F. (1984), 'The Changed World Economy', *US Foreign Affairs Journal*, April.

Lovins, Amory B. (1976), 'Energy Strategy: The Road Not Taken?', *US Foreign Affairs Journal*, October .

Schipper, Lee and Stephen Meyers (1993), 'Using Scenarios to Explore Future Energy Demand in Industrial Countries', *Energy Policy*, March.

6. Asian Structural Interdependency and the Environment[*]

Akihiro Watabe and Kaoru Yamaguchi

1. INTRODUCTION

Recent estimates by the United Nations Population Fund predict that world population will reach at least 8.5 billion by the year 2025 and that about 85 per cent of the world population will be living in the developing countries.[1] The Asian region's population, including Australia and New Zealand, will grow at an average annual rate of 1.3 per cent and is predicted to reach approximately 4.6 billion by the year 2025.[2] Although there is no significant empirical evidence thus far available to support the links between population growth and environmental degradation, population growth in the developing countries obviously requires supporting economic development as in more industrialized economies. As a consequence, more energy and resources will be consumed.

In fact, economic growth rates in the Asian region during the 1990s have been significantly higher than other regions in the world, i.e., they have been at 6.7 per cent in East Asia and 4.7 per cent in South Asia. If these growth rates continue, the Asian region will become a bigger economic bloc than North America and Europe by early next century. Thus, overall energy consumption is projected to increase at the much higher rate of 3.2 per cent and consequently coal consumption will rise to replace declining oil resources. As a result, it is predicted that CO_2 emissions from the Asian region, especially China, India, the Association of South East Asian Nations (ASEAN) countries and the Asian Newly Industrializing Economies (NIEs), will increase by 3.2 per cent annu-

[*]   We are grateful to Ki-joong Kim, Fu-chen Lo and Jacob Park for comments and discussions. In particular, we would like to thank Glen Paoletto for constructive criticism and Global Environmental Forum of Japan for financial support. The views expressed in this chapter are those of the authors and should not be attributed to those of the Institute of Energy Economics, Japan.

93

ally.[3] These predictions tell us that Asia will likely be the most crucial region in the world for global warming and climate change in the twenty-first century.

There is a growing record of industries relocating from the North to the South in several regions in the world. Industrial relocation reflects the comparative advantage of the North in international competition, and at the same time, provides basic needs for economic development to the South. There is clear evidence for this in Asia, for example between Japan and the ASEAN countries and NIEs, whose economies are characterized by structural interdependency. That is, as a result of economic restructuring, industrial production is integrated across several countries. In so doing, each country makes a contribution in order to complete final products and/or intermediate goods and thus each country becomes dependent upon other countries in production processes. Accordingly, structural interdependency involves industrial relocation, division of production and its resulting input–output flows among the countries, and has significant impact on the trade flows of final and intermediate products.

This economic restructuring, however, is not without problems. Economic structural interdependency emerges from the transfer of capital from one country to another and it would stem from comparative advantage in shifting production to the country that incurs lower production costs. Comparative advantage results from cheap labour, abundant natural resource and lower environmental standards of the country. One aspect of environmental concerns is that comparative advantage generates more environmental externalities which may not be fully internalized. In addition, international trade increases competition which forces a reduction in prices of products. Cost reduction therefore is inevitable for reducing prices so as to at least break even, and that encourages more interdependencies of countries between the North and the South. This dynamic could lead to an increasing spiral of environmental costs and impacts.

In fact, there are a number of studies on environmental standards and the migration of dirty industries to developing countries.[4] Previous studies found that there is no significant evidence to support the thesis that environmental regulation leads to the loss of competitiveness. Therefore, higher environmental standards may not necessarily result in the migration of dirty industries to the South (i.e., there is no evidence to support 'pollution havens') although Low and Yeats (1992)[5] find that dirty industries have migrated to the South. Little research on environmental standards and migration of dirty industries, however, has been done for Asia.

In the case of Asia, the economic structural interdependency stated above is initiated primarily through foreign direct investment (FDI) by Japan into the ASEAN countries and NIEs. The appreciation of the Japanese yen against other major currencies, particularly after the Plaza Agreement in 1985, as well as the recent economic growth of Southeast Asian countries accelerated Japan's FDI into the ASEAN countries and NIEs. Hence, it does not seem evident that lower environmental standards alone play a major role in FDI.

It seems plausible that technological progress in the South resulting from economic restructuring by the North, has resulted in more resource-saving as well as less-polluting production processes. Moreover, international trade can generally help the economic growth of countries. None the less, environmental externalities such as CO_2 emissions and the amounts of production are not proportional and both depend on the nature of production processes and abatement technology. It is often the fact that transferred technology is not the most advanced technology but nevertheless meets environmental standards in the South. Thus, even though the shift of production from the North to the South may result in the reduction of a certain amount of CO_2 emissions in the North, it does not mean that the same amount of CO_2 emissions will flow into the South. It seems obvious that shifting production will generate more CO_2 emissions in the South but it is not clear whether this will increase the total amounts of CO_2 emitted at the global level.[6]

When it comes to trade policies and environmental goals, a basic issue is whether the existence of lower environmental standards in less-developed countries implies an advantage in production costs over a country with strict environmental standards. Differences in environmental standards may induce incentives for the country to implement trade measures such as countervailing duties on imported products to offset its disadvantage, if they are not discriminatory under the General Agreement on Tariffs and Trade (GATT) rules. Furthermore, in principle it is impossible to impose domestic environmental polices or to assess the practices of exporting countries under the GATT rules.

In this chapter, we restrict attention to structural interdependency and the environment in Asia by focusing on Japan and NIEs and the ASEAN countries as a regional North–South relationship, and the impact of economic interdependency on the environment through CO_2 emissions. In what follows, we will examine the relationship between Japanese FDI in NIEs and the ASEAN countries leading to structural interdependency, and the amounts of CO_2 emitted by these countries. Thereafter, trade policy for environmental goals will be considered. Regarding regional trade flows in terms of environmental concerns, exports from NIEs and the ASEAN countries to Japan will be taken into account.

The rest of the chapter is organized as follows. In Section 2, we discuss the economic structural interdependency between Japan and NIEs and the ASEAN countries as well as its importance in Asia. Thereafter, the trends in the amounts of CO_2 emitted by countries during the last two decades are examined, using statistics. Section 3 attempts to analyse the link between trade, structural interdependency and the amounts of CO_2 emitted in Asia. Implications for trade policy and environmental goals are discussed in Section 4.

2. STRUCTURAL INTERDEPENDENCY AND THE ENVIRONMENT IN ASIA

Since the late 1960s, Japan has played a major role in the economic restructuring of Asia by making FDI in NIEs and the ASEAN countries. The first FDI boom ceased about 1973 right after the first oil shock. Thereafter, Japanese FDI shifted primarily to the US rather than to Asia. During the 1980s, however, Japanese FDI again shifted back to NIEs and the ASEAN countries.[7] Statistics show that during the last decade, the total values of Japanese FDI to NIEs and the ASEAN countries in US dollars almost tripled (see Table 6.1).[8]

Table 6.1   Japan's FDI into China, NIEs and the ASEAN countries

FDI (million $)	China	NIEs	ASEAN
1983	3	1,117	651
1986	226	1,531	553
1987	1,226	2,580	1,030
1988	296	3,264	1,966
1989	438	4,900	2,782
1990	349	3,355	3,242
1991	579	2,203	3,083
1992	1,070	1,922	3,197

Source: Japan External Trade Organization (1980–94).

There are three major factors affecting the recent growth of Japanese FDI in NIEs and the ASEAN countries: (i) the appreciation of the Japanese yen against major currencies, (ii) the protectionism of industrialized countries, and (iii) the recent economic growth of NIEs and the ASEAN countries. All three factors are linked to international competition, particularly in the manufacturing sector.[9] It should be noted that Japanese FDI aims to promote comparative advantage in international competition. However, there has been an important consequence of Japanese FDI,[10] namely, it expanded industrial belts in NIEs and the ASEAN countries as the complement of industrial production between Japan and those countries. That means that several countries contribute to complete final products and/or intermediate goods by supplying parts and so on, and specific products are assembled in each country as geographically dispersed based manufacturing.

Concerning the protectionism of industrialized countries, the second factor of the recent Japanese FDI growth, Wakasugi (1994)[11] showed that although Japanese FDI induced by the trade restriction was accompanied by a decrease in exports from Japan, Japanese FDI and exports do not substitute for one another. Indeed, a major reason for the increase of Japanese FDI was due to technological innovation which enabled Japanese firms to generate new manufactured products in neighbouring countries, and to export these overseas, as well as back to Japanese domestic markets.

Consequently, Japan's FDI expanded or shifted industrial capacities in the Asian region and comparative advantage in international competition through structural interdependency, while at the same time it promoted the industrialization of Asian countries.[12]

Regarding the environment, our concerns in this chapter are with CO_2 emissions. The amounts of CO_2 emitted by China, Japan, NIEs and the ASEAN countries have been increasing since 1971.[13] All countries except Japan demonstrate rapid increases of CO_2 emissions. In particular, the annual average increase rates of CO_2 emitted by China, NIEs and the ASEAN countries during 1971–90 are 4.9 per cent, 6.5 per cent and 6.35 per cent respectively, while Japan exhibited only 1.55 per cent of its growth rate.[14] Although the total amount of CO_2 emitted by both China and Japan still far exceeds NIEs and the ASEAN countries, these statistics clearly indicate that NIEs and the ASEAN countries are increasing the rates of CO_2 emissions much faster than both China and Japan.

During 1971–80, every year the total amounts of CO_2 emitted by China, Japan, NIEs and the ASEAN countries contributed about 86 per cent of the total CO_2 emissions in the Asian region and about 84 per cent during 1981–90.[15] Taking the shares of CO_2 emitted by the countries, the share of NIEs and the ASEAN countries combined increased from 9 per cent to 15 per cent during 1971–90. Meanwhile, that of China increased from 38 per cent to 45 per cent but that of Japan decreased from 37 per cent to 23 per cent during the same period. Furthermore, the ratio between the share of CO_2 emitted by China, NIEs and the ASEAN countries and that of Japan has increased by approximately one per cent every year since 1971; that is, increasing the share from 47 per cent to 60 per cent. Even excluding China, it increases from 19 per cent to 40 per cent. That means that although Japan is the second biggest generator of CO_2 emissions in Asia behind China, the shares of CO_2 emissions among the countries are gradually shifting from Japan to NIEs and the ASEAN countries. If the growth

Table 6.2   *The countries' shares out of the total amounts of CO_2 emissions in Asia*

CO_2 emission	China (%)	Japan (%)	NIEs+ASEAN (%)
1971	38	37	9
1975	41	34	10
1980	43	29	13
1985	46	24	13
1986	47	24	13
1987	48	23	13
1988	47	22	14
1989	47	23	14
1990	45	23	15

Source: Energy Data Modeling Center (1993).

rates of CO_2 emitted by the countries remain at the same level, then the total amount of CO_2 emitted by NIEs and the ASEAN countries all together will exceed the amount of Japan's CO_2 emissions early in the next century. The important question to be addressed is whether or not a reduction in the share of CO_2 emitted by Japan is replaced by an increase in the share of CO_2 emitted by both NIEs and the ASEAN countries. And if so, does it result from structural interdependency as discussed above? In other words, does structural interdependency result in the geographical shifting of CO_2 emissions from Japan to Southeast Asia with increasing rates in the latter? (see Table 6.2).

3. INTRAREGIONAL TRADE AND THE ENVIRONMENT IN ASIA

Despite the slow economic growth in the world economy, Southeast Asian countries have demonstrated rapid economic growth in recent years and they remain the fastest-growing region in the world. With the exception of the Philippines, all countries in the region achieved over 5 per cent average annual economic growth rates during the 1980s. Such high economic growth rates have been matched by their export performance. The share of East Asian countries in world exports increased from 8.7 per cent to 10.8 per cent during 1986–89. Moreover, trade within the Asian bloc has grown faster than global trade. The share of intraregional trade increased from 33.8 per cent to 38.4 per cent during the 1980s. The increase in intraregional trade has been associated with a growth in intraregional investment flows which are closely linked to the regional production of manufacturing products.[16]

As is stated in the previous section, Japanese FDI has enlarged industrial capacities in Southeast Asia. Expanded industrial capacities in the region have promoted increases in intraregional exports to Japan as well as exports to the rest of the world. Statistics show that industrial products from NIEs and the ASEAN countries increased their share in Japanese markets. During the last decade, Japanese imports from NIEs and the ASEAN countries almost doubled, and their share out of the total Japanese imports has been approximately 50 per cent. Furthermore, CO_2-intensive industries such as chemicals, metal materials, mine fuels, high-tech goods and other industrial products, account for the major share of Japanese regional imports.[17] Therefore, the economic structural interdependency affects not only interregional and intraregional trade flows but also the total amounts of CO_2 emitted by each country, that is, the spatial distribution of CO_2 emissions (see Table 6.3).

Now, let us consider the link between trade and the environment in Asia. As in the above, trade flows as well as regional economies are characterized by structural interdependency and so too are the factors influencing CO_2 emissions.

Table 6.3   Japanese imports from China, NIEs and the ASEAN countries

Imports (million $)	China	NIEs	ASEAN
1983	5,958	8,125	18,254
1986	5,652	12,519	15,054
1987	7,401	18,810	17,531
1988	9,858	25,003	20,119
1989	11,145	27,143	22,857
1990	12,053	25,946	25,689
1991	14,215	27,309	28,345
1992	16,952	26,166	28,482

Source: Japan External Trade Organization (1980–94).

Concerning the effect of North–South economic interactions on the environment within the Asian region, trade flows from NIEs and the ASEAN countries to Japan and investment flows in the opposite direction are likely to reflect the impact of intraregional economic interactions on the environment. It is a fact that in Southeast Asia, Japan was a major supplier of industrial technology and Japanese FDI was a big source of technology transfer. A variety of technology was absorbed from Japan and used to manufacture the products in the recipient countries.[18]

A revealed comparative advantage (RCA) index of the ASEAN countries and NIEs towards Japan in terms of exports has been between 2.0 and 2.5 while the RCA index towards the US has been between 1.0 and 1.5 for the last several years.[19] It implies that the US is the biggest importer from the ASEAN countries and NIEs outside Asia, and the ASEAN countries and NIEs have a comparative advantage in exporting to Japan over the US.

In what follows, we examine the link between intraregional trade and CO_2 emissions by analysing Japanese FDI and imports. The essence of our analysis stems from the characteristics of the regional economies arising from structural interdependency among the countries rather than the phenomenon of 'pollution havens'.[20] Pollution havens include local environmental externalities such as regional destruction of the ecosystem, water pollution, industrial waste and so on. The nature of such pollution is likely to encourage the migration of dirty industries. In that sense, our concerns are with global environmental issues generated in Asia so that pollution havens in a broader sense are given less attention.

The effects of Japanese FDI and imports on the amounts of CO_2 emitted by each country vary across countries. Although about 25 per cent of the total Japanese imports have recently been coming from the ASEAN countries and NIEs, the export shares out of the total values of exports from each ASEAN country and NIEs to Japan still remain small.[21] Therefore, unless we take the total values of exports from the ASEAN countries and NIEs to Japan as a whole, the exports of each individual country do not seem to have a significant impact on CO_2 emissions. Rather, each country's GDP would have a significant impact on CO_2 emissions. It is also expected that FDI has the same consequence as exports. That is, the value of FDI made in the ASEAN countries and NIEs as a whole would have a significant impact on CO_2 emissions; however, the value of FDI made in each country has little impact. The results of regression essentially follow the discussions.[22]

There exist, however, countries where either exports or FDI are significant and countries where neither are significant. For China, exports obtain a significant result but neither FDI nor GDP obtains a significant result. Meanwhile, Indonesia has a significant effect on FDI but not on either export or GDP. None of the independent variables are significant for the Philippines. A possible explanation for these three countries is that both China and Indonesia are the only countries in regression analysis that are categorized as low-income countries by the World Bank. And Chinese exports to Japan far exceeded other countries in terms of the growth rate during the last decade. Moreover, after 1990, China became the biggest exporter to Japan in Asia. In Indonesia, Japanese FDI has been dominant. In 1992, for example, about 50 per cent of Japanese FDI to the ASEAN countries was made in Indonesia. The Philippines is categorized as a lower-middle-income country by the World Bank. Within ASEAN, Japanese FDI is the lowest in the Philippines where exports are among the lowest. Moreover, although manufacturing industries are increasing the percentage of GDP in the Philippines, the economy still relies heavily on the primary industries.

4. IMPLICATIONS FOR TRADE POLICY AND ENVIRONMENTAL GOALS IN ASIA

As is stated in Section 1, over the next decade or so the Asian region will be expecting high economic growth rates as well as high energy consumption rates which rely heavily on coal consumption. As a matter of fact, there are four important elements of the Asian region with respect to environmental concerns: (i) it is the only region where coal is the number one energy source, (ii) Asia has the potential for high increases in energy demands, (iii) increases in energy consumption rates are almost the same as economic growth rates for NIEs and the ASEAN countries, and (iv) it has a decreasing share of oil consumption but an increasing share of coal and natural gas consumption.[23]

Trade policy could change both the international flows of products and the magnitudes of product flows from one country to another. Moreover, it will affect the flows of FDI and thus production locations. Accordingly, trade policy could have significant effects on environmental consequences in the region. Given the prospective high growth of economies as well as environmental matters in the Asian region specified in the above four elements, it is clear that the region needs more energy-efficient production and advanced technology for reducing CO_2 emissions. One of our concerns here is whether or not environmental goals can be achieved with a trade policy. If there is any way of implementing a regional trade policy for environmental objectives, Japan, as the only country of the North in Asia, needs to develop a role of leader–follower relationships with the ASEAN countries and NIEs.

Analytically, trade policy and environmental goals give rise to two main issues: (i) different environmental standards in countries and trade measures, and (ii) characteristics of trade policy to reach environmental goals and their possible conflict with the GATT.[24] The first issue relates to international competition among countries with different environmental standards. That is, industries in higher standard countries may impose countervailing duties on imports against an exporting country with lower environmental standards to offset their disadvantage if they are non-discriminatory under GATT rules. The second issue relates particularly to the GATT rules regarding 'nature of products' and 'production processes', and Article XX of the GATT (public policy exception) which allows signatories to deviate from their basic obligations for public policy goals.

The result of the analysis in the previous section suggests that a trade policy, in general, would be ineffective for the control of CO_2 emissions since Japanese imports from each ASEAN country and NIEs have an insignificant effect on CO_2 emissions. But for China, a trade policy can have an effect on CO_2 emissions. Furthermore, a unilateral trade policy against China would not create any barriers in an international society since China is (as yet) a non-signatory of the GATT.[25] It is, however, widely discussed that unilateral restrictions on trade would never be the most efficient instrument for dealing with environmental problems.[26] Unilateral sanctions can lead to the imposition of unilaterally perceived values across countries with marginal benefits with respect to the global environment. In the context of an international trade system, it is likely to do more harm than good.[27] Regarding the use of sanctions against non-signatories, there are three basic choices for the compatibility of the GATT: (i) Article XX could be interpreted to allow for trade sanctions under international treaties if they are judged necessary, (ii) GATT signatories could waive their GATT obligations case by case in the event of any GATT inconsistent measure, and (iii) GATT could be amended to cater for the environmental concerns of its signatories.[28] These issues, however, are not tested yet. As a consequence, we need to seek multilateral cooperation among the countries. The study on trade and the environment by the GATT (1992)[29] is clear on this point:

> When an environmental problem involves a transborder physical spillover, the only alternative to unilateral actions based on economic and political power is for countries to cooperate in the design, implementation and enforcement of an appropriate

multilateral agreement for dealing with the problem at hand.

Regardless of the nature of an environmental problem, the contribution of multilateral cooperation is to reduce the possibility that solutions are affected by differences in the economic and political strengths of the parties involved.

Regional economic cooperation among Asian countries was initiated by the ASEAN countries as an external security measure and led to the regional concentration of trade. In 1992, the ASEAN countries agreed to implement over the next 15 years an ASEAN Free Trade Area with a common external preferential tariff. The establishment of an East Asian Economic Caucus has also been discussed in various regional forums where the Asian trade group would be under Japan's leadership. There are indeed fears that the emergence of an East Asian trade bloc is moving the world economy into an era of increasing trade barriers and would lead to an increase in tension towards North American and European blocs. Nonetheless, such fears seem to be overstated and regional cooperation is essentially aimed at opening market access within the region.[30]

Regional cooperation in Asia is, in essence, reinforced by structural interdependency of the region, which makes it harder to design and implement an intraregional trade policy for environmental goals. In other words, it seems to be the fact that an intraregional trade policy itself is not an effective economic instrument to achieve the control of CO_2 emissions in Asia. In addition, it is evident that protectionism is still practised, and moreover markets outside the region account for the major share of the exports of the ASEAN countries and NIEs. It follows, therefore, that in order to achieve an environmental objective such as the reduction of CO_2 emissions, regional multilateral cooperation is more important than the manipulation of trade policies. Repetto (1993)[31] argues in a similar vein that eliminating quantitative restrictions on the export of labour-intensive manufactures from developing countries would have significant economic as well as environmental benefits. Output would expand in labour-intensive processing industries to add more value to their exported primary materials for the export of natural-resource-based commodities and also reduce rural population growth which can cause ecosystems to deteriorate.

The Climate Change Convention which entered into force in March 1994 committed developed countries to take measures to keep their greenhouse gas emissions to 1990 levels by the year 2000. Furthermore, developed countries must take practical steps to promote and finance the transfer of environmentally sound technologies to developing countries. Ratifications of the Convention through June 1994 were made by 75 countries, of which those in our concern include only China, Japan and Korea.

The Convention indeed disputes some issues. First, it aims at stabilizing the greenhouse gas emissions of developed countries and not global emissions. Therefore, commitments of developed countries (i.e., ratified developed countries) will not be sufficient to achieve a stabilization of the concentration of greenhouse gases in the atmosphere. The second issue envisaged by the Convention is joint implementation. That is, countries could limit emissions through cooperative activities in other countries, including financial and technological transfers. In order to avoid abatement expenditures under joint implementation, developed countries may try to reduce emissions in developing countries which are inefficient energy consumers. In particular, developed countries with high emissions per capita would try to fulfil their obligations under the Convention by paying developing countries to take measures which are not necessarily in the interest of the developing countries. In effect, joint implementation becomes an alternative to development cooperation.[32]

Japanese CO_2 emissions per capita are slightly below the average of G7 countries and are significantly higher than China, the ASEAN countries and NIEs, except for Singapore.[33] Moreover, given her advanced abatement technology and its high efficiency, it would not be surprising if Japan initiates joint implementation within Asia so as to reduce her CO_2 emissions as required by the Convention. In the above, structural interdependency in Asia was primarily initiated by Japanese FDI following the appreciation of the Japanese yen against major currencies and the high economic growth of Southeast Asian countries. In addition, its structure was well established long before the Climate Change Convention. Hence, it does not necessarily follow that joint implementation among Asian member states such as China, Japan and Korea would replace intraregional development cooperation in Asia. None the less, it is inevitable that various kinds of assistance from Japan to NIEs and the ASEAN countries, such as technology, finance, infrastructure, education and so on, will be needed in the future.[34]

Lastly, the present chapter focused on North–South economic interactions within Asia and the resulting environmental consequences. However, it is a fact that Asian structural interdependency is of relevance not only for intraregional economic and environmental consequences, but also for those outside the region, especially in North America and Europe. Hence, from our analysis, although Japanese trade policy towards the ASEAN countries and NIEs may have little effect on CO_2 emissions, it is necessary that trade policy for environmental goals associated with CO_2 emissions by Asian countries be evaluated in the broader global context in which ASEAN trade is embedded. In addition, oil-exporting countries and the associated energy trade will have to be taken into account.

NOTES

1. World Resources Institute 1990.
2. Japan Environment Agency 1994.
3. Japan Environment Agency 1994. Countries of NIEs consist of Hong Kong, Korea, Singapore

and Taiwan.

4. See Birdsall and Wheeler 1992; Dean 1992; Leonard 1988; Low and Yeats 1992; and Tobey 1990.

5. Low and Yeats 1992.

6. This issue is related to the dispute on joint implementation envisaged by the Climate Change Convention. We will discuss it with reference to the Asian case in Section 4.

7. Lall 1993.

8. Statistics on how Japanese FDI has been allocated in industrial sectors in each country are not available at this time.

9. Expansion or shifting industrial capacities differ from industry to industry. Labour-intensive industries were shifted primarily to the ASEAN countries and capital-intensive industries were expanded to NIEs. But capital-intensive industries have recently been expanded to the ASEAN countries as well.

10. Needless to say, FDI in NIEs and the ASEAN countries has also been provided by the US and Europe. Also, NIEs have recently become major contributors of FDI to the ASEAN countries. None the less, Japan has been the biggest contributor of FDI during the 1970s and 1980s.

11. Wakasugi 1994.

12. Nangaku 1989.

13. See Energy Data and Modeling Center 1993. Indeed, there are some years when the amounts of CO_2 emitted go up and down by small percentages for every country. General trends of the amounts of CO_2 emitted are, however, rising since 1971.

14. Energy Data and Modeling Center 1993.

15. Australia, India and New Zealand are included in the total amounts of CO_2 emissions in the Asian region.

16. Kirkpatrick 1994.

17. Japan External Trade Organization 1977–93.

18. See Wakasugi 1994. It should be noted that industrial products produced in NIEs and the ASEAN countries are certainly exported to countries other than Japan and some of them are intraregionally exported. Recently, trade among NIEs and the ASEAN countries, particularly trade within NIEs, has had a growing share of world trade. Therefore, trade and investment flows to and from Japan may not necessarily reflect the amounts of CO_2 emitted in the region as a whole. Since the primary purpose of this chapter is to consider intraregional trade policy and the trend in CO_2 emissions under structural interdependency with focus on the North–South economic interactions only in Asia, we disregard the effects of the rest of the world on the region.

19. See Japan External Trade Organization 1980–94. The RCA index is defined by $RCA_{AB} = (EX_{AB}/EX_{AT})/(EX_{BT}/EX_W)$ where EX_{AB} is the value of country A's export to country B, EX_{AT} is the total export of country A, EX_{BT} is the total export of country B and EX_W is the total value of world export. The RCA index measures the comparative advantage of exports within a specific region and if the RCA index exceeds one, the country's exports have revealed comparative advantage in the region.

20. Leonard (1988) examined industrial-flight and pollution-haven hypotheses of the US towards Mexico and Brazil by foreign investment and import trends. In doing so, he tried to identify four trends in foreign investment and import figures: (i) the high-pollution manufacturing sectors should be increasing their foreign direct investment more rapidly than other manufacturing industries; (ii) US imports of chemical and processed mineral products should be expanding faster than overall manufactured imports; (iii) less-developed countries should be receiving an increasing share of the total foreign direct investments made by US firms in the high-pollution sectors; and (iv) an increasing share of US imports of goods produced by high-pollution industries should be coming from the less-developed countries (Leonard, pp. 93–4). He found that there is no significant evidence to support the four trends.

21. Japan External Trade Organization 1977–93.

22. The following estimates resulted from OLS for each country in ASEAN and NIEs with the amounts of CO_2 emissions as a dependent variable and Export, FDI and GDP as independent

variables. The quantities in parentheses are the *t*-statistics of the regression coefficients at the 5 per cent level. Taiwan is excluded from the regression since data on GDP were not available.

	Exports	FDI	GDP	Adjusted R^2
China	132.56	0.03	−0.03	0.89
	(3.89)	(0.91)	(−0.12)	
Hong Kong	1.13	−0.00006	0.074	0.85
	(1.97)	(−0.791)	(4.20)	
Korea	1.06	−0.001	0.192	0.99
	(1.50)	(−0.31)	(23.50)	
Singapore	0.25	0.003	0.128	0.77
	(0.87)	(0.47)	(4.10)	
Indonesia	−1.74	0.024	−0.211	0.69
	(−1.45)	(3.90)	(−0.95)	
Malaysia	0.20	0.004	0.349	0.95
	(0.91)	(1.40)	(2.06)	
Philippine	−0.24	0.009	0.096	0.91
	(−0.77)	(1.86)	(1.49)	
Thailand	0.97	0.00002	0.23	0.91

23. Japan Science and Technology Agency 1991.
24. Office of Technology Assessment 1992.
25. This is indeed not so simple. If China pays heed to the GATT, then GATT will want to encourage China to sign.
26. This is also impossible.
27. Baumol 1971.
28. Sorsa 1992.
29. General Agreement on Tariffs and Trade 1992, p. 22.
30. Kirkpatrick 1994.
31. Repetto 1993.
32. Cutajar 1994.
33. Energy Data and Modeling Center 1993.
34. MacDonald 1992.

REFERENCES

Baumol, William (1971), 'Environmental Protection, International Spillovers and Trade', *The 1971 Wicksell Lectures*, Stockholm.
Birdsall, Nancy and David Wheeler (1992), 'Trade Policy and Industrial Pollution in Latin America: Where are the Pollution Havens?', in *International Trade and the Environment*, ed. by P. Low, Discussion Paper #159, Washington, DC: The World Bank.
Cutajar, Michael Zammit (1994), 'The Climate Change Convention: What Role Can Business Play?', *UNEP Industry and Environment*, 17, 11–13.
Dean, Judith (1992), 'Trade and the Environment: A Survey of the Literature', Working Paper #WPS966, Washington, DC: The World Bank.
Energy Data and Modeling Center (1993), *Survey on World Oil Demand and Supply: 1993*, Tokyo.

General Agreement on Tariffs and Trade (1992), *International Trade 90–91*, Geneva: GATT.

Japan Environment Agency (1994), *Report of International Workshop on Eco-Asia Long-Term Project*, Tokyo.

Japan External Trade Organization (1977–93), *White Paper on International Trade: Japan Trade Statistics*, Tokyo: JETRO.

Japan External Trade Organization (1980–94), *World and Japanese Trade*, Tokyo: JETRO.

Japan Science and Technology Agency (1991), 'Analysis of Structure of Energy Consumption and Dynamics of Emission of Atmospheric Species Related to the Global Environmental Change (SO_x, NO_x, CO_2) in Asia', NISTEP Report #21 (in Japanese), Tokyo.

Kirkpatrick, Colin (1994), 'Regionalisation, Regionalism and East Asian Economic Cooperation', *World Economy*, 17, 191–202.

Lall, Sanjaya (1993), 'Foreign Direct Investment in South Asia', *Asian Development Review*, 11, 103–19.

Leonard, Jeffrey (1988), *Pollution and the Struggle for the World Products*, New York: Cambridge University Press.

Low, Patrick and Alexander Yeats (1992), 'Do Dirty Industries Migrate?', in *International Trade and the Environment*, ed. by P. Low, Discussion Paper #159, Washington, DC: The World Bank.

MacDonald, Gordon (1992), 'Technology Transfer: The Climate Change Challenge', *Journal of Environment and Development*, 1, 1–39.

Nangaku, Masaaki (1989), 'Japanese Economic Cooperation to Support the Industrialization of Asian Nations', in *Global Adjustment and the Future of Asian–Pacific Economy*, ed. by M. Shinohara and F. Lo, Tokyo: Institute of Development Economics.

Office of Technology Assessment (1992), *Trade and the Environment: Conflicts and Opportunities*, US Congress, Washington, DC: OTA.

Repetto, Robert (1993), 'Trade and Environmental Policies: Achieving Complementarities and Avoiding Conflicts', *Issues and Ideas*, Washington, DC: World Resources Institute.

Sorsa, Piritta (1992), 'The Environment: A New Challenge to GATT?', Working Paper #WPS980, Washington, DC: The World Bank.

Tobey, James (1990), 'The Effects of Domestic Environmental Policies on Patterns of World Trade: An Empirical Test', *Kyklos*, 49, 191–209.

Wakasugi, Ryuhei (1994), 'Is Japanese Foreign Direct Investment a Substitute for International Trade, *Japan and the World Economy*, 6, 45–52.

World Resources Institute (1990), *World Resources 1990–91*, New York: Oxford University Press.

7. A Comparison of Energy Economics in Two Alternative Systems: Conventional Enclave Development and Community-based Sustainable Settings

Sixto K. Roxas

1. INTRODUCTION

The market is an age-old mechanism through which people and institutions have exchanged products, services and assets to maximize the utilities and satisfactions they derive from material goods and services. Economists have used the maximization and perfect market logic to establish norms of production and distribution efficiency. But in real life, allocations through markets and the priorities established by the prices they set have not reflected the optimum welfare that economists' models predict. They fail in two major areas: in establishing appropriate priorities among human needs, and in reflecting the imperatives of environmental sustainability.

The first was recognized earlier even by economists and project evaluators in Multilateral Development Banks. The practice of calculating economic rates of returns through shadow pricing of costs and benefits, recognizes the divergence, particularly in developing countries, between private and social returns. The second has been catapulted into global attention in more recent times. Work is in progress to reflect environmental costs in national income accounting and, although at somewhat earlier stages, in project evaluation as well.

The wider requirement of environmental impact assessments and social impact assessments[1] as well as the even more recent introduction of 'Social Acceptability' criteria for development projects reflect the rising level of awareness. This is the context in which the propositions advanced in this chapter are presented.

Project economics and project appraisal methods are grounded in an economic theory in which enterprise-centred, profit-maximizing logic in a free competitive market has become the norm for efficiency. The logic underlying the calculation of economic or social as opposed to merely private rates of return was addressed in 1951 by Alfred Kahn when he proposed the use of a social marginal productivity test as the basis for establishing investment criteria in developing countries. It recognized in the allocation of capital resources that private rates of return were not a sufficient guide for efficiency.

The benefit from an investment project was to be measured from the viewpoint of the economy, meaning the nation state. So the first approximation was the contribution to national income. Since these were priced at market, then adjustments needed to be made in the benefits to reflect: premiums on certain results not reflected in the market price, such as employment of labour where the opportunity cost was zero; balance of payments effects; and external economies. In an article written two years after Kahn's, Hollis Chenery formulated a more 'operational' application of the social marginal productivity criterion to include as well adjustments for effects on income distribution, employment and balance of payments equilibrium. This approach was admittedly based on a partial equilibrium method with heavy *ceteris paribus* assumptions. More refined application of shadow-pricing techniques then began to be introduced, with the use of general equilibrium models, and optimization programmes using linear or non-linear programming techniques.

Economic rates of return (ERR) calculations are based on measurements of social productivity of projects and are calculated as adjustments in private rates of returns. These adjustments take into account the macro impact of projects from which shadow prices are derived, which are substituted for market prices in calculating benefits and costs. The adjustments, however, are to numbers derived from an accounting system that is informed by the same postulates as provide the theoretical underpinning of the present system of national accounts (SNA). The SNA continues to be basically neoclassical in its theoretical basis. The hard-core propositions of this theory are:

- the ultimate unit of economic activity is the enterprise, and the enterprise Chart of Accounts is the framework within which transactors and transactions are classified;
- the basis of valuation is market price in product and factor markets;
- adjustments for non-marketed products and services are appended at the margin through imputations. Over time, revisions have attempted to encompass more of these non-market activities.

The present paradigm leaves economic optimization at a first instance at the individual and enterprise levels, and there is no intervention to effect intermediate tradeoffs until the nation-state level. The question we pose is: what would be the effect if we defined a unit of management, where a balance sheet and income statement manager would intervene to optimize community welfare long before state intervention at the national level and in-between the enterprise and the nation state. National accounts would then be a consolidation primarily of community accounts reflecting effective social optimization at that level, instead of primarily, as at present, enterprise accounts reflecting their profit-maximizing decisions.

What would be the impact of such a perspective on the comparative economics of energy projects? The assumption of perfect knowledge and equal bargaining power such that communities effectively register their valuations and the resulting orders of priority in a virtual market would provide a set of derived demand prices for energy. The change-path of demand configuration for electric power would reflect a difference from the 'colonization' mode of development. Maximum capacity, average per unit usage small and scattered, and load factors would be low. But the demand price would be relatively high because the priority of the needs from which the demand is derived will have a high marginal valuation. These valuations would be reflected in the shadow pricing of natural resources, capital and manpower, which would show higher opportunity costs for alternative usage. The alternative usage would then show lower rates of economic returns.

Scientific research and technology development, now following the dictates of a community-based and ecologically sustainable imperative, would move in the direction of consumption and production systems involving lower energy usage and generating less material throughput. And over a longer horizon, as communities developed along a trajectory defined by their own choice of style and pace, they would design their own modes of balancing dispersed settlement with degrees of concentration dictated by convenience and scale-economies.

2. FROM MARKET TO VIRTUAL VALUATION

Economists have long recognized that market failures are more or less normal in developing countries. It is taken for granted then that private rates of return will deviate from economic rates of return. In project feasibility studies, the practice is fairly well established of adjusting private rates to reflect economic rates of return. This is accomplished through a process of setting 'shadow prices'[2] for specific cost items and for measurement of product benefits.

These calculations recognize the concept of what we might call in more contemporary terms 'virtual market prices'. Such prices are no longer the result of real but calculated market prices. The market remains the standard. But the adjustments are made on a notional basis for imputing virtual markets. The process is then deeply dependent on the theory that forms the basis for constructing the virtual markets and the prices derived from them.

It is from this consensus that there has emerged quite a literature on the formulation and application of 'investment criteria' in investment programmes of developing countries.[3] One of the earliest formulations was by Alfred Kahn in 1951, followed by Hollis Chenery in 1953. The World Bank has incorporated shadow pricing into its manuals on project evaluation, in which financial values are adjusted to reflect 'economic' values. Thus in Gittinger's *Economic Analysis of Agricultural Projects*, published by the Economic Development Institute of the World Bank (Second Edition, revised, 1982), 'Determining Economic Values' (Chapter 7) prescribes the process of going from 'financial prices' to the 'value to the society as a whole of both the inputs and outputs of the project', the 'opportunity cost to the society' which is the 'shadow price' or 'accounting price'.[4]

Chenery's article states the theoretical premise that underlies the practice:

> In developed countries, perfect competition provides a standard for judging such a distribution of resources without the necessity of measuring the marginal productivity save in exceptional cases. . . . In underdeveloped areas, it is generally recognized that both private value and private cost may deviate from social value and social cost. In such cases perfect competition cannot even be used as a standard for many sectors of the economy; rather it is necessary to measure social productivity and to provide for some form of government intervention to achieve more or less efficient distribution of investment resources.[5]

The practice is standard, particularly in the evaluation of power projects. Dr Mohan Munasinghe of the World Bank devotes a chapter to 'Shadow Pricing' in his study of *The Economics of Power System Reliability and Planning*, published by the World Bank in 1979. Munasinghe is somewhat more specific in stating the theoretical justification for shadow pricing.

> In the idealized world of perfect competition, the interaction of atomistic profit-maximizing producers and atomistic utility-maximizing consumers yields a situation called Pareto-optimal. In this state, prices reflect the true marginal costs, scarce resources are efficiently allocated, and for a given income distribution, no one person can be made better off without someone else worse off.[6] (p. 105)

He then lists the distortions that make conditions in the real world deviate substantially from the rigorous assumptions of the perfect market. And then he proceeds to discuss various methods for calculating shadow prices.[7]

My chapter takes its point of departure from this generally accepted assumption: that the perfect competition criterion needs to be modified to reflect some concept and measurement of social opportunity costs and benefits. But my approach takes a different tack from that of conventional, neoclassical economics.

Shadow pricing clearly takes the valuation exercise out of the realm of actual markets and real world valuation into the realm of theory. The late Professor

Tinbergen used a most felicitous term for the exercise. These 'accounting prices' are those derived not from the real plan but from the 'shadow plan'.[8] His 1958 development manual *The Design of Development*, prepared for the Economic Development Institute of the World Bank, still bears reading. In this work, Professor Tinbergen still advocates the contribution to national income as a first approximation of benefits from a project. But to compensate for market failures the values need to be adjusted through estimated 'accounting prices'.

It is interesting to read his 1958 manual in the light of articles Professor Tinbergen wrote just before his death in July 1994. I refer particularly to the piece written jointly with Roefie Hueting on the distorted signals given by the markets to relative scarcities and values. 'Market prices and economic indicators based on them, such as national income and cost–benefit analyses, misleadingly signal to society and therefore must be corrected. The factor for which correction is most urgently needed is the environment'.[9]

In undertaking the 'correction' it is essential to understand where precisely the market breakdown occurs and to visualize the process of remedying what (in the 1958 work) Tinbergen called 'fundamental disequilibria'. The failure, I believe, would be at two points in the system:

- Perfect knowledge on the part of the market players—knowledge of the full range of alternative options and the cost–benefit relationship of each option. The shadow-pricing process fills this knowledge gap by making the options explicit and assuming that the values will settle on those established by the options that are optimal from the viewpoint of the transactors.
- Equality of bargaining power. The players have equal bargaining power, so that the choice of options is backed by sufficient bargaining power so that no one party is able to impose an option that is unduly advantageous to it and override the choice of the others.

The practice of shadow pricing fills the imperfect knowledge gap with a neoclassical model of efficiency—calculating the optimal shadow prices from an approximation of an equilibrium condition under perfect competition among atomized individual consumers maximizing utility and atomized enterprises maximizing profits. This is done either through partial or general equilibrium methods, rigorously optimized through linear programming or roughly approximated by sectoral criteria (shadow exchange rate or shadow wages, etc.). This is the exercise which Tinbergen would call 'shadow programming'.

The theory precisely takes no account of either equity or ecological and sustainability criteria. It is a problem to introduce these criteria precisely because of the choice of decision units in the model: atomized individuals and profit-maximizing enterprises. These units exclude from their responsibility either communal welfare or ecological integrity, which are externalities, falling outside the mainstream concern of the players.

Modern economic policy in fact attempts to remedy this failing but only at the level of the nation-state. The practice may be interpreted in the following manner. It notionally makes an omniscient and omnipotent state a market player. The calculated shadow prices represent the valuations given by its omniscience to the relevant items in costs and benefits. The state's omnipotence then gives it the bargaining power to reflect its valuations on the project costs and benefits.

This interpretation then poses the question: upon what sort of theoretical framework does this omniscient state make its valuation judgement? It is here that alternative methodologies represent options from which practice selects one. But why should the option selected be the 'right' one? And what is so sacred about a system that assumes atomized individuals and enterprises and their maximizing logic to be the proper base on which the adjustments are then introduced at the level of the nation state? Why should not the notional reconfiguration take place much earlier than the nation state, at some level between the atomized individuals and the country?

Both from the viewpoint of appropriate theory and effective organization and management, intervention at the country level is too late. It is interesting that John Maynard Keynes in his 1926 essay on 'The End of Laissez-Faire' advances the notion that there should be a level of decision-making somewhere between the individual and the state. But he thought this might be the large public corporation then coming into prominence (public here meaning really endowed with a public purpose, like 'public utilities', rather than publicly listed in the stock exchange).

The notion that I advance is the community as a unit of integration and decision-making. The concept of community must include both the human settlement and its territory as habitat. The community is posited as a transactor in the market reflecting then its valuations which are the results, in the first instance, of the optimization of its objective function which is defined as the 'highest and best sustainable use (HABSU)' of its resources. The two primary indicators of the community welfare would be a concept of *net community income* and *community networth*.

3. SHADOW PROGRAMMING FOR ENERGY ECONOMICS: TWO PERSPECTIVES

Let us return to the term proposed by Tinbergen: 'shadow programming'. The set of shadow prices we derive will depend on the nature of the shadow programming exercise that we adopt.

A national power company looks at the configuration of demand, its composition, daily pattern, cyclical periods and secular trends in relation to the effects on capacity requirement, peak loads, fluctuations during the day, average loads and load factor. The activist demand management strategy will be directed at getting a base load, peak and average loads which will be optimal from the viewpoint of the project economics. Thus the project economics dictates a preference for high density of usage since transmission and distribution costs are functions of space density of demand, high ratio of average to peak loads, and large-volume economic usage.

What would the significance be of a genuinely demand-driven perspective? The power supply is seen from the viewpoint of the user and the question is not what mode of development would produce the demand configuration that favours the economics of power supply projects? But rather what system evolution path would be optimal given the choice of communities for a particular lifestyle and a capital development strategy that fits the lifestyle and its evolution over time?

These two perspectives correspond to two different views of the development process. One I would call the 'colonization' view. The term 'colonization' is used without value and political overtones but purely as an apt and precise description of a particular approach to development.[10] The other is the evolutionary view, the idea of development as springing from an inner force in society instead of being imposed from outside.

In both, the term 'development' is taken to mean much more than mere growth in output. It is in fact distinguished from 'growth' which is left to denote merely the physical expansion of capital, production, incomes and consumption. 'Development' encompasses all the institutional, cultural, behavioural and psychological structures, patterns and processes that emerge from a transformation of societies.

Colonization is used in a meaning that recalls its origins in the Greek αποικια or the Latin *colonia* meaning a transplanted segment of a human society. In the post-industrial revolution period, the phenomena we refer to is the transplanting of a segment of industrialized society in a preindustrialized community. This creates an enclave which is systemically linked to its parent and therefore transforms the host community into an ancillary subsystem of it.

Evolutionary development is an inner-determined (as opposed to outer-determined) development. The outside influences are controlled and digested organically by the society which pursues its own development according to a pattern that its own constituents choose. The prime example in Asia is Japan, which deliberately protected itself from the cooptation of its development pattern and path by the already industrialized nations, and adopted a strategy of catching up with the Western industrialized nations on its own terms and at its own pace.

Inner-directed development invokes what I would call an 'infant community argument' for mounting community defences against cooptation of a community's evolutionary path.[11]

How would a community's choice to pursue an inner-directed, human-centred, sustainable development path be reflected in valuations and become meaningful in the calculus of project appraisals? This is the problem I pose.

- Those valuations would have to be registered in the resource allocation process. Power projects appropriate natural, capital, foreign exchange and human resources.
- Natural resources: depending on the mode, power projects need land, water, fossil fuel, and part of the territory's waste-absorbing capacity (we assume now that this is limited as well).
- Capital resources may be current domestic savings or from the stock of past savings embodied in foreign assets, or from future savings through the use of scarce external borrowing capacity.
- Human resources will range from manual labour to technical and professional personnel for design, construction and operation.

Resources will be needed during the operating period in the form of water, fuels, human resource services and environmental services.

Suppose that households all over the country, as organized stakeholders of their respective habitats, had the perfect knowledge that is essential to perfect markets, in the sense of a full awareness of the alternative development configuration that would earn for them sustainable and 'higher quality' earnings than being garment workers, or construction labourers, or domestic servants and entertainers abroad. Suppose that they also had the equal bargaining power that perfect competition prescribes, and could bid effectively for alternative uses of natural, capital and human resources. Their valuations then would reflect the marginal utilities of their satisfactions and they would show higher yields on natural resources and capital.

But since markets are in fact imperfect—both from the viewpoint of awareness and bargaining powers (because of skewed distribution of resources)—then the values reflected do give higher priority to needs that have lower marginal utilities. The solution is shadow pricing in interventions of governments and international financial institutions. But the shadow-pricing approaches do not at all compensate for the knowledge or bargaining power gaps. On the contrary, by truncating analysis they merely reinforce the fundamental defects of the real-life imperfections of the market system.

4.   COMMUNITY-CENTRED VALUATION AND ALLOCATION PATTERNS

Let us then examine what the impact of such a shadow-pricing approach would be on the economics of energy systems. In the absence of primary empirical work, we would have to deduce the shifts in patterns of resource allocation that are likely to result. For the purpose, let us review some of the familiar relationships in energy projects.

In general the tradeoff is between large capital investments per kilowatt capacity and current operating costs. Larger fixed capital investments can result in lower current capital costs. Thus hydroelectric plants entail large fixed investments per kW capacity but zero fuel costs and negligible maintenance. Gas turbine plants entail smaller capital costs per kW capacity but very high operating expenses. Within a range of specifications, the same is true of steam-turbine plants. Generation of high-grade steam will involve larger costs in boilers per pound-hour capacity. But the higher pressure makes it possible to generate higher temperatures at lower station steam rates and therefore at lower BTU expense.

The heaviest costs are therefore related to investments, followed by fuel and other operating expenses. The higher the cost of fuel at given costs of capital, the more favourable it is to go for the more capital-intensive but fuel-saving specifications. A higher cost of capital, however, would shift the specifications to less fixed capital-intensive and more operating capital-intensive specifications.

What happens when community valuations are brought in which reflect alternative development paths that raise the opportunity cost of both man-made capital and natural resources?

Let us apply marginal productivity analysis to community-centred development. The analysis must be in real rather than monetary terms. At the community level, consumer baskets to meet basic needs, building on the complementarity of resources, is the essential matter. Natural resources and labour must be complemented with energy supplying capital resources. Resource usage needs to be intensified over a wide diversity of sectors and simultaneously over many communities in order to produce the real production base for effective exchange to take place, internally among households and among communities and externally between local and outside communities. This is the world of Say's Law where only real supply can generate effective demand.

If complementarity is being achieved over a large enough and diverse enough range of populations and resources, then the incremental resources are inevitably yielding high marginal rates of returns. Thus projects that are liberating rural wives from the task of gathering firewood and fetching water, and enabling them to turn to biointensive gardening and raising livestock and poultry or fish in aquaculture, will reflect high marginal productivity yields. The availability of complementary energy and human resources that make possible the more intensive use of land resources, will then create rent value for land which raises the opportunity cost of diverting land to other uses such as commercial centres and export-processing zones which yield lower marginal utility real incomes for enclave populations.

The important point is to make it possible for this internally driven development process to take place without being aborted by cooptation of the development patterns to render the communities subservient to the system demands of an outside economic process with priorities of its own.

This is the real key to the whole authentic, sustainable and human-centred transformation process: to set up an effective defence against cooptation until adequate internal solidarity can be built up which will enable the communities to hold their own in the open global arenas and then be able to compete on equal terms and achieve complementarity with other systems on a mutually advantageous basis.

5. IMPLICATIONS FOR PROJECT DESIGN CONCEPTS: INDUSTRIAL ECOLOGY

The advantages of power projects using renewable sources of energy have been increasingly recognized. Even the World Bank in its 1992 *World Development Report* highlighted the recent technological developments that have made the economics of renewables extremely competitive.[12] Still, the flow of financial resources either to further research and development and certainly to actual installations has been relatively small, particularly in comparison with the funds that go to the more conventional coal-fired steam turbine, hydro and internal combustion-driven generation.

Part of the problem is scale. Since each unit installation is small, it is not as interesting for financial institutions. But part of the argument made in this chapter is that the energy economics of power projects in community-based systems draw their advantage precisely from the fact that the projects are integrated into interrelated community-based production systems: biogas generation with animal husbandry, thermal units using agricultural wastes for fuel, hybrid solar-windmill systems in isolated agro-forestry settlements, and so on.

The design of these complexes falls right in with the more recent trends in industrial-complex engineering, a field that has become known as 'industrial ecology'.[13] This means designing entire production networks in a manner that apes nature's way of establishing complete metabolic chains where the waste of one process becomes the feedstock of the others. There are few examples to date (see below). The one most often cited is Kalundborg in Denmark. Let us first consider a few characteristics of industrial ecology.

As an analogue, nature points to designs that are cyclical rather than linear in their process flows. Natural systems have zero waste in the sense that the cycle of birth–death–decay–birth makes all outputs inputs of other natural processes in a perennial cycle. Modern industrial design is linear in the sense of taking low-entropy matter, processing it, turning out a product which is consumed, and leaving both production and consumption waste as a permanent residual. The sustainability of the process assumes unlimited supplies of low-entropy matter and an unlimited capacity of the earth to absorb waste without permanent damage to its carrying capacity.

In recent years there have been examples of industrial complex design which is cyclical in the sense that the output and waste of production and consumption processes become feedstock inputs of other processes. For example, the Danish Kalundborg case in which a petroleum refining plant, a coal-fired electric power utility, a pharmaceutical company specializing in biotechnology, a sheetrock plant, concrete producers, a producer of sulphuric acid, the municipal heating authority, a fish farm owned by the utility, some greenhouses, local farms and enterprises worked cooperatively to design such a complementarity and carry it out.

The Asnaes Power Plant started this process in the 1980s by recycling its waste heat in the form of steam. It had formerly condensed the steam and returned it as water to a nearby fjord; now it sends the steam directly to the Statoil refinery and the Novo Nordisk pharmaceutical company. It also provides surplus heat to greenhouses, a fish farm owned by the utility, and the residents of the local town, allowing 3,500 oil-burning systems to be shut-off.

The Statoil refinery produces surplus gas, which was not used prior to 1991 because it contained excessive amounts of sulfur. The refinery installed a process to remove the sulfur, so that a cleaner burning gas is sold to Gyproc, the sheetrock factory, as well as to the coal-fired utility (saving 30,000 tons of coal); the sulfur that is being retrieved is sold to Kemira, a chemical company. The process that removes the sulfur in the smokestacks of Asnaes Power Plant also yields calcium sulfate, which they will be selling to Gyproc as a substitute for mined gypsum. The fly ash from coal generation is used on road construction and concrete production. Waste heat from the refinery is used to warm the waters of a fish farm that produces 200 tons of turbot and trout sold into the French market, while its fish sludge goes to local farmers as fertilizers. Meanwhile, Novo Nordisk has developed a process to make the sludge generated in its fermentation process useful for local farmers through the addition of chalk-lime and processing at 90$C for an hour to kill any remaining microorganisms. (Hawken, 1993, pp. 62–3)

Hawken quotes Hardin Tibbs (1993, p. 20):

It is significant that none of the examples of cooperation at Kalundborg was specifically required by regulation, and that each exchange or trade is negotiated independently. Some were based strictly on price, while others were based on the installation of infrastructure by one party in exchange for a good price offered by the other. In some cases mandated cleanliness levels, such as the requirement for reduced nitrogen in waste paper, or the removal of sulfur from flue gas, have permitted or stimulated reuse of wastes, and have certainly contributed to a climate in which such cooperation becomes feasible. The earliest deals were purely economic, but more recent initiatives have been made for largely environmental reasons and it has been found that these can be made to pay, too.

Hawken points out that

> Geographical proximity of the industries was critical to some of the exchanges (heat, water, steam), but fly ash is exported out of the area . . . the Kalundborg success speaks to the wealth of exchange that are possible between industries, without design or preplanning. Imagine what a team of designers could come up with if they were to start from scratch, locating and specifying industries and factories that had potentially synergistic and symbiotic relationships. (p. 63)

> Tibbs goes beyond complementary siting and interaction of industrial processes . . . he actually proposes that industrial ecology recalibrate its inputs and outputs to adapt to the carrying capacity of the environment . . . to accomplish which industrial design would emphasize 'dematerialization,' using less material per unit of output; improving industrial processes and materials employed to minimize inputs; and a large-scale shift away from carbon-based fuels to hydrogen fuel, an evolution already under way that is referred to as 'decarbonization'. (pp. 63–4)

Tibbs describes the strategy as 'linking the metabolism of one company with that of others' (quoted in Hawken, note on p. 229).

What would make companies adopt this strategy as a matter of course? In the case of Kalundborg, it did not happen in the neoclassical market order. It took the leadership of the power utility; it entailed a tremendous amount of negotiating. It circumvented the linear perspective built into mainstream enterprise thinking.

A theoretical paradigm tends to become a potent influence on the way people think and behave, it becomes part of organization philosophy and mode of operations, becomes embodied in planning processes and the detailed operating philosophy of organizations. It becomes ideology on the basis of which men and organizations actually refashion reality.

This is what happened to neoclassical economics. It passed from being an analytical tool to becoming a blueprint for designing actual organizations and societies and educating manpower; it becomes ideology and a culture and civilization. This is what the enterprise system has become in the modern world. Markets evolved naturally. But the enterprise system was an artefact of the nineteenth century. This artefact made the organizational paradigm a-natural and then anti-nature as part of its philosophical underpinnings. The logic of the enterprise operations leaves out any concern for natural values.

6. IMPLICATIONS FOR INTERNATIONAL FINANCIAL INSTITUTIONS' OPERATING STRATEGY: COMMUNITY 'PORTFOLIO' FINANCING

In February 1992, Lewis Preston, the new President of the World Bank, constituted a 'Portfolio Management Task Force' to examine the problems affecting the quality of the Bank's active portfolio of loans and creditors. The report of this team was entitled 'Effective Implementation: Key to Development Impact' and went into circulation as the Wapenhams Report. After examination of the financial portfolio and the assessment of development impact, one of its key recommendations was to 'Introduce the Concept of Country Portfolio Performance Management Linked to the Bank's Core Business Process'.[14]

The formalization of valuation exercises of the sort proposed in my chapter may have a persuasive effect on the management of loan portfolios of multilateral development banks. It would fit in with the thrust of the Wapenhams Report's suggestion that the World Bank view the management of its programmes in terms of country portfolios instead of single projects, to get a more integrated and systemic view of development impact. This perspective would bring the view down to subcountry territories and look at subcountry, community portfolios to evaluate development impact. This suggests that the nation state is not a meaningful unit for evaluating system impact of integrated project clusters.

The requisite scale for purposes of portfolio administration economics in a financial institution would be achieved precisely by looking at ecologically-engineered production networks. In other words, portfolios would not only depart from single-project but also from single-sector approaches. A serious rethinking, in the international financial institutions, of operating department approaches to project design would in fact provide empowerment finance to communities, move their participatory planning processes from shadow to reality, and give needed support to the project engineering of the future: 'industrial ecology'.

NOTES

1. For example, the World Bank guidelines proposed earlier this year set forth the rationale for a 'Social Assessment and Participation Strategy' to guide 'Operational Departments'. Social assessment is needed to:
   (a) Ensure the appropriateness and acceptability of project objectives and activities to the range of people who are intended to benefit (including women and vulnerable groups);
   (b) Enhance the involvement of beneficiaries in project design and implementation;
   (c) Ensure that institutional mechanisms (for the delivery of services, participation, etc.) are sustainable, and appropriate to project beneficiaries;
   (d) Anticipate, minimize and mitigate any negative social effects of projects.

Internal World Bank Memorandum dated 14 February 1994 addressed to Social Policy Thematic Team on the subject: 'Guidelines for Incorporating Social Assessment and Participation into Bank Projects'.

2. Shadow price is

the opportunity cost to a society of engaging in some economic activity. . . . In a perfectly functioning economy, market prices will be equal to MARGINAL COST, which itself represents the true costs to society of producing one extra unit of a commodity; it is equivalent to the value of the items that could have been made as alternatives to the last unit of the commodity produced, with the same resources. In the competitive economy, therefore, the market price of an item is equal to the opportunity cost of producing that item. In an economy which does not function perfectly, however, this is not so. . . . More generally, shadow prices are used in valuing any item which is implicitly rationed or constrained in some way. Shadow prices can be derived using LINEAR PROGRAMMING techniques, and can be used in social COST–BENEFIT ANALYSIS, which attempts to achieve an optimal RESOURCE ALLOCATION in the absence of an effective PRICE SYSTEM. (Graham Bannock et al. 1987, pp. 372–3)

3. For an excellent survey of the literature, see United Nations 1961.
4. Gittinger 1982.
5. Chenery 1953.
6. Munasinghe cites Francis J. Bator's simplified geometry on welfare maximization in the March 1957 issue of *The American Economic Review* (pp. 22–59). He quotes a different title for the article, however; the title of the article in the Review is 'The Simple Analytics of Welfare Maximization'.
7. He cites the following distortions: (a) monopoly practices, (b) external economies and diseconomies not internalized in the private market, (c) interventions in the market process through taxes, duties, and subsidies, (d) large income disparities which may be socially and politically unacceptable (Munasinghe 1979, p. 106).
8. He describes the calculation as 'the application to all physical elements of net income (i.e., output of products and input of factors) of accounting prices representing the "true value" of these products and factors. . . . In principle this calculation requires a "shadow development program," differing from the "real" program in that equilibria would be obtained by flexible pricing instead of, as may be the case in reality, by quantitative restrictions and rigid pricing' (Economic Development Institute 1958, p. 82).
9. 'GNP and Market Prices: Wrong Signals for Sustainable Economic Success that Mask Environmental Destruction', Chapter 4 in Robert Goodland et al. (eds), *Environmentally Sustainable Development: Building on Brundtland,* The World Bank, Environment Working Paper No. 46, July 1991, pp. 36–42.
10. In fact S. Herbert Frankel (1953), in an essay written in 1953, applied the term, meaning not so much a form of territorial expansion, but as a social unit in process of transformation.
11. James Fallows (1994), in his recent book underscores this aspect of Japanese national strategy from the sixteenth century. They sought a double objective: protection from cooptation of their development by the West, and catchup on their own terms with Western technology. See particularly Chapter 2, pp. 72–116.
12. World Bank 1992, pp. 122–4.

The costs of all commercial forms of renewable energy have declined remarkably over the past two decades (as they did in the earlier part of this century for electric power generation from fossil fuels) . . . The costs of solar energy may well fall further. In high solar-insulation areas the costs of electric power from solar energy seem likely to become competitive with those of nuclear power within the next ten years or so (even ignoring their advantages in reducing environmental costs) and probably with those of fossil fuels over the long term. . . . The commercial development of renewables may thus be justified on nonenvironmental grounds.

The report then proceeds to recommend measures to promote the wider use of renewables.

13. The term, according to Paul Hawken, was first coined by Robert Frosch and Nicholas Gallopou-

los in 1989, in an article in *Scientific American* entitled 'Strategies for Manufacturing'.
14. Internal World Bank document, Report of the Portfolio Management Task Force, 'Effective Implementation: Key to Development Impact', 1992.

REFERENCES

Bannock, Graham et al. (1987), *Dictionary of Economics*, Fourth Edition, The Economist Books, London: Hutchinson Business Books.
Chenery, Hollis (1953), 'The Application of Investment Criteria', *The Quarterly Journal of Economics*, February, p. 76.
Economic Development Institute (1958), *The Design of Development*, International Bank for Reconstruction and Development, Baltimore: Johns Hopkins Press.
Fallows, James (1994), *Looking at the Sun: The Rise of New East Asian Economic and Political System*, New York: Pantheon.
Frankel, S. Herbert (1953), 'The Concept of Colonization', *The Economic Impact on Under-Developed Societies: Essays on International Investment and Social Change*, Cambridge, Mass: Harvard University Press, Essay I, pp. 1–17.
Gittinger, J. Price (1982), *Economic Analysis of Agricultural Projects*, Second Edition, EDI, Baltimore and London: Johns Hopkins University Press, pp. 243–84.
Hawken, Paul (1993), *The Ecology of Commerce: A Declaration of Sustainability*, New York: Harper & Row.
Munasinghe, Mohan (1979), *The Economics of Power System Reliability and Planning: Theory and Case Study*, Published for the World Bank, Baltimore and London: Johns Hopkins University Press, p. 106.
Tibbs, Hardin (1993), 'Industrial Ecology: An Environmental Agenda for Industry', *Annals of Earth*, Vol. XI, No. 1, p. 20.
United Nations, ECAFE (1961), 'Criteria for Allocating Investment Resources among Various Fields of Development in Underdeveloped Countries', *Economic Bulletin for Asia and the Far East*, June.
World Bank (1992), *Development and the Environment World Development Report 1992*, Oxford University Press, pp. 122–4.

8. Quality of Life Indicators for Interregional Planning and Distributional Decisions

Ben-Chieh Liu, Maw Lin Lee and Chich-Ping Hu

1. INTRODUCTION: DSS, GNP AND QOL

Decision analysis (DA) and decision support system (DSS) focus thinking on objectives and alternatives, and the decisions that can help achieve those objectives. They deal in the real world with subjects full of risk and uncertainties which sometimes can disrupt even the best conceptualized plans. They provide an explicit role for each or a group of decision makers, and a framework for evaluating each decision logically and intelligently. DA and DSS are positive, action-oriented, computer-based approaches to problem solving and policy prioritization. Decision analysis, seemingly, is the best combination of computer power with some semi-structured or formally established scientific methods to focus and complement good judgement. Thus, analysts become decision facilitators in management. They help their associates and organizations overcome the difficulty and confrontation that constrain efficient and effective decision-making in operations and production management.

Ever since the Great Depression, industrialization and urban development through technological progress and economic growth as measured by gross national product (GNP) or real income per capita have elicited nearly total acceptance in the world as national policy goals. A healthy GNP has provided an ever-increasing standard of living and enabled more people to pursue their material well-being by. exercising their consumptive choices over more and better goods and services, including energy and information resources, and urban and environmental amenities. Since most of the technological developments have been tied either directly or indirectly to energy and electrical power, including the latest developments of computer hardware and software, varying energy and electricity production and consumption patterns have shaped our urban or suburban lifestyle and affected our strategic decisions on our quality of life (QOL) determination and environmental management.

The increasing dependence of any economy and urban community on an uninterrupted power supply has made the availability, accessibility and reliability of the supply of power and information resources the most critical issues, respectively, in interregional systems planning, power generation and overall environmental protection. All of these issues, in turn, have made the managerial tasks of public decision-making difficult, especially when all the performance and evaluation criteria—'efficiency' in industrial production and energy generation, 'reliability' in freedom from power shortage and information system strike-out, and 'equity' in goods and services distribution among different urban–rural and socioeconomic strata—are to be met. In the midst of post-industrialization and suburbanization and high- tech development, public decision makers have also been faced with such subtle national or global problems as natural resource depletion, environmental quality deterioration, nuclear proliferation, information exploration and global market mechanism distortion (see Liu, 1988; Heidenheimer et al. 1990; Hsieh and Liu 1988, 1993).

In Taiwan, as well as in many newly developed countries, the tradeoff effects between economic growth and environmental degradation resulting from additional urban and social infrastructure development, energy production and consumption are so intricate that they have been neither scientifically analysed nor statistically documented. The primary objective of this chapter is to illustrate a simple computer-based decision support system (DSS) as a planning and evaluation tool for community QOL improvement in general, and for investigating the technological and urban and environmental development impacts in particular (see Liu and Hu 1992a,b and Liu et al. 1992). The island country of Taiwan, ROC, where economic miracles were brought about by a series of public policies and programmes of energy, industrial and urban-socioinfrastructural developments at the expense of environmental deterioration will serve as an illustration in this chapter (see Lee et al. 1994).

2. DEVELOPMENT OF THE DSS MODEL FOR PLANNING AND MANAGEMENT

Public policies are generally made as the result of complex political processes and most decisions are usually highly unstructured and often depend heavily on the personal judgement of some not-always identifiable decision-making experts. Although policy evaluations frequently called for multidisciplinary team efforts for inputs, many planning and controlling aspects are viewed differently by different managers with different levels of responsibilities and perceptions (see Miller and Katz 1986; Minch and Sanders 1986; Schoner and Wedley 1989, among others). Therefore, the DSS proposed here should be objective-oriented

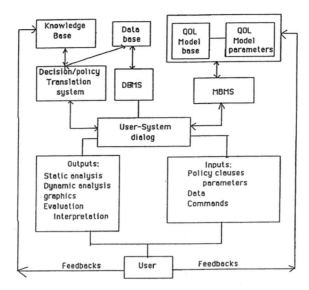

Figure 8.1   Proposed DSS–QOL framework

and user-driven, and equipped with built-in flexibility, adaptability and inter-face/ communication capability (see Dos Santos and Bariff (1988).

According to Alter (1977), Bennett (ed.) (1983), Perry (1984), Henderson and Schilling (1985), Harmon et al. (1988) and Young (1989), any computer-based decision support systems should provide the means for interactive, user-controlled, human-computer dialogue to assist decision makers coping with semi-structured or unstructured decision-making processes. As shown in Figure 8.1, this proposed computer-based interactive DSS encompasses the following three major sub-modules: the data base, the model-base and the knowledge, and decision-base systems. While the database is a system designed for data organi-zation, storage, retrieval, communication and reprocessing, the model-base system contains quantitative/econometric and statistical models for computation and simulation, inductive and deductive inferences, and most importantly, for quality of life assessment. The third is the least structured system in which the users or decision makers can play highly unstructured roles either in input-fitting, or in output-extracting from various policy outcomes or solutions per-taining to the question or problem being addressed.

Although the model base may incorporate a number of quantitative software packages, such as the Statistical Package for Social Sciences (SPSS), Statistical Analysis Software (SAS), Quick Quant, Fast QM, etc., the backbone of the

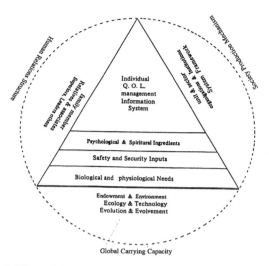

Global Carrying Capacity

Figure 8.2   QOL model system

model base in this study is the Quality of Life (QOL) Model originally developed by Liu (1975) and Fox (1983) and elaborated by Liu et al. (1986), Lee and Liu (1988), Liu and Hu (1992a,b), and Hsieh and Liu (1993) among others. The QOL model is an econometric model characterized by its input–output relationships. In a productive or consumptive framework, the 'measured' quality of life attainment, rather than the 'perceived' level of satisfaction, is hypothesized as a collection of variable factor inputs contributing to our overall macro-, not the individual micro-well-being, under a democratic society, which consists of three major sectors—household, business and government—and the natural environment in which we all live, work and enjoy. To capture realistically the progress or retrogression of our society, we have included in the QOL model those components other than the traditional economic measures, such as the social, political, environmental, health-education and welfare components. Under each component, there are categorical variables, factors and attributes injecting positive or adverse effects into our social well-being mainstream.

It should be noted that the level of our QOL attainment is measured only by those quantifiable elements while holding as constant the psychological components. Furthermore, the QOL indexes are aggregate indicators for a given community at a particular point in time. Although the QOL items are collective and ordinal measures, they can be used for policy-specific impact assessment as well as for targeted decision objective and/or goal analysis. With a much broader application than the traditional income or employment measures adopted in the GNP or national income accounting system, the QOL model also attempts to cope with factors characterized by their non-marketability and externality. For example, a mandated Environmental Impact Statement (EIS), between a coal-burning and another nuclear-powered plant, always calls for social cost–benefit justification and community risk assessments far beyond the forecasted impacts on income and/or employment alone. A comprehensive EIS must provide information on community QOL for public decision analysis (see Figure 8.2).

Although more than 100 QOL factors are incorporated in the model base of the system, the user is allowed to change any factor relationship in existence, add new, or delete any existing factors. To increase the flexibility such that the proposed system can tailor an individual decision maker's personality, capability, preference, environmental state and so on, a model-base management system (MBMS) should be established to handle the generation of the final model for calculating the QOL indexes. The model generated will be stored in the model base, and information about the relationships among identified factors should be maintained in the model parameter base, or something similar to the knowledge base in a modern expert systems framework.

One of the areas open to users when using this model is the relative importance of each factor, or variable weights, in QOL components, for that can vary from one decision maker to another. To facilitate operations, our system provides the decision maker with several alternatives. The first alternative is to reach a consensus among decision makers via the use of certain commercial software packages, such as Expert-Choice developed by Decision Support Software, Inc. The results then are fed into the database of a proposed DSS, which in turn works together with MBMS to complete the final task. Decision makers may also use a factor analysis to generate the weights for each QOL variable included in the model base, or simply adopt all weights as provided in the parameter base.

As expected, the database should have comprehensive inventory files on the population at risk. Such characteristics as man-made and natural environmental conditions, energy production and consumption, income, employment and demographic accounts, among others, should be developed. Deterministic and probabilistic models should be built for data generation, parameter estimation and policy and decision impact simulation. Through the user-system interface dialogue and the networking linkages between the three subsystems just delineated, questions like 'what is' and 'what if', as well as 'why' and 'how to' inquiries, can be accommodated under varying assumptions on uncertainty and risk.

3. URBAN–SUBURBANIZATION AND ENVIRONMENTAL QUALITY MANAGEMENT

The economic miracle of Taiwan has been well recognized and internationally acknowledged not only for her impressive rate of growth in real income per capita, about 7.0 per cent annually, but also for her remarkable accomplishment in narrowing the gap of income distributed between the richest and the poorest families, from a ratio of 11.56 in 1961 to 5.18 in 1990, with a Gini coefficient between 0.28 and 0.31 in the 1980s. Meanwhile, Taiwan has maintained price stability and full employment. The aggregate wholesale and consumer price indexes rose about 2–3 per cent per year for 1963–72, and levelled off at 5–6 per cent since 1973 with a global energy crisis signified by the first oil embargo; and the annual unemployment rate has always been less than 4 per cent for the entire period under study. With per capita GNP in Taiwan growing from US$1511 in 1968 to US$7512 in 1990, energy consumption per capita also increased proportionally from 638 to 2507 litres of oil equivalent (kloe), of which imported energy also increased sharply from 46.1 per cent to 93.5 per cent of the total energy supply in Taiwan.

Along with Taiwan's alarming dependency on imported energy for industrial development, and on export-oriented trades for economic growth, public policy decision makers in Taiwan are also confronted with threatening issues of skewed and unbalanced urban development. In 1990, Taiwan's population totalled 20.4 million and 75 per cent of them were urban; Taipei and Kaohsiung cities alone accounted for one-third of the total urban population. Because of environmental deterioration and damage caused by the development projects, environmentalists and special interest groups in Taiwan are fighting against any industrial plant construction, be they petrochemical or nuclear powered. A 1985 survey of 4,650 families on Taiwan revealed that two-thirds of them ranked environmental protection as their first-order priority and only 27.0 per cent of those surveyed still consider economic growth in general and housing development in particular as, their foremost important goal.

The aforementioned information extracted from the database management system (DBMS) clearly indicates that energy, foreign trade and economic growth are positive factors and air pollution and hazardous or nuclear wastes are negative elements in the QOL model base. The family survey traces a non-monotonic transformation function between economic growth as represented by real income per capita and social well-being as expressed by the QOL indexes. Factor or variable weights and the tradeoff relations required in the QOL model parameter base may be gathered from the general public or from a group of experts. Once the QOL model is specified with the direction and magnitude among the various contributing factors, the relational linkage and impact coefficients could technically be estimated through econometric tools such as regression analysis or a simultaneous-equations simulation which are enlisted in the QOL model-based-management systems. Some empirical results are illustrated in the following section.

4. EMPIRICAL RESULTS AND FINDINGS

Relevant QOL variables were selected from the 23 regional areas consisting of prefectures and cities throughout Taiwan. The domains of these variables range from demographic, educational, socioeconomic and environmental issues to public policy concerns. Because of data paucity only the following 36 variables were selected and employed to construct a preliminary QOL indicator set for Taiwan: (1) Population density, (2) Illiteracy rate, (3) Number of hospital beds per 10,000 population, (4) Dustfall-tons per month and km^2, (5) Sulphur dioxide, (6) Carbon monoxide, (7) Nitrogen dioxide,(8) Offender rate, (9) Juvenile delinquents as percentage of offenders, (10) Number of households affected from fire per 10,000 houses, (11) Estimated losses from fire, (12) Book stock of local Cultural Centre, (13) Piped water supply, (14) Highway density, (15) Number of newspapers and magazines per 1,000 population, (16) TV sets per 1,000 population, (17) Local government expenditure per capita, (18) Final statements of expenditure of education, science and culture, (19) Employment by commerce, (20) News agencies' distribution, (21) Education and recreation, (22) Saving as percentage of income, (23) Employed persons as percentage of civilian population aged 15 and over, (24) Social increase rate, (25) Dependency ratio, (26) Average current income, (27) Local government revenue per capita, (28) Daily refuse generation production per capita, (29) Amount per worker, (30) Average family housing expenditure, (31) Doctors per 10,000 population, (32) Automobiles per 10,000 population, (33) Subscribers per 100 population, (34) Monthly per capita electricity consumption, (35) Daily water consumption per capita, and (36) Population in urban planned districts as percentage of total population. The direction, source and unit of measurement of those variables are shown in Appendix 8A.

In this chapter, QOL indicators are created through two multi-criteria models for comparing alternative solutions to problems concerning QOL development and management decisions. As an application, both the bottom-up factor-generating procedures (built up from individual variable data sets) along with the top-down component-categorization identification procedures were employed to highlight some critical factors jointly affecting the QOL levels in Taiwan, ROC. While some 36 socioeconomic, demographic, urban and environmental variables were inputted originally, only 5 independent QOL indicators or components were developed by the bottom-up factor-analysis for the 23 cities and prefectures (see Table 8.1).

The bottom-up patterns of QOL indicators developed among the 23 observations in Taiwan were evaluated initially through factor analysis, fuzzy dominance matrix modelling and fuzzy clustering modelling (see Liu and Hu 1992a). In this study, variables were first simplified and reduced to some independent factors through factor analysis. The common indicators employed to identify the priority and similarity of QOL among cities were the normalized factor

Table 8.1   Data matrix of factor scores

District	Factor 1	Factor 2	Factor 3	Factor 4	Factor 5
Taipei City	4.105	−0.613	−0.34	−0.591	−0.676
Kaohsiung C.0	1.145	0.461	−0.966	0.033	0.607
Taipei Prefecture	0.483	−0.12	2.829	1.038	0.04
Ilan P.0	−0.683	0.643	0.097	−0.258	−0.869
Taoyuan P.0	0.06	−0.569	2.937	−0.208	0.102
Hsinchu P.0	−0.439	−0.011	−0.037	−0.648	−1.543
Miaoli P.	−0.405	−0.374	−0.311	0.932	−0.989
Taichung P.	−0.33	−1.218	−0.45	1.26	−0.913
Changhua P.	−0.547	−1.082	−0.339	−0.248	0.748
Nantou P.	−0.324	−0.109	−0.731	−0.404	−0.787
YuanlinP.	−0.398	−1.66	−0.939	−0.315	1.61
Chiayi P.	−0.399	−1.406	−0.72	−0.536	0.398
Tainan P.	−0.491	−0.693	0.153	−0.06	0.787
Kaohsiung P.	−0.132	−0.521	−0.303	0.266	−0.383
Pingtung P.	−0.464	−0.865	−0.428	−0.351	−1.037
Taitung P.	−0.498	0.676	0.022	−0.112	−1.354
Hualian P.	−0.427	2.122	−0.436	−1.286	−1.149
Penghu P.	−0.388	0.062	0.934	−2.608	0.989
Keelung C.	−0.189	1.277	−0.027	1.426	−0.016
Hsinchu C.	−0.342	0.854	−0.027	0.025	1.005
Taichung C.	0.857	1.528	−0.108	−0.136	1.092
Chiayi C.	−0.254	1.336	−0.551	0.407	1.861
Taina C.	0.133	0.332	−0.258	2.375	0.479

Note: C = City; P = Prefecture.

scores. The second approach (top-down) ranks alternatives based on pairwised comparison. The QOL levels were further measured by dominance matrix among factors. The third model identifies similarity relationships among alternatives, and also by some pre-defined distance functions, it provides additional information for cluster grouping with similarity relations. Tables 8.1–3 show some of the empirical results from the aforementioned transformation processes.

In short, 5 common factors or 5 substitutive QOL indicators were extracted from the aforementioned 36 variables, to achieve the independent status through factor analysis. Thus, 5 total common factor scores acted as evaluation criteria in the fuzzy modelling (as shown in Table 8.2). Following the fuzzy dominance matrix model, based on factor scores, a dominance relationship among 5 common factors (indicators) was defined. As an application on fuzzy modelling I, in this chapter, QOL was then ranked by score, S_i and component, C_j. From the fuzzy dominance matrix shown in Table 8.3, we note that the most superior ranking city, for example, for the QOL evaluation on Taiwan is Taichung City (District No. 21) where the dominance relationship score is the highest, 80 points; and the worst ranking QOL level is focused in Taitung Prefecture (District No. 16) whose dominance relationship score is the lowest, only 35

Table 8.2   Five common factor loadings

Variable	Factor 1	Factor 2	Factor 3	Factor 4	Factor 5	Communalities
1	0.721	−0.5512	−0.1195	−0.2288	0.078	0.8964
2	−0.5134	0.3009	0.414	−0.137	0.4207	0.7213
3	0.1848	0.0837	−0.5913	−0.1975	−0.2848	0.5109
4	0.2255	−0.5514	0.0872	0.4693	−0.2239	0.6329
5	0.2866	0.1195	0.621	−0.3079	−0.076	0.5826
6	0.5847	−0.6333	0.0409	0.2639	−0.1349	0.8324
7	0.3589	0.1371	0.0894	0.1634	−0.5925	0.5334
8	0.5004	−0.3376	−0.5956	−0.2576	0.0096	0.7855
9	−0.0295	0.1702	−0.3895	0.3786	−0.6898	0.8006
10	0.3655	0.3977	−0.4184	−0.1696	−0.3221	0.5994
11	0.029	−0.0772	−0.0653	0.8879	−0.239	0.8
12	0.2759	−0.8776	−0.0593	0.0098	−0.0456	0.8520
13	0.5742	−0.0774	−0.1973	−0.0069	0.3432	0.4924
14	0.0854	0.2519	0.0226	0.0963	0.7391	0.6269
15	0.8613	−0.2974	−0.1231	0.2103	−0.1754	0.9205
16	0.7877	−0.3701	−0.3612	0.1435	−0.1145	0.9217
17	0.3364	−0.6792	−0.4929	−0.1818	0.0278	0.8512
18	0.3656	−0.835	0.117	0.2214	−0.724	0.8989
19	0.7308	−0.492	−0.3142	−0.1087	−0.1584	0.9118
20	0.3943	−0.8797	−0.0817	−0.0313	−0.0055	0.937
21	0.7566	0.025	−0.1313	−0.0817	−0.2248	0.6475
22	−0.0407	−0.0967	0.7038	−0.0061	0.0999	0.5164
23	−0.4137	0.3212	0.1082	0.0348	0.59	0.6354
24	0.1926	0.4693	0.5045	0.495	−0.261	0.7576
25	0.6938	0.0646	0.2391	0.5471	−0.2261	0.8923
26	0.8379	−0.2803	−0.0177	0.1815	−0.1555	0.838
27	0.3341	−0.655	−0.5331	−0.1582	0.0354	0.8511
28	0.3649	−0.2597	−0.616	0.1856	0.2375	0.6709
29	−0.4096	0.5258	−0.0812	0.3491	0.3314	0.6826
30	0.8471	−0.4668	0.014	0.1264	−0.0524	0.9543
31	0.8859	−0.2404	−0.2578	−0.1351	−0.0345	0.9285
32	0.7973	−0.2041	0.03162	0.1508	0.0439	0.802
33	0.9264	−0.2348	−0.1106	−0.056	−0.0082	0.9289
34	0.8794	−0.431	−0.0162	0.0841	−0.0249	0.9669
35	0.8317	−0.2869	−0.1726	0.0021	−0.0698	0.8087
36	0.891	−0.0912	−0.0434	−0.0597	−0.3139	0.9062
Proportion	0.4356	0.2339	0.1395	0.0916	0.0994	
Cumulative Proportion	0.4356	0.6695	0.809	0.9006	1	

points.

Based on the power matrix (shown in Table 8.4), 5 common factor scores become the clustering criteria of QOL on Taiwan. The relative distance power of the 23 observations are: 0.9986, 0.9985, 0.9971, 0.9952, 0.9949, 0.9926, 0.9910, 0.9828, 0.9817, 0.9789, 0.9781, 0.9765, 0.9738, 0.9692, 0.9683, 0.9622,

Table 8.3   Fuzzy dominance matrix–relative dominance of QOL on Taiwan

District	1	2	3	4	5	6	7	8	9	10	11	12	13	14	15	16	17	18	19	20	21	22	23	S	R
Taipei City	0	2	3	4	3	3	4	4	4	3	3	4	4	4	4	4	2	2	3	3	3	2	3	70	4
Kaohsiung C.	3	0	5	3	4	4	4	5	3	4	3	4	3	5	4	3	3	3	4	2	2	3	5	79	2
Taipei P.	2	0	0	2	3	2	3	4	2	2	2	2	2	3	3	2	2	1	3	1	0	1	2	44	17
Ilan P.	1	2	3	0	3	2	2	2	2	1	2	1	3	2	2	2	1	2	1	1	1	1	2	39	20
Taoyuan P.	2	1	2	2	0	2	3	4	2	2	2	2	3	3	3	3	2	1	3	2	1	2	1	48	14
Hsinchu P.	2	1	3	3	3	0	2	2	3	2	2	2	4	2	3	3	0	1	2	2	2	1	1	46	15
Miaoli P.	1	1	2	3	2	3	0	2	2	0	1	1	3	2	3	3	2	1	2	1	1	0	2	38	21
Taichung P.	1	0	1	3	1	3	3	0	2	2	2	2	1	3	3	4	2	2	2	1	0	2	0	40	19
Changhua P.	1	2	3	3	2	3	3	3	0	1	1	2	2	3	1	3	1	1	3	2	2	1	3	46	15
Nantou P.	2	1	3	4	3	3	5	5	4	0	3	3	4	3	5	4	3	2	2	3	2	2	2	68	5
Yuanlin P.	2	2	3	3	3	3	4	3	4	2	0	3	4	3	3	4	3	2	3	3	3	2	2	65	7
Chiayi P.	2	1	3	4	3	3	4	3	3	2	2	0	3	3	4	4	3	1	3	2	2	2	3	59	10
Tainan P.	1	2	3	2	2	1	2	3	3	1	1	2	0	2	2	2	1	1	2	1	0	1	2	37	22
Kaohdiung P.	1	0	2	3	2	3	3	4	2	2	2	2	3	0	3	3	2	2	3	2	1	2	2	49	13
Pingtung P.	1	1	4	3	2	2	2	4	0	2	1	3	2	0	0	4	1	1	2	2	2	1	2	42	18
Taitung P.	1	2	3	3	2	2	2	2	2	1	1	1	3	2	1	0	0	2	1	1	0	1	2	35	23
Hualian P.	3	2	3	4	3	5	3	1	4	2	2	2	4	3	4	5	0	2	3	3	3	2	2	66	6
Penghu P.	3	2	4	3	4	4	4	3	4	3	3	4	4	3	4	3	3	0	2	1	1	1	3	65	7
Keelung C.	2	1	2	4	2	3	3	3	2	3	2	2	3	2	3	4	2	3	0	2.5	0	1	2	51.5	12
Hsinchu C.	2	3	4	4	3	3	4	3	3	2	2	3	4	3	3	4	2	4	2.5	0	0	1	3	62.5	9
Taichung C.	2	3	5	4	4	3	4	4	3	3	3	4	3	5	4	3	5	2	4	5	0	4	3	80	1
Chiayi C.	3	2	4	4	3	4	5	5	4	3	3	4	3	4	4	3	4	4	4	2	3	0	4	79	2
Tainan C.	2	0	3	3	4	4	3	3	2	3	2	3	3	3	3	3	2	3	3	2	1	1	0	56	11

Note: C=City; P=Prefecture; S=sum; R=rank.

0.9533, 0.9347, 0.9293, 0.8963 and 0.8416. We may note, from Table 8.4, that if R (a) = R (0.9986) all observations are dependent, except Ilan and Penghu Prefectures; if R (a) = R (0.8416) all observations are independent, and the 23 prefectures and cities would be in one single cluster.

The clustering of QOL on Taiwan was analysed using the fuzzy clustering relation–partition tree and population density as shown respectively in Figures 8.3 and 8.4; when R (a) = R (0.9533), five clusters were established. Based on the fuzzy clustering model, the empirical results on Taiwan can be summarized as follows:

1. Members in Cluster 4 are mostly highly urbanized metropolises, and their QOL are comparatively better than others, showing a greater level of similarity or homogeneity of QOL. Major cities in Taiwan which have benefited mostly from the planned construction and public investment projects of governments are, as expected, much more dominant than their rural counterparts.
2. Members in Clusters 1, 2 and 3 are mostly small cities and rural areas, which have received less concentrated public policy effects than Cluster 4. These

Table 8.4   Fuzzy resemblance relation-power matrix on Taiwan

District	1	2	3	4	5	6	7	8	9	10	11	12	13	14	15	16	17	18	19	20	21	22	23
Taipei City	1	0.968	0.896	0.842	0.968	0.842	0.842	0.842	0.842	0.842	0.842	0.842	0.842	0.842	0.842	0.842	0.842	0.842	0.968	0.968	0.962	0.962	0.962
Kaohsiung C.	0.968	1	0.869	0.842	0.968	0.842	0.842	0.842	0.842	0.842	0.842	0.842	0.842	0.842	0.842	0.842	0.842	0.842	0.968	0.976	0.962	0.962	0.962
Taipei P.	0.896	0.869	1	0.842	0.896	0.842	0.842	0.842	0.842	0.842	0.842	0.842	0.842	0.842	0.842	0.842	0.842	0.842	0.896	0.896	0.896	0.896	0.896
Ilan P.	0.842	0.842	0.842	1	0.842	0.935	0.993	0.979	0.979	0.935	0.979	0.935	0.929	0.995	0.935	0.991	0.993	0.999	0.842	0.842	0.842	0.842	0.842
Taoyuan P.	0.968	0.968	0.896	0.842	1	0.842	0.842	0.842	0.842	0.842	0.842	0.842	0.842	0.842	0.842	0.842	0.842	0.842	0.968	0.968	0.962	0.962	0.962
Hsinchu P.	0.842	0.842	0.842	0.935	0.842	1	0.935	0.935	0.935	0.969	0.935	0.842	0.842	0.842	0.935	0.935	0.935	0.935	0.842	0.842	0.842	0.842	0.842
Miaoh P.	0.842	0.842	0.842	0.993	0.842	0.935	1	0.979	0.979	0.935	0.979	0.935	0.929	0.935	0.935	0.991	0.997	0.993	0.842	0.842	0.842	0.842	0.842
Taichung P.	0.842	0.842	0.842	0.979	0.842	0.935	0.979	1	0.982	0.935	0.995	0.935	0.929	0.979	0.979	0.979	0.979	0.979	0.842	0.842	0.842	0.842	0.842
Changhua P.	0.842	0.842	0.842	0.979	0.842	0.935	0.979	0.982	1	0.935	0.982	0.935	0.929	0.979	0.935	0.979	0.979	0.979	0.842	0.842	0.842	0.842	0.842
Nantou P.	0.842	0.842	0.842	0.935	0.842	0.969	0.935	0.935	0.935	1	0.935	0.969	0.929	0.935	0.953	0.935	0.935	0.935	0.842	0.842	0.842	0.842	0.842
Yuanlin P.	0.842	0.842	0.842	0.979	0.842	0.935	0.979	0.995	0.982	0.935	1	0.935	0.929	0.979	0.953	0.979	0.979	0.979	0.842	0.842	0.842	0.842	0.842
Chiayi P.	0.842	0.842	0.842	0.935	0.842	0.998	0.935	0.935	0.935	0.969	0.935	1	0.929	0.935	0.953	0.935	0.935	0.935	0.842	0.842	0.842	0.842	0.842
Tainan P.	0.842	0.842	0.842	0.929	0.842	0.929	0.929	0.929	0.929	0.929	0.929	0.929	1	0.929	0.929	0.929	0.929	0.929	0.842	0.842	0.842	0.842	0.842
Kaohsiung P.	0.842	0.842	0.842	0.995	0.842	0.944	0.993	0.979	0.979	0.935	0.979	0.935	0.929	1	0.935	0.991	0.993	0.995	0.842	0.842	0.842	0.842	0.842
Pingtung P.	0.842	0.842	0.842	0.935	0.842	0.953	0.935	0.935	0.935	0.953	0.953	0.953	0.929	0.935	1	0.935	0.935	0.935	0.842	0.842	0.842	0.842	0.842
Taitung P.	0.842	0.842	0.842	0.991	0.842	0.935	0.991	0.979	0.979	0.935	0.979	0.935	0.929	0.991	0.935	1	0.991	0.991	0.842	0.842	0.842	0.842	0.842
Hualian P.	0.842	0.842	0.842	0.993	0.842	0.935	0.997	0.979	0.979	0.935	0.979	0.935	0.929	0.993	0.935	0.991	1	0.993	0.842	0.842	0.842	0.842	0.842
Penghu P.	0.842	0.842	0.842	0.999	0.842	0.935	0.993	0.979	0.979	0.935	0.979	0.935	0.929	0.995	0.935	0.991	0.993	1	0.842	0.842	0.842	0.842	0.842
Keelung C.	0.968	0.968	0.896	0.842	0.968	0.842	0.842	0.842	0.842	0.842	0.842	0.842	0.842	0.842	0.842	0.842	0.842	0.842	1	0.968	0.962	0.962	0.962
Hsinchu C.	0.968	0.976	0.896	0.842	0.968	0.842	0.842	0.842	0.842	0.842	0.842	0.842	0.842	0.842	0.842	0.842	0.842	0.842	0.968	1	0.962	0.962	0.962
Taichung C.	0.962	0.962	0.896	0.842	0.962	0.842	0.842	0.842	0.842	0.842	0.842	0.842	0.842	0.842	0.842	0.842	0.842	0.842	0.962	0.962	1	0.974	0.983
Chiayi C.	0.962	0.962	0.896	0.842	0.962	0.842	0.842	0.842	0.842	0.842	0.842	0.842	0.842	0.842	0.842	0.842	0.842	0.842	0.962	0.962	0.978	1	0.974
Tainan C.	0.962	0.962	0.896	0.842	0.962	0.842	0.842	0.842	0.842	0.842	0.842	0.842	0.842	0.842	0.842	0.842	0.842	0.842	0.962	0.962	0.982	0.974	1

Note: C = City; P = Perfecture.

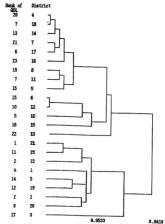

Note: District Unit: see Table 8.1.

Figure 8.3   Fuzzy clustering relation—partition tree of QOL on Taiwan

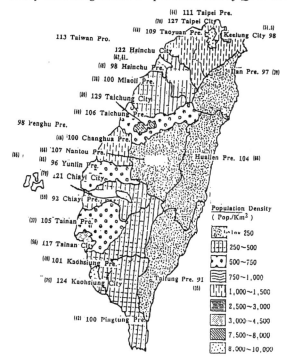

Figure 8.4   Empirical results of QOL model in Taiwan

cities and prefectures were observed to have relatively less planned public investment and construction endeavours by governments.

On the other hand, the top-down QOL model is processed by standardization and regression analysis (see Liu and Hu 1992b). With point scores and standardized normal Z scores, the empirical results of this model with Taiwan's data as the norm are shown in Tables 8.5 and 8.6. Comparing results obtained from both the bottom-up and top-down models, one notes that very similar QOL patterns exist among them, despite the fact that there are, in a cardinal sense, somewhat different QOL scales and scores for the cities and prefectures.

The empirical results from our regression analysis are interesting and worth noting with respect to policy implication. By regressing QOL scores on such selected demographic, socioeconomic and environmental policy variables as population density, offender rate, carbon dioxide, housing expenditure as per-

Table 8.5   Z-value and P-value of quality of life on five components in Taiwan

	Economic		Environment		Health and Education		Society		Social Infra-structure	
	Z-Value	P*	Z-Value	P*	Z-Value	P*	Z-Value	P*	Z-Value	P*
Taipei City	2.9531	5	3.4404	5	−1.7428	1	0.2280	3	0.1972	3
Kaohsiung C.	1.0413	5	0.7770	4	−1.6020	1	0.5430	4	−0.2889	2
Taipei P.	0.4198	4	−0.3120	2	0.5157	4	−2.9854	1	−1.4972	1
Ilan P.	−0.4878	2	−0.5401	2	0.4795	4	0.5215	4	−2.0073	1
Taoyuan P.	0.1474	3	−1.8429	1	1.6006	5	−2.7201	1	−0.4834	2
Hsinchu P.	−0.7558	2	−0.6652	2	1.2593	5	0.5861	4	−0.1563	3
Miaoli P.	−0.6067	2	−0.3401	2	0.3944	4	0.5501	4	0.3201	4,
Taichung P.	−0.4570	2	0.0244	3	1.0305	5	0.3591	4	−0.0816	3
Changhua P.	−0.7495	2	−0.1470	3	1.7259	5	0.2375	3	0.3105	4
Nantou P.	−0.4650	2	0.5162	4	0.0650	3	0.3670	4	−0.1474	3
Yuanlin P.	−0.7686	2	−0.1572	3	0.9323	5	0.5312	4	2.1013	5
Chiayi P.	−1.0539	1	0.5616	4	−0.9396	1	0.5807	4	1.4018	5
Tainan P.	−0.8202	2	0.0650	3	0.0739	3	−0.6464	2	1.1576	5
Kaohsiung P.	−0.4886	2	−0.1354	3	−0.7309	2	0.5332	4	−0.5471	2
Pingtung P.	−0.7824	2	0.2399	3	0.3324	4	0.5713	4	−0.3991	2
Taitung P.	−0.8882	1	0.1216	3	−0.3116	2	0.5544	4	−1.2734	1
Hualian P.	−0.3219	2	−0.0926	3	1.0008	5	0.0192	3	−0.2518	2
Penghu P.	−0.8492	1	1.2458	5	−0.8135	2	−1.7677	1	1.4697	5
Keelung C.	0.1887	3	−1.4097	1	−1.5600	1	0.5889	4	−1.5091	1
Hsinchu C.	0.8886	5	−0.5103	2	−1.3195	1	0.5770	4	1.0272	5
Taichung C.	2.1349	5	1.0294	5	−0.6858	2	−0.0458	3	0.3514	4
Chiayi C.	0.8898	5	−1.0476	1	0.6084	4	0.4679	4	1.0689	5
Tainan C.	0.9025	5	−0.7179	2	−0.5596	2	0.3492	4	−0.0594	3
Taiwan Prov.	−0.0713	3	−0.0932	3	0.2468	3	0.0	3	−0.7040	2

Note: C=City; P=Prefecture.
    *P-Value

Table 8.6   P-value, Z-value and rating of quality of life indicator in Taiwan

Area	Measured Value of QOL Indicator		
	Sum of P- Value	Z- Value	Rating
Taipei City	127	1.829600	A
Kaohsiung C.	124	1.556300	A
Taipei Prefecture	111	0.371998	B
Ilan P.	97	−0.90340	E
TaoyuanP.	109	0.189798	C
Hsinchu P.	98	−0.81230	D
Miaoli P.	100	−0.63010	D
Taichung P.	106	−0.08350	C
Changhwa P.	100	−0.63010	D
Mantou P.	107	0.007597	C
Yunlin P.	96	−0.99450	E
Chiayi P.	92	−1.35890	E
Tainan P.	105	−0.17460	C
Kaohsiung P.	101	−0.53900	D
Pingtung P.	100	−0.63010	D
Taitung P.	91	−1.45000	E
Hualien P.	104	−0.26570	D
Penghu P.	98	−0.81230	D
Keelung C.	98	−0.81230	D
Hsinchu C.	122	1.374100	A
Taichung C.	129	2.011801	A
Chiayi C.	121	1.282999	A
Tainan C	117	0.918599	A
Taiwan Province	113	0.554198	B
Mean Value	106.9166	0.043247	
Standard Deviation	10.9769	0.999301	

Note: C=City; P=Prefecture.

centage of income, and income per capita, our simple model clearly indicates that housing expenditure as a percentage of income is a very significant and dominating explanatory variable in both linear ($t = 1.98$) and log-linear ($t = 2.46$) forms of QOL analysis. And the impact coefficients of housing expenditure as a percentage of income are estimated at 0.001 and 0.22 respectively. As a result, various patterns on housing development and distribution should become our focal point for further public policy decision and QOL improvement on Taiwan (see Tables 8.7 and 8.8).

5. CONCLUDING REMARKS

The fact that QOL does not increase monotonically with that of GNP or income per capita has been well recognized and received in many newly developed

Table 8.7   *QOL model of constructed regression analysis (linear) on Taiwan*

	Variable					
	Popula-tion Density	Offender Rate	Carbon Monoxide	Housing Expenditure /Income	Income/ Year	QOL Index
Taipei City	9944.58	62.41	5.98	115.37	712.62	127
Kaohsiung C.	8946.65	73.08	1.44	72.39	592.53	124
Taipei P.	1447.03	35.95	4.08	77.07	594.46	111
Ilan P.	209.8	39.28	0.01	44.28	466.4	97
Taoyuan P.	1081.4	24.33	2.22	54.68	574.56	109
Hsinchu P.	259.7	43.96	0.41	45.93	564.98	98
Miaoli P.	299.91	30.75	0.6	47.09	574.56	100
Taichung P.	599.99	20.1	0.51	54.97	506.44	106
ChanghuaP.	1151.52	25.96	0.8	45.07	453..55	100
Nantou P.	130.1	40.24	0.1	44.39	450.61	107
Yuanlin P.	586.6	29.06	0.35	33.2	399.41	96
Chiayi P.	290.27	33.8	0.55	31.73	380.98	92
Tainan P.	503.7	30.37	0.55	38.13	426.91	105
Kaohsiung P.	385.81	44.72	1.6	44.33	472.02	101
Pingtung P.	320.49	29.79	0.31	41.01	454.96	100
Taitung P.	73.4	37.1	0.11	30.43	372.78	91
Hualian P.	75.72	44.43	0.7	38.93	454.16	104
Penghu P.	759.25	51.63	0.11	31.79	449.51	98
Keelung C.	2638.49	48.07	2	48.93	548.29	98
Hsinchu C.	3066.36	48.53	0.8	68.88	647.33	122
Taichung C.	4569.54	68.7	1.6	94.87	661.63	129
Chiayi C.	4267.6	49.32	1.4	54.96	550.45	121
Tainan C.	3846.87	33.57	1.9	67.86	543.87	117
Taiwan Prov.	450.62	37.69	2	53.14	514.7	113
Total	45915.4	982.83	30.13	1275.31	12352.82	2566
Mean	1913.1420	40.9613	1.2554	53.1379	514.7009	106.9167
Std. Dev.	2704.6660	13.4607	1.3782	20.7914	89.1831	11.2130

			Regression Results			
Variable	Coeffici-ent	Mean	Standard Deviation	Correlation x vs. y	t	Probability
Income/Year	0.0262	514.7009	89.1831	0.8178	0.8230	0.5760
Population Density	0.0011	1913.1420	2704.6660	0.7836	1.1717	0.2522
Housing Expend--iture/Income	0.3701	53.1379	20.7914	0.8573	1.9807	0.0568
Carbon Monoxide	−2.3642	1.2554	1.3782	0.5718	−1.5793	0.1244
Offender Rate	−0.0009	40.9513	13.4607	0.5942	−0.0072	0.9902
QOL Index		106.9167	11.2130			

Intercept: 74.6613   Coefficient of Determinant: 8000   F Statistic: 14.39
Number Observations: 24   Standard Error Estimate: 5.6680   Probability: 0.0000

Note: C=City P=Prefecture.

Table 8.8 *QOL model of constructed regression analysis (Log-Linear) on Taiwan*

	Variable					
	Population Density	Offender Rate	Carbon Monoxide	Housing Expenditure /Income	Income/ Year	QOL Index
Taipei City	3.9576	1.7953	0.7767	2.0621	2.8529	2.1038
Kaohsiung C.	3.9517	1.8638	0.1584	1.8597	2.7727	2.0934
Taipei Prefecture	3.1605	1.5557	0.6107	1.8869	2.7741	2.0453
Ilan P.	2.3218	1.5942	−2	1.6462	2.6688	1.9868
Taoyuan P.	3.0340	1.3801	0.3464	1.7378	2.7593	2.0374
Hsinchu P.	2.4145	1.6430	−0.3872	1.6621	2.7520	1.9912
Miaoli P.	2.4770	1.4878	−0.2218	1.6730	2.7409	2
Taichung P.	2.7781	1.3032	−0.2924	1.7401	2.7045	2.0253
Changhua P.	3.0613	1.4143	−0.0969	1.6539	2.6566	2
NantouP.	2.1143	1.6047	−1	1.6473	2.6624	2.0294
Yuanlin P.	2.7683	1.4633	−0.4559	1.5211	2.6014	1.9823
Chiayi P.	2.4628	1.5289	−0.2596	1.5022	2.5809	1.9638
Tainan P.	2.7022	1.4824	−0.2596	1.5579	2.6303	2.0212
Kaohsiung P.	2.5975	1.6505	0.2041	1.6467	2.6740	2.0043
Pingtung P.	2.5058	1.4741	−0.5086	1.6129	2.6580	2
Taitung P.	1.8657	1.5694	−0.9586	1.4833	2.5715	1.9590
HualianP.	1.8792	1.6477	−0.1549	1.5674	2.6572	2.0170
Penghu P.	2.8804	1.7129	−0.9586	1.5023	2.6527	1.9912
Keelung C.	3.4214	1.6819	0.3010	1.6898	2.7390	1.9912
Hsinchu C.	3.4866	1.6860	−0.0969	1.8381	2.8111	2.0864
Taichung C.	3.6599	1.8370	0.2041	1.9762	2.8206	2.1106
Chiayi C.	3.6302	1.6930	0.1461	1.7400	2.7407	2.0828
Tainan C.	3.5851	1.5260	0.2788	1.8316	2.7355	2.0682
Taiwan Province	2.6538	1.5762	0.3010	1.7254	2.7116	2.0531
Total	69.4092	38.1772	−4.3240	40.7640	64.9288	48.6438
Mean	2.8921	1.5907	−0.1802	1.6985	2.7054	2.0268
Std. Dev.	0.6138	0.1395	0.6069	0.1511	0. 0749	0.0446

Regression Results						
Variable	Coefficient	Mean	Standard Deviation	Correlation x vs. y	t	Probability
Income/Year	−0.0464	2.7054	0.0749	0.8101	−0.2778	0.7798
Housing Expenditure/Income	0.2157	1.6985	0.1511	0.8763	2.4637	0.0206
Population Density	0.0116	2.8921	0.6138	0.7660	0.8801	0.6082
Carbon Monoxide	0.0034	−0.1802	0.6069	0.5814	0.3221	0.7486
Offender Rate	0.0469	1.5907	0.1395	0.4989	1.1802	0.2488
QOL Index		2.0268	0.0446			

Intercept: 1.678627   Coefficient of Determinant: 0.799827   F Statistic: 17.18
Number Observations: 24   Standard Error Estimate: 0.0225362 Probability: 0.0000

Note: C=City; P=Prefecture.

countries, including Taiwan (Tables 8.7 and 8.8). To reverse the trends of environmental deterioration brought about by urbanization and industrialization, and to develop energy alternatives urgently needed for sustaining economic growth and QOL enrichment, the public decision makers on Taiwan should be better assisted with some micro-based DSS in order to complete their planning, implementation and controlling tasks effectively and efficiently.

This chapter has outlined in a simple and rudimentary form, a mini- or personal computer-based system to help strategic managers make better and more intelligent decisions on semi-structured or unstructured tasks (see Sprague and Carlson 1982 and Mclean and Sol (eds) 1987 for similar system development). Problems and potential solutions concerning tradeoff analysis among economic growth, energy production, urban development, environmental protection and overall quality of life management in Taiwan or elsewhere can be briefly illustrated through the linkages between the QOL model-base, the database, and the knowledge-base system operations.

Some preliminary output produced from the proposed DSS has reconfirmed empirically, though tentatively, that the QOL experienced in Taiwan by region and sector has not risen monotonically as a function of real income per capita and urbanization status because of the negative impacts observed in the natural and man-made environmental sector. Using the traditional economic indicators, such as income and/or employment, alone for policy decision analysis would be misleading, as suggested by Lee and Liu (1988). Present results show that cities with more balanced urban planning and well-thought-out housing development projects tended to have enjoyed better QOL in Taiwan.

The historical growth path of Taiwan's economic miracle has been revisited (Lee et al. 1994) and chronologically associated with a number of central government policies such as the 'land reforms' in the fifties, the 'import–export substitution' and 'extended educational investment' in the sixties, the 'public construction projects' in the seventies, the 'high-tech' and 'internationalization' policies in the eighties, and the 'great national re-vitalization projects' thereafter. However, the relationship between fiscal policy, especially income tax, economic growth and income distribution, urban development and environmental protection, and quality of life enrichment patterns, has not been thoroughly investigated because the governments in Taiwan have rarely encountered any financial difficulties or been threatened with a prolonged budgetary deficit until the 1980s. Nevertheless, several local governments and even the central government in Taiwan now have significant budget problems. Financing of the 'great national re-vitalization projects' including the energy, transportation, environmental cleaning, interregional development, and privatization and globalization projects, will certainly incur public debt, which in turn will have significant impacts on the country's distribution of social-economic well-being and the overall QOL between urban and rural populations.

Following arguments developed by Hammond (ed.) (1980), Fishburn (1984),

Amadio (1989) and Liu and Hu (1992a,b), this chapter thus recommends that a micro-based functional DSS be provided for public officials to undertake strategic planning and public policy decision analysis in order to understand and improve the overall quality of life of their citizens, interregionally as well as intertemporally.

APPENDIX 8A

Table 8A.1   Variables and measurement unit of QOL indicator on Taiwan

Source & Sign	Indicator — Variable	Unit
1an	Population density	Population/km^2
2a–	Illiteracy rate	%
3a+	Beds/10,000 population	Number of beds/10,000Population
4a–	Dustfall	Tons/Km^2/Month
5a	Sulphur dioxide	ppm
6a	Carbon monoxide	ppm
7a–	Nitrigen dioxide	ppm
8a–	Offender rate	Population/10,000 population
9a–	Juvenile delinquents	%
10a–	Households affected by fire per 10,000 houses	Household
11a–	Estimated losses from fire	1,000,000 New Taiwan Dollar
12b+	Book stock of local Cultural Centre	#
13b+	Piped water supply	%
14b+	Highway density	Km/Km^2
15b+	Newspaper and magazines per 1,000 population	#/1,000 population
16b+	TV Sets/1,000 population	#/1,000 population
17b+	Local government expenditure per capita	1,000 New Taiwan Dollar,
18b+	Final statements of education, science and culture	100,000,000 New Taiwan Dollar
19a+	Employment by commerce	%
20a+	News agencies' distribution	#
21b+	Education and recreation	#
22b+	Saving as % of income	%
23b+	Employed persons as % of civilian population aged 15+	%
24bn	Social increase rate	%
25bn	Dependency ratio	%
26b+	Average current income	New Taiwan Dollar
27b+	Local government revenue per capita	New Taiwan Dollar
28b–	Daily refuse production per capita	Kg
29b+	Amount per worker	Ton/Day
30b+	Average family housing expenditure	New Taiwan dollar
31b+	Doctors per 10,000 population	#/10,000 Population

Table 8A.1   Continued

32b+	Automobiles per 1,000 population	#
33b+	Subscribers per 100 population	Subscribers
34b+	Monthly kWh per capita	kWh
35b+	Daily water consumption per capita	Litre
36b n	Population in urban planned districts as % of total population	%

Key: + Positive Indicator, – Negative Indicator, n Neutral Indicator.
Sources: a: Directorate-General of Budget, Accounting and Statistics, Social Indicators in Taiwan of ROC 1989, ExecuteYuan, 1989.
          b: Council for Economic Planning and Development, Urban and Regional Development Statistics 1990, Execute Yuan, 1990.

REFERENCES

Alter, S. (1977), 'A Taxonomy of Decision Support Systems', *Sloan Management Review*, Autumn, 39–56.
Amadio, W. (1989), *Systems Development: A Practical Approach*, Santa Cruz, CA: Mitchell Publishing, Inc.
Arrow, K. (1974), 'Limited Knowledge and Economic Analysis', *American Economic Review*, March.
Bennett, J.L. (ed.) (1983), *Building Decision Support Systems*, Reading, MA: Addison Wesley.
Centeno, M.A. (1995), 'Software Review: Criterium Decision Plus', *ORMS Today*, August, pp. 62–3.
Cook, T., P. Falchi and R. Mariano (1984), 'An Urban Allocation Model Combining Time Series and Analytic Hierarchical Methods', *Management Science*, Vol. 30, No. 2, February, 198–208.
Dos Santos, B. and M. Bariff (1988), 'A Study of User Interface Aids for Model-Oriented Decision Support Systems', *Management Science*, Vol. 34, No. 4, April, 461–8.
Fishburn, P. (1984), 'Foundations of Risk Measurement', *Management Science*, Vol. 30, No. 4, April, 396–406.
Fox, K. (1983), 'The Geo-Behavioral View of Human Societies and Its Implications for System Science', *International Journal of Systems Sciences*, Vol. 14, No. 6.
Hammond, K. (ed.) (1980), 'Judgment and Decision in Public Policy Formation', AAAS Selected Symposium Proceedings, Boulder, CO.
Harmon, P., R. Maus and W. Morrissey (1988), *Expert Systems: Tools and Applications*, New York: John Wiley & Sons.
Heidenheimer, A., H. Heclo and C.T. Adams (1990), *Comparative Public Policy: The Politics of Social Choice*, New York: St. Martins.
Henderson, J.C. and D. Schilling (1985), 'Design and Implementation of Decision Support Systems in the Public Sector', *MIS Quarterly*, Vol. 9, No. 2, June, 157–69.
Hsieh, C.T. and B.C. Liu (1988), 'A Group Decision Support System for Public Policies', Proceeding of Southwest Decision Science Institute Conference, 168–70.
Hsieh, C.T. and B.C. Liu (1993), ' Educational and Geographical Inequality in Life Quality Management: An MIS Approach', *Quarterly Journal of Business Ideology*,

Vol. 15, Spring.

Huber, G. (1984), 'Issues in the Design of Group Decision Support Systems', *MIS Quarterly*, Vol. 8, No. 3, September, 195–204.

Lee, M. L. and B. C. Liu (1988), 'Measuring Socioeconomic Effects When Using Income as Life Quality Indicators', *American Journal of Economics and Sociology*, Vol. 47, No. 2, 167–74.

Lee, M.L., B.C. Liu and P. Wang (1994), 'Growth and Equity with Endogenous Human Capital: Taiwan's Economic Miracle Revisited', *Southern Economic Journal*, Oct.

Liu, B.C. (1975), 'Net Migration Rate and the Quality of Life', *Review of Economics and Statistics*, Vol. 57, No. 3.; also in Ramanathan, *Introductory Econometrics*, 3rd Edition, New York: The Dryden Press, 1995.

Liu, B.C. (1976), *Quality of Life Indicators in the US Metropolitan Areas, 1970: A Comprehensive Statistical Assessment*, Washington, DC: USGPO, and New York: Praeger Publishers.

Liu, B.C. (1988), *Energy, Income and Quality of Life Management in U.S.A., An Information Systems Approach to Decision Analysis*, Taipei, Taiwan: Tamkang University Press.

Liu, B.C. (1991), 'Industrial Planning and Environmental Quality Management: A Decision Support System,,' paper presented at the ORSA/ TIMS Joint Annual Meetings, Anaheim, California: November.

Liu, B.C. and C.P. Hu (1992a), 'Quality of Life Indicators for Urban Development Decisions: A Multivariate Study on Taiwan', Proceedings of the Tenth Conference on Multiple Criteria Decision Making, Taipei, Taiwan: 9–24 July.

Liu, B.C. and C.P. Hu (1992b), 'Quality of Life Indicators for Urban Policy: A Decision Support Analysis for Taiwan', Proceedings of American Statistical Association, Social Statistics Session, Boston.

Liu, B.C., T. Mulvey and C.T. Hsieh (1986), 'Effects of Educational Expenditures on Regional Inequality in the Social Quality of Life', *The American Journal of Economics and Sociology*, Vol. 45, No. 2, April.

Liu, B.C., K.S. Tzeng and C.T. Hsieh (1992), 'Energy Planning and Environmental Quality Management: A Decision Support System', *Energy Economics*, October.

Mclean, E.R. and H.G. Sol (eds) (1987), 'Decision Support Systems: A Decade in Perspective', Proceedings of IFIP WG 8.3, 5–18 June, 1986, Noordwijkerhout, The Netherlands, Amsterdam: North Holland.

Miller, L. and N. Katz (1986), 'A Model Management System to Support Policy Analysis', *Decision Support Systems*, March, 55–64.

Minch, R. and G.L. Sanders (1986), 'Computerized Information Systems Supporting Multicriteria Decision Making', *Decision Sciences*, Vol. 17, No .3, 395–413.

Perry, W.E. (1984), 'How to Maintain Control in the Data Base Environment', *Journal of Information System Management*, Vol. 1, No. 2, Spring, 46–54.

Savage, S.L. (1985, 1994), *What's Best and Fundamental: Analytic Spreadsheet Tools for Quantitative Management*, New York: Osborne McGraw Hill.

Schoner B. and W.C. Wedley (1989), 'Ambiguous Criteria Weights in AHP: Consequences and Solutions', *Decision Sciences*, Summer, 462–75.

Sprague, R. and E. Carlson (1982), *Building Effective Decision Support Systems*, Englewood Cliffs, NJ: Prentice-Hall.

Young, L.F. (1989), *Decision Support and Idea Processing Systems*, Dubuque, IA: W.C. Brown Publisher.

PART III

The Public: Client or Decision Maker?

9. Siting Hazardous Facilities: Lessons from Europe and America

Howard C. Kunreuther, Joanne Linnerooth-Bayer and Kevin Fitzgerald

1. INTRODUCTION

With growing concern over environmental and health protection, siting controversial facilities, from prisons to power plants, has become increasingly difficult
and has emerged as a policy problem of major significance in North America
and Europe. In the United States, this problem is acute. A national survey
revealed in 1990 that 62 per cent of the US public oppose placing a new landfill
in their community and a 53 per cent majority believes that current land disposal
technologies are inadequate to protect groundwater (Cambridge Reports 1990).

The situation is also acute in many European countries although there are
some successes to report. Switzerland is struggling to find host communities for
solid waste landfills with some limited success (Renn 1994). In Austria, a
private firm has gained permission to locate a hazardous waste landfill in one
Austrian state, although Austria's overall programme to locate facilities in each
state is partly stalemated (Linnerooth and Davy 1994).

The siting impasse has been the subject of extensive analysis (Kunreuther and
Linnerooth 1982; O'Hare et al. 1983; Greenberg et al. 1984; Kasperson 1986;
Colglazier and Langum 1988; English and Davis 1987; Kasperson et al. 1992).
At a National Workshop on Facility Siting in the United States in 1990 a group
of practitioners and researchers developed a set of guidelines for siting noxious
and/or hazardous facilities. These guidelines were formalized in a Facility Siting
Credo which focused on developing fair procedures and outcomes for locating
facilities (Kunreuther et al. 1993).

No analysis, however, can lead to a blueprint for a siting procedure that will
be acceptable to all parties, in all cases, and in all countries. The intent of this
chapter is (1) to review siting procedures that have been tried or proposed in
North America and Europe, and (2) to analyse these procedures with respect to
the perceived fairness of the process. Without labelling any siting procedures

as more or less desirable or suitable, we will point out their differentiating characteristics with respect to the fairness of the procedures and the outcome. We begin by discussing common features of siting problems that need to be considered before contrasting different procedures. Section 3 characterizes the process in terms of who has the authority to make decisions and how open and accessible the procedures are to the public.

Section 4 discusses what we mean by a fair outcome by focusing on two broad criteria: efficiency, whether some overall societal goal is met at lowest social cost, and equity, where distributive features of the solution are considered to be fair. After summarizing in Section 5 what we have learned from North American and European experiences, in Section 6 we pose a set of questions related to siting for consideration by Asian countries, most of whom face critical siting problems today. Throughout the chapter we will illustrate similarities and differences through examples of actual siting experiences.

2. COMMON CHARACTERISTICS OF SITING PROBLEMS[1]

2.1. Many Interested Parties

In any siting controversy there are a set of interested parties, each of which has its own values and goals. There are those groups who would like to see the facility built because it yields sufficient benefits to them; others are likely to have serious concerns about the facility. Some of the key stakeholders are the applicant, normally a private firm or government agency interested in having the facility built; public interest groups, such as local citizen organizations and environmental groups; government regulatory agencies for developing and enforcing regulations; and finally the general public where there may be a wide spectrum of attitudes about the facility.

Some of the interested parties may feel the same way about the facility but for different reasons. For example, an environmental group may oppose the construction of a high-level nuclear waste repository primarily because it would like to end the use of nuclear power and recognize that this will happen if there is no place to store the waste. Citizens' groups may oppose the facility because of strong fears of an accident either to themselves or to future generations.

When one lines up all the different interested parties on a particular siting question there is likely to be considerable conflict on whether the facility is needed and, if so, where it should be placed. The fact that different groups may have the same attitude towards a proposed facility but for very different reasons suggests that it is important to understand the nature of the controversy before making policy recommendations.

2.2. Uncertainty About the Risks

Even in the unlikely case that risk is defined in the same way by all the stakeholders there are likely to be significant discrepancies in estimates. For new technologies there are limited statistical data on how well the facility is likely to perform in practice. In the case of a proposed high-level nuclear waste (HLNW) repository in the United States, one has to rely entirely on theoretical or prototype analyses since there is no historical record to consult. Scientists may disagree on the assumption on which their analysis was based, and thus come up with very different estimates of probabilities and consequences.

In situations where stakeholders are talking about the same event (e.g. groundwater contamination from a landfill) they may still disagree on the consequences of the event both in time and place. Kasperson et al. (1988) have pointed out that the consequences of risk events go far beyond direct harms to include many of the indirect impacts such as loss of confidence in institutions and the perceived fairness of the risk-management process. For example, the accident at Three Mile Island did not kill any individual but wrought enormous social consequences in the form of stricter regulations, greater opposition to nuclear power and an increased concern with other complex technologies such as chemical plants and genetic engineering. This potential social amplification of risk needs to be taken into account when designing the decision process and strategies for siting and managing new facilities.

Scientific experts and the general public are likely to define the nature of the risk differently. Scientists tend to focus on the probability of the event occurring and define the consequences as the fatalities, injuries and property damage while laypersons will focus on other dimensions of risk such as fear and dread (Slovic 1987). Thus facilities where experts feel that they pose little risk may be strongly opposed by the general public who are concerned with other features of the risk which are not part of the expert's model.

2.3. Prerequisites for Successful Siting

Each siting case has its own unique characteristics and dynamics. Recognizing that political and legal culture in each country will influence the siting process, there are two prerequisites that are important for achieving success independent of the type of facility and where it is to be located:

Prerequisite 1: Achieve sufficient agreement that there is a need for a new facility
A facility siting process must begin with general agreement by the relevant interested parties that there are severe consequences of maintaining the status quo and that the proposed facility is needed. When there is disagreement on the issue of *need* then it may be difficult to site the facility as illustrated by the

controversy that is now raging in the United States regarding the storage of high-level radioactive waste (HLNW):

The Proposed Nevada Repository In the United States, nuclear wastes are currently stored in holding ponds at the reactor site; however, the storage capacity of on-site facilities will be exceeded in the next few years. The nuclear industry and the federal government have argued that long-term geologic disposal is the solution to the HLNW problem. Yucca Mountain in the state of Nevada has been chosen as the site of a repository where the waste will be buried for 10,000 years. Those opposed to the repository feel that interrum storage of spent fuel is now feasible and desirable using new technologies such as dry-cask storage and multi-purpose canisters (Easterling and Kunreuther 1995).

Prerequisite 2: Achieve sufficient agreement that the proposed facility is acceptably safe
Unless the affected parties feel that the proposed facility does not impose significant health and safety risks it will be difficult to site a facility. Sufficiently rigorous design standards for mitigating future risks should be set and enforced. In some countries, as the following example illustrates, showing that the facility is acceptably safe from an expert point of view is sufficient justification to proceed with the facility:

Siting Hazardous Waste Facilities In Austria The federal government obtained an explicit agreement with the local community that expert judgments of acceptable risk for affected population and the environment would be valid grounds for siting a facility. The local citizens were part of the process of choosing the experts (Linnerooth and Davy 1994).

3. ALTERNATIVE SITING PROCEDURES

3.1. Criteria for Evaluation

In describing different siting processes it is useful to specify two criteria, *efficiency* and *equity*, which have a long history in the social sciences and are useful for characterizing both the siting process and the outcomes.

   Process efficiency is a measure of the expenditures in terms of time and money associated with finding a home for a particular type of facility. *Process equity* refers to the perceived fairness of the procedure from the viewpoint of the different interested parties concerned with the final outcome. Easterling (1992) is one of the few researchers who has tried to operationalize this concept. He stresses the importance of the legitimacy of a siting strategy in determining whether a facility will actually be built. In addition there is a need to establish trust between the interested parties in order for the siting process to be perceived as a fair one (Kasperson et al. 1992; Slovic 1993; Kunreuther et al. 1994).

A highly efficient siting process might be one where experts first find a low-cost/low-risk location for a facility and then the developer arbitrarily announces that it will be located there, often defending the decision in a climate of escalating public protest. This approach is classified as the Decide–Announce–Defend (DAD) model.

The DAD approach is generally viewed by the affected public as being highly inequitable because they feel excluded from the process. O'Hare et al. (1983) describe the end stage of this process as follows:

> At the end of a process already far along, the developer thus faces a hostile population, composed of people who feel duped—informed of a project in the eleventh hour, and told by government and industry alike, 'love it or leave'.

At the other extreme members of the Berger Commission, in trying to determine whether a pipeline should be sited in northern Canada, travelled over 17,000 miles interviewing residents of affected small communities and villages. Millions of dollars were spent in the process, after which it was decided not to construct the pipeline (Gamble 1979). This process was viewed as procedurally fair by many of the affected parties, although the developer was uncomfortable with it. This process was a highly efficient one since it required enormous amounts of time and money.

3.2. A Typology of Siting Processes

One way to categorize differences in siting processes is by looking at *decision authority* and the *openness of the process*. Decision authority specifies which organization or group has the right to make the final selection of the site(s). This is a question of entitlement or property rights, where the property right in this case can be thought of as the right to impose risk (Whitehead 1991).

At one extreme is the case where the federal government has the authority to make a final decision independent of whether the community residents or the general public agree with it. The concept of *eminent domain*[2] or takings is the classic example of the ability of government to take private property for public use without consent. At the other extreme is the ability of residents of the proposed host community to determine whether or not to accept a facility through some type of social consensus process such as a referendum.

An open process is one where there is active public participation, and the different interested parties have standing in the siting debate and access to relevant information about the site. In a closed process decisions are made with little public involvement and can not usually be challenged by the affected citizens.

The adversarial process, which characterizes most siting debates today in the United States, best illustrates an open process. For example, in Massachusetts a private firm called Clean Harbors proposed a site for a hazardous waste incinerator costing $42 million. The firm was required to carry out a very detailed risk assessment study. Several local citizen groups then spent over $700,000 to critique this study and presented their findings to the Department of Enviromental Protection (DEP). Based on these findings DEP recommended against approval of the facility because they felt it posed unacceptable health risks to the large surrounding population (Brion 1991).

The French system epitomizes this process since official decisions on where to site a noxious facility appear to be made by government officials behind closed doors,[3] as illustrated by the decision process utilized by Gaz de France in determining where they should locate a liquified energy gas facility (Kunreuther and Linnerooth 1982).

Figure 9.1 depicts a typology for characterizing siting processes by crossing Decision Authority (x-axis) with Openness of the Process (y-axis). In each of the four resulting quadrants are examples of cases from Europe and North America which characterize these siting processes today. In some cases, there is an associated line which extends to one of the other quadrants, indicating that the process has changed over time. For example, the controversy over siting a high-level nuclear waste repository in the United States, has moved from open process with some local local control to a closed process with government authority. Brief case histories of siting processes which fall in one or more of the four quadrants provide a perspective on the advantages and challenges associated with using different strategies for attempting to site new facilities.

Open process with local rights
A process with public participation and local rights has only recently been tried in North America. This process is illustrated with two cases: one in Canada and one in the United States.[4]

Siting a hazardous waste facility in Alberta[5] In 1979, the province of Alberta, Canada initiated a process to site an integrated hazardous waste facility that includes treatment, incineration and landfilling (of non-hazardous residues). The two innovative features of the process were that only communities that satisfied technical criteria of feasibility would be eligible and then only if they volunteered to be considered as a possible candidate.

Planning grants were given to the nine communities that expressed an interest in hosting the facility and satisfied the technical criteria without any commitment on their part. These funds were used for feasibility studies, public information efforts and other public outreach efforts.

Two towns expressed an interest in hosting the facility. Swan Hills was

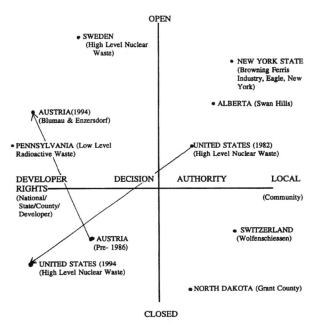

OPENNESS OF PROCESS

OPEN

• SWEDEN
(High Level Nuclear
Waste)

• NEW YORK STATE
(Browning Ferris
Industry, Eagle, New
York)

• ALBERTA (Swan Hills)

AUSTRIA(1994)
(Blumau & Enzersdorf)

• PENNSYLVANIA (Low Level
Radioactive Waste)

UNITED STATES (1982)
(High Level Nuclear Waste)

DEVELOPER
RIGHTS
(National/
State/County/
Developer)

DECISION   AUTHORITY

LOCAL
(Community)

• SWITZERLAND
(Wolfenschiessen)

AUSTRIA
(Pre- 1986)

UNITED STATES (1994
(High Level Nuclear Waste)

• NORTH DAKOTA (Grant County)

CLOSED

Figure 9.1   A typology of siting

ultimately chosen by the province to host the facility because this community, in contrast to the other, did not have fierce opposition from the surrounding rural population. The hazardous waste treatment centre in Swan Hills promised 55 new jobs, which convinced town leaders that other new developments such as a new hospital would now be feasible. The other town, Ryley, was disappointed with the outcome and placed a newspaper advertisement indicating that they should have won.

Siting a landfill in New York State In 1990, William Ruckelshaus, the Chief Executive Officer of Browning–Ferris Industries (BFI) made an unusual offer to virtually every municipality in New York State. He established a community partnership programme in which each town had an opportunity to consider hosting a solid waste landfill in return for a share of the benefits from its operation.

The process was entirely voluntary with the company requiring an official invitation by the community to even begin the process, at which time it began an educational campaign of open houses and tours of other BFI facilities. One community, Eagle (with 1300 residents) agreed to this process and eventually held a referendum in which the citizens turned down the facility. True to its word, BFI left town. Only after a grassroots movement organized another referendum which overwhelmingly favoured community partnership did the company return. By August 1993 a preliminary site had been identified and a benefits package which included tipping fees, local jobs and free trash disposal was agreed upon. In the subsequent months other companies, in addition to BFI, were invited by Eagle to make proposals for constructing a landfill. In February 1995, the town decided to proceed with one of these other companies (Raylman 1995).

Closed process with local rights
The juxtaposition of a closed process with local rights seems somewhat contradictory. If a community has the right to decide whether or not it wants a facility, then one would expect a fair amount of discussion as was the case in Alberta and Eagle, New York. We did find two cases falling in this category which are described below.

Siting an underground repository in Switzerland[6] The community of Wolfenschiessesn has 500 households and 1800 inhabitants. It agreed to host an underground repository for storing low- and mid-level nuclear waste without much public discussion, most likely because the Swiss government made it clear that scientific experts considered the facility to be safe and offered the community 2.5 million Swiss francs for the next 25 years.

Since most residents of the community were convinced that the facility would not pose health and safety risks, they did *not* treat the compensation as a bribe. It is not clear how the money will be used by the community but if it was distributed to the residents then each individual would receive a sizeable sum per year for the next 25 years.

Siting a monitored retrieval storage (MRS) facility in North Dakota In 1987 a voluntary siting process was initiated in the US for temporarily storing high-level waste in MRS facilities until a permanent repository is built. Non-binding grants were provided by the federal government to enable communities to investigate the risks and benefits of hosting an MRS.[7]

Three county commissioners in sparsely populated Grant County, North Dakota decided to apply for a grant in 1990 to study the possibility of hosting an MRS facility. They apparently initiated the process with little public awareness or involvement. The following March, residents voted all three county commissioners out of office in a recall election because they accepted this grant even though they knew it was not binding in any way.

Open process with government rights
By far the most common process in both Europe and the United States is an open

process where the federal, state or local government have the right to make a final decision. This process is illustrated with two cases from Europe and one from the United States.

Siting a hazardous waste facility in Austria Like most European countries, Austria faces a hazardous waste crisis. Today most wastes are disposed of illegally or shipped to neighbouring countries (especially Slovakia and the Czech Republic). The federal government is required to identify and designate sites relying primarily on technical expertise but also listening to the opinions of residents, landowners and firms within the identified communities.

The siting process in Austria has moved from a closed to an open process as shown in Figure 9.1. Prior to 1986 citizens were given almost no information on the proposed facility and siting decisions were made with little public input. In 1986 the province of Lower Austria initiated a process that gave more discretionary latitude to local governments and citizens.

In 1987, Blumau and Enzersdorf were selected as possible candidates for the hazardous waste facility. A public participation process was initiated in both communities where citizen representatives were given broad responsibility in choosing the experts and monitoring the siting process. The final decision is legally in the hands of the federal government, whereby approval must be based on the results of the expert investigations assessing the risks of the proposed facility for the public health and environment. The experience and the outlook for this approach are rather different at Blumau, where this approach appears to have lost all legitimacy with the public, and Enzersdorf, where there is cautious optimism that the public will accept the facility.

Siting a high-level nuclear waste repository in Sweden There is political consensus in Sweden that it is necessary to store high-level nuclear waste from Sweden's twelve nuclear power stations in Sweden and not to export the waste to another country for final disposal. A process for identifying an appropriate disposal site will proceed in two stages:

1. First, the utility-owned Swedish Nuclear Fuel and Waste Management Company (SKB) will develop a small demonstration of direct disposal, for which construction would start around 2005, with emplacement of encapsulated spent fuel starting by 2008. At this state, the waste would be in a retrieveable mode.
2. After evaluation of suitability for final disposal, the demonstration facility would be extended to a full repository, with disposal of spent fuel beginning around 2020.

In the meantime, SKB is constructing a rock laboratory for basic studies close to the Oskarshamn nuclear power station and the operating interim storage facility (CCAB). This laboratory is scheduled for completion during 1995.

Political leaders in two communities in the North have volunteered their areas as potential sites by agreeing to preliminary investigations, and discussions are in progress with several other northern communities. The willingness of the local community to accept the facility is an important consideration in the siting decision. Primary licensing authority rests with the Nuclear Power Inspectorate (SKI) and the National Institute of Radiation Protection. The siting process in Sweden has been characterized by openness and active public participation. with financial resources given to community and environmental groups (Ahlstrom 1994; *Nuclear News* 1994).

Siting a low-level radioactive waste (LLRW) facility in Pennyslvania As host state for the disposal of LLRW for the Appalachian Compact states, Pennsylvania has passed legislation and regulations outlining a screening process which would identify three of the best potential locations for a disposal facility, based on the administrative record. Legislation also requires that the Department of Environmental Protection (DEP) establish an open and public process to locate a regional facility in the Commonwealth. The system is thus similar to the Austrian system for locating a hazardous waste facility described above.

Chem-Nuclear System Inc. (CNSI) was selected by the Pennsylvania Department of Environmental Resources (DER) in 1989 to site, license, construct, operate and close an LLRW facility in the Commonwealth. Legislation further requires the DEP to appoint an LLRW Advisory Committee to review draft regulations pertaining to the siting, design, construction, operation and closure of the facility. The site selection process is completed through the local disqualification phase. In July 1994, the DEP announced a policy to seek a volunteer community to host the facility, thus allowing for real public involvement in deciding what is acceptable risk (Rue 1995).

Closed process with national/state rights

The most salient closed process today relates to the storing of high-level nuclear waste (HLNW) in the United States. Interestingly enough the process twelve years ago was a much more open one, but legislation in 1987 changed the character of siting. In this case, the United States has moved in the opposite direction from Sweden, as will be noted by comparing this case with the Swedish one described above.

Storing HLNW in repositories in the United States The Nuclear Waste Policy Act (NWPA) of 1982 was the principal legislation for finding feasible sites to store HLNW in underground repositories for the next 10,000 years. The Act recognized the need to find sites that would be both technically and politically feasible and called for a number of candidate areas to be characterized before making a final choice.

Under the Act, strict safety standards would be employed and regional equity would be sought. States would have an opportunity to disapprove of having a repository, but a negative vote could be overridden by Congress and the President. The system was thus identical to the Swedish programme described above.

The NWPA was amended in December 1987 when Congress chose Yucca Mountain to be characterized, thus singling out Nevada, the least populated state in the country. The repository is scheduled to be constructed there by 2010 unless the site is shown to be unsafe or new legislation is passed by Congress putting the repository 'on hold' and requiring temporary storage of HLNW in dry-cask or multiple-purpose canisters, as discussed above.

As shown in Figure 9.1, the process for siting a repository has moved from one that was relatively open in 1982 to one that resembles the closed Decide–Announce–Defend (DAD) approach. Today there is considerable public distrust in the siting process, which overshadows experts' claims that the proposed repository will safely bury waste for 10,000 years (Flynn et al. 1992; Ericksen 1994).

4. FAIR OUTCOMES FOR SITING HAZARDOUS FACILITIES

In all parts of the world it will be increasingly difficult to find sites for hazardous facilities without the cooperation of the local citizens. This cooperation will not be forthcoming if public groups and other stakeholders do not consider the siting process and outcome to be fair.

4.1. What is a Fair Outcome?

Is it fair, for instance, to put a hazardous waste facility in an industrial area where the residents are poor and otherwise disadvantaged? Alternatively is it fair to choose a site in an environmentally pristine area in order to spread the burdens of industrial society more equally among the population? If one site is technically superior by minimizing the population and environmental risks, should the distribution of the risk burden matter at all? Do regions and even countries have a responsibility to deal with their own wastes and not to export them? Should the host community have the right of refusal? Should the community be compensated for hosting a facility?

As these questions suggest, fair process and fair outcomes are closely interlinked. In the last section, we examined two fundamental characteristics of siting procedures, decision authority and openness of the process. The outcome of the process is, of course, not independent of these characteristics. If the local community has the right to veto a siting proposal, then the developer will be motivated to offer compensation in order to gain the approval of the community. This may lead to a different outcome than if the central government imposes the facility on the community.

Regardless of the approach taken for allocating hazardous facilities, explicit or implicit judgements about the fairness of the site are unavoidable in justifying the choice. Two types of justification are usual. The first concerns the efficiency of the site choice, which in its broadest meaning refers to the optimization of some overall social objective given limited budget constraints. The welfare of society or the environment might be thought of as global efficiency, whereas some intermediate or partial goal, such as the maximization of the welfare of a group of communities, might be considered local efficiency (Elster 1992).

The second type of justification concerns equity, or what individuals and groups consider to be appropriate, reasonable and customary for the distribution of the burden (Young 1994). Efficiency and equity are not necessarily competing objectives, although emphasis on one or the other leads to different procedural designs and outcomes.

Ideas of what is fair in any different context are by no means unanimous in society. As controversies on siting hazardous facilities illustrate, what one group considers a fair process and outcome will be vehemently opposed by another group. This controversy cannot be explained fully by self-interest (i.e., 'Not In My Back Yard') but appears to be linked to strong social norms and 'world-views' that characterize different social groups. It is crucial to recognize and understand this plurality in designing institutions and procedures that promote trust and that accommodate competing ideas of what is a fair process and outcome for siting hazardous facilities (Linnerooth and Thompson 1993).

4.2. Technical and Welfare Efficiency

Technical efficiency

A siting outcome is said to be technically efficient if the costs and risks of the facility as specified by experts are at a minimum at the chosen site. The implicit objective of this approach is to minimize the construction, operating and transport costs of the facility, while taking into account the probability of a leakage or escape of toxic substances and the consequences of this escape on the public and environment.

Factors such as geology, hydrology, neighbouring land uses, environmental surroundings and population are important factors in determining the technical efficiency of alternative sites. So is the length of time that the facility is likely to be in place. If one treats future generations as part of a definition of efficiency then it is important to evaluate the long-run benefits and costs of mitigation measures as well as monitoring and control procedures in specifying an efficient outcome.

Siting a hazardous waste facility in Austria Technical efficiency was the *raison d'être* for selecting Blumau and Enzersdorf as potential sites for a hazardous waste facility in Austria. The procedures incorporated elaborate public partici- pation processes for the stated purpose of confirming the technical suitability or efficiency of the candidate sites.

The technical efficiency approach to siting facilities works best, therefore, in hierarchical, top-down political systems (the more centralized approaches shown in Figure 9.1), where technical experts enjoy a position of trust and authority. The appeal of this approach lies in the notion of equal treatment of all communities since the selection depends only on technical conditions. Since the goal of technical efficiency is minimizing the societal risk burden, the approach might be regarded (by some) as inherently fair regardless of which community ultimately receives the facility.

Trust in expert authority, a prerequisite for this approach, is eroding in most Western countries. The authority and effectiveness of government policies for regulating and managing hazardous activities are often questioned when scien- tists disagree on the nature of the risks. These disagreements have led to a disturbing loss of public confidence in public sector institutions and their viability in the siting process is more likely to depend on building public trust with the different stakeholders than in managing risks efficiently (Wynne 1983).

Welfare efficiency
Welfare economists argue that it is not expert estimates of risks that should be the main criterion in siting decisions, but rather how people feel about the risks. Hence a welfare-efficient solution locates a site where the public's perceptions of risk and costs are lowest. Using this criterion it is necessary to ascertain the nature of citizens' preferences for avoiding the burden of a hazardous waste facility in their back yard.

One possible way to proceed is to identify the technically qualified sites and then to determine how much compensation the residents of each community would require to be willing to accept the facility. In contrast to the technical- efficiency criterion, which deemed the best site to be where the costs and risks are lowest, this welfare-efficiency criterion imputes the best site to be the one with the lowest required compensation.[8]

4.3. Outcome Equity

Both technical and welfare efficiency (without compensation) award the full burden of the hazardous waste facility to one community but it does not have to be that way. For example, a number of smaller facilities can be sited rather than locating just one large one. This is the idea behind the Austrian hazardous waste legislation which requires each Austrian state to provide a waste disposal infrastructure (Linneroth and Davy 1994). But short of putting a 'barrel of waste in every community' it is hard to imagine an equal spread of the burden. If equality is the goal, a novel approach might be to choose a site among qualified communities by lottery, thus achieving a sort of *ex ante* equality.

An alternative criterion for determining where to site a facility is the extent to which the community has contributed to the hazardous waste problem. This might imply locating hazardous facilities at the same site where the wastes are produced. In a recent questionnaire to the Austrian public, contribution to the waste problem ranked highest among twelve different criteria for siting a hazardous waste facility (Linneroth and Davy 1994). This idea of responsibility for one's own wastes is a strong motivation behind recent European legislation to require countries to deal with their own wastes and not export them to other countries.

The most obvious, and most discussed, way of spreading the burden across society is to compensate the host community by sharing the benefits of the new facility with it. This compensation might be paid by the waste-disposing industry which will then pass on the added costs to waste producers. Alternatively, it might be paid by central government thus passing the costs on to the taxpayers. Compensation can take many forms ranging from direct monetary payments to the community (e.g. tipping fees) to in-kind payments such as providing the community with a new hospital or perhaps 'green' improvements such as parks or bicycle trails (Gregory et al. 1991).

Pareto improvement

The notion of compensation underlies a key concept in thinking about equity, that of a Pareto improvement. An allocation of a good is said to be a Pareto improvement if everybody is better off with the new allocation and nobody is worse off. In the case of a hazardous waste facility, a Pareto improvement can be understood only by considering movements from the status quo. For example, the status quo might be a situation where the wastes are improperly disposed of and are threatening the environment. If the citizens are willing to pay to reduce or eliminate this threat, and if a community is willing to accept a facility for an amount less than the total willingness to pay, then a Pareto improvement is possible.

A Pareto improvement requires that the compensation be paid. The payment can be negotiated between the developer and the community.[9] In such a market-based approach, the community or local government 'sells' its permission to site the facility and the developer 'buys' this permission. Naturally, this requires that the right to give permission lies with the local community. This is the basis of voluntary siting approaches such as the negotiated deal between Eagle, New York and Browning–Ferris Industries discussed in the previous section. The citizens of Eagle agreed to 'sell their permission' to BFI in return for a benefits package.

Local authority, preferably in the form of a referendum, is viewed as necessary for reaching a mutually agreed and beneficial siting choice. As suggested by the Eagle, New York, case, negotiated compensation has had a few successes, but mainly with respect to siting solid waste facilities. In the US, it is common to impose 'host fees' or fees on the wastes that go to the community budget, and these can be rather significant (reducing property taxes as much as 20 per cent). An Austrian community (Frommleiten) has benefited enormously from a waste fee from their solid waste facility, and this experience appears to be having a positive influence on other Austrian communities which would like to consider hosting a facility (Linnerooth and Davy 1994).

Others are sceptical of compensation because it explicitly and visibly places health and safety on the market. While economists point out that these kinds of trades are made in the context of hazardous jobs and other activities, evidence suggests that *ex ante* bargaining over the health and safety of families and children is not acceptable to many people. In fact, many residents view *ex ante* compensation as nothing less than a bribe. For example, in a recent study of attitudes to compensation in both Hungary and New York, Vari (1993) noted a marked reluctance to accept this quasi-market approach. Typical comments were: 'Human life cannot be compensated'; 'Compensation is bribery'; and, 'We cannot be bought'. Interestingly, *ex post* agreements to compensate victims appears more socially acceptable (Linnerooth, in press).

Environmental justice

For many people the Pareto improvement is not viewed as leading to fair outcomes, since facilities are often located in low-income and otherwise disadvantaged areas. Because of their economic circumstances, these areas will likely have a lower 'reservation price' for exposure to health risks than wealthy communities. This means they will sell their permission to site the facility for less than more advantaged communities. Therefore, it is less costly for developers—and more efficient in the Pareto sense—to locate waste facilities in the disadavantaged areas.

To the extent that minority populations, those in poor health, and other vulnerable groups live in poor areas, the process may be viewed as a breach of environmental justice since there will be a predominance of hazardous and otherwise undesirable facilities close to these groups (Bullard 1993). Experience with regard to hazardous waste facilities indicates that many citizens are reluctant to negotiate a price for a facility (Portney 1985; Kleindorfer et al. 1988). If the majority of citizens in a community refuse to bargain for *ex ante* compensation, even the most fervent advocates of market approaches would agree that the process is not politically viable.

What is more controversial is the case where a poor or otherwise disadvantaged community does agree to negotiate for compensation. Some Native

American tribes, for instance, are entering negotiations with the federal government on siting high-level nuclear waste repositories on their reservations. Environmental justice advocates are generally against such bargains on moral grounds. The following article in a local news bulletin illustrates the controversy:

> Caught between tribal leaders desperate to lure investments to their reservations and federal and corporate officials desperate to find new waste dumps are the thousands of Indian families who simply want a safe homeland to pass on to their children . . . the MRS program is a classic example of environmental racism: the targeting of non-white communities for waste dumps, nuclear and otherwise. (*Ethnic News Watch*, p. 8)

Market advocates argue that an informed negotiation between the US government and tribal leaders is a legitimate and fair way to go about finding an appropriate site for storing spent nuclear fuel. If the site is proved to be technically suitable, and if the tribes have full authority to make the final decision, then they contend that a compensated deal should be viewed as both fair and morally correct. Forcing the wastes on an affluent community would be Pareto inferior or 'Pareto pessimal' in that both communities would feel themselves worse off than if the tribes had taken the waste with the agreed-upon compensation.

Yet many people may be willing to accept Pareto-pessimal outcomes and paternalistic processes to promote valued social ideals (Calabresi and Bobbit 1978). One such valued ideal may be that health and safety are inherent rights similar to the Rawlsian argument that certain individual rights—which might include health and safety—should never be traded off against material goods (see Elster 1992, p. 224). To those opposed to the market approach, allowing the poor to sell their health and safety is not a legitimate way of improving their economic condition (or even their health). As Frey and Oberholzer (1994) point out, the market approach accepts the status quo as given, whereas many people refuse to accept negotiated bargains, even among willing partners, based on what they see as an unfair starting point. As such, the siting of hazardous waste facilities in poor areas is viewed as an exploitation of those in poverty and not as a means of improving their economic condition.

Global efficiency and the no site option
No discussion on the efficiency and equity of siting regimes would be complete without mention of those who advocate doing nothing, even for hazardous wastes that already exist. To some this position appears void of any fairness considerations, especially if doing nothing means leaving the wastes in environmentally inferior locations which expose people to high risks.

This seeming Pareto-pessimal position may, however, look different when viewed from the lens of long-term, global efficiency (Thompson 1994). If the whole siting issue is linked with the long-term objective of changing production processes towards lower-waste economies, then the local Pareto-pessimal solution may be globally Pareto superior. The reason is that wastes that are 'out of sight' may lull institutions into a more passive mode with regard to industrial restructuring.

This argument often surfaces in siting debates. For instance, there is concern that the proposed underground storage of nuclear wastes at Yucca Mountain will inadvertently advance the nuclear option as a source of power which many consider nothing less than immoral. From this perspective, the proposal by Easterling and Kunreuther (1995) to store wastes at nuclear power plants in the medium term would allow the continued social dialogue on the desirability of nuclear power. Many view the phasing out of this technology as promoting long-term social welfare.

5. SUMMARY

If there is one thing to take away from this chapter it is that a good siting process and a fair outcome will vary across individuals, interested parties and regions. What one group views as morally justifiable may be seen as iniquitous by another group. Those who view Pareto improvements and market-based solutions as inherently fair and correct will judge voluntary siting procedures with negotiated settlements as the most appealing process. Disallowing these negotiated deals will be considered both paternalistic and unfair to poor communities that wish to improve their status.

Other groups are strikingly opposed to these kinds of deals. In their view health and safety cannot be (at least not visibly) bought and sold, and there can be no fair agreements based on unjust starting positions. These groups appear willing to accept an allocation where 'everyone is (materially) worse off' in order to protect cherished social values.

Still other groups may be attracted to more hierarchial, top-down approaches to siting hazardous facilities, where the choice of the site is justified on technical criteria. Whereas this approach has been the most prevalent in Western countries, declining trust in expert authority is necessitating more open siting procedures.

Finally, some people take a position based on ideas of long-term social efficiency. These groups find that even the undesirable status quo—keeping hazardous wastes in unsuitable facilities—is superior to the 'out of sight, out of mind' alternative of long-term disposal. Their implicit goal is to restructure economies towards more sustainable uses of resources and less waste.

Each of these views is legitimate and should be respected in the policy process. Indeed, if social conflicts regarding technology and siting processes are not to become more polarized, then it is important to create mutual respect among those holding different concepts of fair procedures and outcome. This will require building institutions based upon mutual respect for the competing concepts and ideas of fairness.

6. RELEVANCE TO ASIAN SITING EXPERIENCES

We conclude this chapter with an open set of questions on siting which should serve as a basis for comparing the Asian experience with Europe and North America.

6.1. Political Culture

- What are the special features of political culture that affect siting processes in different Asian countries?
- How will these features affect the criteria used to judge the fairness of the siting outcome?
- Are there strong forces in some countries that favour the 'no site' option?

6.2. Current Situation (Status Quo)

- How does one characterize the current situation (status quo) with respect to the magnitude of the wastes problem and availability of storage facilities?
- What are the rationales for determining whether there is a need for new sites?

6.3. Trust

- Who has to be trusted in the siting process of your country?
- Is there a large amount of distrust today with respect to institutions involved in siting?
- How can one create trust in your culture?

6.4. Policy Tools

- What are the relevant policy tools that are appropriate for sharing the burden when siting new facilities?
- What policy tools are appropriate for redistributing benefits between winners and losers?

6.5. Criteria for Judging

* What are the relevant criteria for judging fair siting processes and outcomes in your country?
* How would you characterize a fair process and outcomes in siting a new facility?

NOTES

1. This section is based on material which has appeared in Kleindorfer and Kunreuther (1994).
2. For a comprehensive analysis of the eminent domain clause in the context of the United States Constitution see Epstein (1985).
3. It is possible that informal discussions took place between community officials and the developer to determine whether the facility would be acceptable under a certain set of conditions including some type of compensation arrangement. No public documents were available for us to determine whether this process actually occurred.
4. We could not find any examples of open siting processes with local rights in European countries.
5. For more details on this case see Rabe (1991) and Linnerooth and Davy (1994).
6. The following account is based on personal discussions with Bruno Frey and Felix Oberholzer, 24 May 1994.
7. The grants were divided into three phases. Phase I grants of $100,000 gave the community an opportunity to learn about the technical aspects of high-level waste storage and determine whether there was a real interest in hosting the facility without any formal commitment to do so. Phase II and III grants were for larger amounts and required more focused investigations.
8. The compensation need not actually be paid out. In fact, to be effective the government cannot always redress redistributional inequities, but it must operate with the authority to redistribute wealth and risks (Kneese and Pawlowski 1992).
9. The well-known Coase theorem in microeconomics suggests that if a facility has large overall benefits for society, but imposes a (lesser) negative externality on identifiable groups, then private negotiation and trades can lead to an outcome where all members of society consider themselves better off with the facility than without it.

REFERENCES

Ahlstrom, P.E. (1994), 'Sweden Takes Steps to Solve Waste Problem', *Forum for Applied Research and Public Policy*, Fall, 9:119–21.

Angell, P. (1993), Personal communication regarding Browning–Ferris Industries programme for siting landfills, Houston, Texas: BFI, April.

Brion, D.J. (1991), *Essential Industry and the NIMBY Syndrome*, New York: Quorum Books.

Bullard, R.D. (1993), 'Waste and Racism: A Stacked Deck?', *Forum for Applied Research and Public Policy*, Spring: 29–35.

Calabresi, G. and P. Bobbit (1978), *Tragic Choices*, New York: Norton Press.

Cambridge Reports (1990), *Window on America: Solid Waste*, Cambridge, Mass.: Cambridge Reports.

Colglazier, E.W. and R.B. Langum (1988), 'Policy conflicts in the process for siting nuclear waste repositories', *Annual Review of Energy*, 11:317–57.

Douglas, M. and A. Wildavsky (1982), *Risk and Culture*, Berkeley: University of California Press.

Easterling, D. (1992), 'Fair Rules for Siting a High Level Nuclear Waste Repository', *Journal of Policy Analysis and Management* 11:442–75.

Elster, J. (1992), *Local Justice: How Institutions Allocate Scarce Goods and Necessary Burdens*, New York: Russell Sage Foundation.

English, M. and G. Davis (1987), 'American Siting Initiatives: Recent State Developments. Appendix 4', in B.W. Piasecki and G.A. Davis, *America's Future in Toxic Waste Management*, New York, NY: Quorum Books.

Epstein, R. (1985), *Takings*, Cambridge, Mass.: Harvard University Press.

Ericksen, K. (1994), 'Out of Sight, Out of Our Minds', *N.Y. Times Magazine*, 6 March:34–41, 50, 63.

Ethnic News Watch, 'How the Feds are Pushing Nuclear Waste on Reservations', 14:8.

Flynn, J., R. Kasperson, H. Kunreuther and P. Slovic (1992), 'Time to rethink nuclear waste storage', *Issues in Science and Technology*, Summer:42–8.

Frey, B. and Oberholzer (1994), 'Procedural Fairness and Ex-Post Acceptance of Noxious Facilities: A Case Study', Paper presented at the IIASA Workshop on Fairness and Siting, 21–22 May, International Institute for Applied Systems Analysis, Laxenburg, Austria.

Gamble, D. (1978), 'The Berger Inquiry: An Impact Assessment Process', *Science* 199:946–52.

Greenberg, M.R., R.F. Anderson and K. Rosenberger (1984), 'Social and Economic Effects of Hazardous Waste Management Sites', *Hazardous Wastes,* 1:387–96.

Gregory, R., H. Kunreuther, D. Easterling and K. Richards (1991), 'Incentives Policies to Site Hazardous Facilities', *Risk Analysis*, 11:667–75.

Kasperson, R.E. (1986), 'Hazardous Waste Facility Siting: Community, Firm, and Governmental Perspectives', in National Academy of Engineering, *Hazards: Technology and Fairness,* Washington, DC: National Academy Press, pp. 188–244.

Kasperson, R.E., S. Emani and B.J. Perkins (1990), 'Global Environmental Change, the Media and Publics: Preliminary Data and Observations', in *Sustainable Development, Science and Policy*, Bergen: Norwegian Research Council for Science and the Humanities, pp. 457–86.

Kasperson, R.E., D. Golding and S. Tuler (1992), 'Siting Hazardous Facilities and Communicating Risks under Conditions of High Social Distrust', *Journal of Social Issues*, 48:161–7.

Kasperson, Roger E., Ortwin Renn, Paul Slovic, Halina S. Brown, Jacque Emel, Robert Gobel, Jeanne X. Kasperson and Samuel Ratick (1988), 'The Social Amplification of Risk: A Conceptual Framework', *Risk Analysis*, 8(2):177–97.

Kleindorfer, P., M. Knez, H. Kunreuther and D. MacLean (1988), 'Valuation and Assessment of Equity in the Siting of a Nuclear Waste Repository', Project Report prepared for Nevada Agency for Nuclear Projects/Nuclear Waste Projects Office.

Kleindorfer, P. and H. Kunreuther (1994), 'Siting of Hazardous Facilities', in S. Pollack, Barnett and M. Rothkopf (eds), *Handbook of Operations Research*, Amsterdam: Elsevier, Chapter 11.

Kneese, A. and J. Pawlowski (1992), 'Benefit–Cost Analysis: The Historical and Ethical Context', Draft Paper, Resources for the Future, Washington DC.

Kunreuther, H., K. Fitzgerald and T.D. Aarts (1993), 'Siting noxious facilities: A test of the facility siting credo', *Risk Analysis*, 13:301–18.

Kunreuther, Howard and Joanne Linnerooth (1982), *Risk Analysis and Decision Processes; The Siting of Liquified Energy Facilities in Four Countries*, Berlin: Springer-Verlag.

Kunreuther, H., P. Slovic and D. MacGregor (1994), 'Risk Perception and Trust: Challenges for Facility Siting and Risk Management', Paper presented at the IIASA Workshop on Fairness and Siting, 21–22 May, International Institute for Applied Systems Analysis, Laxenburg, Austria.

Linnerooth, J. and B. Davy (1994), 'Fair Siting of Hazardous Waste Facilities in Austria', Paper presented at the IIASA Workshop on Fairness and Siting, 21–22 May, International Institute for Applied Systems Analysis, Laxenburg, Austria.

Linnerooth, J. and M. Thompson (1993), 'Risk and Fairness', *Options*, June.

Linnerooth-Bayer J. and B. Davy (1994), 'Hazardous Waste Cleanup and Facility Siting in Central Europe: The Austrian Case', Final Report (GZ 308.903/3–43/92), Bundesministerium fuer Wissenschaft und Forschung, Vienna, Austria.

Mitchell, R. and R. Carson (1986), 'Property Rights, Protest, and the Siting of Hazardous Waste Facilities', *AEA Papers and Proceedings*, 76:285–90.

Nuclear News (1994), 'Two Northern Areas Want Repository', February, 37:54.

O'Hare, M., L. Bacow and D. Sanderson (1983), *Facility Siting and Public Opposition*, New York: Van Nostrand Reinhold.

Portney, K. (1985), 'The Potential of the Theory of Compensation for Mitigating Public Opposition to Hazardous Waste Treatment Facility Siting: Some Evidence from Five Massachusetts Communities', *Policy Studies Journal*, 14:81–9.

Rabe, B. (1991), 'Beyond the NIMBY Syndrome in Hazardous Waste Facility Siting: The Alberta Breakthrough and the Prospects for Cooperation in Canada and the United States', *Governance*, 4:184–206.

Raylman, R. (1995), Personal communication regarding Browning–Ferris Industries programme for siting solid waste landfills, New York, BFI, October.

Renn, O. (1994), 'Fairness and Competition in Siting a Landfill in Switzerland', Paper presented at the IIASA Workshop on Fairness and Siting, 21–22 May, International Institute for Applied Systems Analysis, Laxenburg, Austria.

Rue, J. (1995), Personal communication regarding siting of low-level radioactive waste (LLRW) disposal facility in Pennsylvania, Harrisburg, PA, Department of Environmental Protection, October.

Slovic, P. (1987), 'Perception of Risk', *Science*, 236:280–85.

Slovic, P. (1993), 'Perceived Risk, Trust, and Democracy: A Systems Perspective', *Risk Analysis*, 13:675–82.

Swedish Dialogue Project (Hallencreutz) (1994), 'An Outline Based on the Report of the Project Group', Swedish Nuclear Power Inspectorate.

Thompson, M. (1994), 'Unsiteability: What Should It Tell Us?', Paper presented at the IIASA Workshop on Fairness and Siting, 21–22 May, International Institute for Applied Systems Analysis, Laxenburg, Austria.

US Office of Technology Assessment (1983), *Technologies and Management Strategies for Hazardous Waste Control*, Washington, DC: US Government Printing Office.

Vari, A. (1993), 'Public Perceptions about Equity and Fairness Siting Low-Level Radioactive Waste Disposal Facilities in the United States and Hungary', Paper presented at the Workshop on Risk and Fairness, 20–22 June, International Institute of Applied Systems Analysis, Laxenburg, Austria.

The Public: Client or Decision Maker?

Whitehead, B. (1991), 'Who Gave You the Right? Property Rights and the Potential for Locally Binding Referenda in the Siting of Hazardous Waste Facilities', John F. Kennedy School of Government, Harvard University, Boston.
Wynne, B. (1983), 'Redefining the Issues of Risk and Acceptance: The Social Viability of Technology', *Futures,* 15:13–32.
Young, P. (1994), *Equity In Theory and Practice*, Princeton, New Jersey: Princeton University Press.

10. An Economic Framework for Analysing Facility Siting Policies in Taiwan and Japan[*]

Daigee Shaw

1. INTRODUCTION

A common problem that has been faced by many countries for many years finally reached Taiwan in the 1980s. As a result of the accelerating deterioration in the quality of the environment which had occurred in the 1970s, there was a sharp rise in the number of 'Not In My Back Yard' (NIMBY) protests staged by various citizens' groups all over the island. Among the casualties of this movement were a nuclear power plant, a coal-fired power plant, a titanium dioxide plant (TiO_2) plant, a pesticide plant and two petro-chemical complexes. Several siting proposals were either killed outright or delayed and, in addition, some existing plants also have had to be closed or forced to compensate victims or every individual living in the polluted community in order to continue operations.

Among the 259 cases of environmental conflicts which occurred between 1988 and 1993 and were recorded in EPA's database (EPA 1993), the incident of the Lin-Yuan petro-chemical industrial complex is a milestone case. The petro-chemical industrial complex, which is the most important industrial base in Taiwan, was forced to close by local residents after an incident of waste-water overflow caused by heavy rainfall in September 1988. Minister Chen of the Ministry of Economic Affairs, on behalf of all firms of the Lin-Yuan petro-

* I am grateful for helpful comments from my colleagues at the Institute of Economics, Academia Sinica and Chung-Hua Institution for Economic Research, participants at the 1990 Chung-Hua Institution for Economic Research/Korea Development Institute Conference on Industrial Policies, participants at the 1990 AERE Workshop on Natural Resource Market Mechanisms, and participants at the Conference on Energy, Environment and the Economy: Asian Perspectives.

chemical industrial complex, was forced to agree to pay a huge compensation package of 1,270 million NT dollars to local residents before production could be resumed and the economic losses from production interruption could be stopped. The two most important features of the incident are that the money was distributed to everyone in the local community and that the government or the firms easily fell victims of the environmental conflict. As a result of the incident, the number of NIMBY confrontations has increased rapidly since then and peaked in 1989 (Table 10.1).

Its sharp decrease after 1989 could be attributed mainly to the change in the government's strategy, in addition to the greater attention paid by polluters to pollution control after the Lin-Yuan incident. Under a new prime minister, the government vowed not to yield again to any illegal demonstrations. The EPA announced ten unacceptable terms for the settlement of environmental conflicts in February 1989. At about the same time, the EPA pressured for the adoption of the Environmental Conflict Resolution Act , proposed in 1988, and this was finally passed by the Legislative Yuan (Congress) in 1992.

Table 10.1   Numbers of environmental conflicts in Taiwan between 1988 and 1992

Year of first appearance	before 1988	1988	1989	1990	1991	1992	Total
No. of conflicts	7	45	101	38	44	24	259

Source: EPA, *The White Book of Environmental Conflicts Resolution,* 1993.

In order to resolve the social unrest brought about by the NIMBY problem, the traditional approaches of regulation and environmental impact assessment (EIA) have been utilized in Taiwan and almost every country. Regulation is the basic approach for resolving siting and operational problems that emerge as a result of polluting facilities. Here, the government formulates specific rules, regulations or standards that set the requirements for siting and operation permits. The logic behind the system is quite straightforward but the results obtained are usually inefficient since the external cost is quite often not fully internalized and it is usually poorly enforced. The system also tends to breed conflict and mistrust since the interests of the residents in the area are not adequately taken into consideration.

Faced with a serious pollution problem, the EIA approach was first adopted by the US to supplement the regulatory approach in 1970, and it later spread to other countries. Taiwan has adopted the EIA system since 1985. The approach is designed primarily to make sound decisions about development and the environment through an informed decision-making process. Through better public participation, the EIA approach is also designed to solve the problem of siting polluting facilities. However, based on the vast experience of the US in this area and the relatively lesser experience in Taiwan, it cannot solve the problem of siting polluting facilities since the influence of public participation comes too late and is virtually negligible. Also, the information required for the public to understand the issues involved and make a clear decision is either inaccessible or incomprehensible to the lay reader and, as a result, they feel threatened and out-matched. They are also mistrustful of the information that is provided to them by the EIAs. Another problem associated with the EIA approach, noted by Livingston (1987), is that it employs an adversarial negotiation process which results in greater divergence and polarized negotiating positions. Thus EIA processes have done little more than create more confusion and confrontation and waste an enormous amount of time and resources.

The problem common to both approaches is that economic incentives that are necessary to induce polluters and residents to behave in a manner compatible with maximization of social net benefit are not present.

Economists have a long tradition of advocating economic incentive systems for pollution control, namely, effluent charges on polluters and emission trading among polluters. In these ways, private markets are stimulated to economize on pollutant emissions, just as they are stimulated to economize on other costly resources. However, these two economic-incentive systems are not sufficient to resolve the NIMBY problem since they are only appropriate when the property rights are such that the neighbours of a polluter can do nothing but accept the externality. Otherwise, the residents would just stage NIMBY protests since there is still a (so-called efficient) level of pollutants being emitted by the polluter despite the fact that he or she is levied the optimal effluent charges or that he or she pays the optimal price for emission permits in an open market. Thus, economic incentives—both for residents and polluters—are required for the resolution of the NIMBY problem. Some new approaches now utilized by various countries are based on this principle. However, to some extent they all have flaws that make them function inefficiently.

The list of NIMBY protests is expected to be longer in the future if the general quality of the environment is not improved significantly, if the government's policies for siting facilities are not revised, and if the incentive for lumping private compensation is not stopped. In this chapter, a policy instrument is designed which may resolve the NIMBY confrontations which embody the dissatisfaction with the present property rights system and the conflict between environmental protection and economic development. The instrument entails negotiated pollution-prevention agreements between residents, local governments and polluters, and also encompasses the missing link in the environment management market mechanism which traditionally includes only such instruments as effluent charges and emission trading when there are a lot of people involved. The chapter proposes a process for negotiating pollution-prevention agreements which may solve the conflict by directing incentives to the causes which gave rise to the NIMBY problem in the first place.[1]

In Section 2 of the chapter the theories for understanding and analysing the facility-siting issues are developed. With these theories in mind, environmental negotiating, and related practices and laws of the ROC and Japan are reviewed in Sections 3 and 4. Finally, as the conclusion of the chapter, Section 5 contains a proposal for institutional change that tries to address the long-term facility-siting problem.

2. THEORETICAL BACKGROUND

2.1. Environmental Rights

The development of any system of rights or entitlement results from social demand which is, in turn, determined by social benefit–cost considerations.[2] For example, in the developed countries during the 1950s and 1960s, environmental concerns were highly debated topics and the notion of environmental rights or, simply put, the people's right to a clean environment, emerged. A few states in the United States—Michigan, Minnesota, to name two—passed laws or amendments that provided for and protected the people's environmental rights. Following the lead of some of the states in the US, both the International Social Science Council, in their Tokyo Resolution of 1970, and the United Nations Conference on the Human Environment held in Stockholm in 1972, adopted a concept of the people's right to a clean and healthy environment. At about the same time, the Japanese Federation of Bar Associations passed a Proposal for an environmental right. The Resolution states:

> Above all, it is important that we urge the adoption in law of the principle that every person is entitled by right to an environment free of elements which infringe upon human health and well-being as well as nature's endowments, including its beauty, which should be the heritage of the present to future generations.

Furthermore, the Japanese Federation of Bar Association pronounced:

> the environment should be common to all people. . . . It must be completely separated from the ownership of the real estate. The right to utilize the environment must be a common property to be distributed equally to everyone regardless of whether or not he is an owner of real estate. . . . . The Environmental Right, therefore, must be established as a community's collective right, giving the people a position substan-tially equal to that of industry. (Gresser et al. 1981, pp. 146–7)

Thus, the right to a pollution-free environment or environmental right can be characterized as a constitutional right, a physical property right common to all, and as a basic human right which is non-transferable.[3]

However, if the proposal for the traditional environmental right were followed, environmental problems still would not be solved. This is because environmental problems tend to have a high degree of uncertainty when trying to determine their associated benefits and costs, and tend to be locally oriented, technical, and interest-conflicting. Thus, the mechanical assignment of a non-transferable ownership of a pollution-free environment to all of a country's citizens may result in severe inefficiency in resource allocation, and in severe unfairness of the distribution of costs and benefits associated with the right. Property rights without transferability cannot solve the problem. Consequently, this traditional environmental right has not been successfully incorporated into any country's constitution[4] and has not been fully exercised.

From an economic point of view, an environmental right is considered as an institutional property right (with the physical property right as its subset) that is transferable, which allows for efficiency in determining the use of environmental resources.[5] A system of property rights with an efficient transaction system can therefore allocate these resources thereby maximizing the citizens' welfare and internalizing the external costs and benefits. The transaction system takes the form of decentralized negotiations for cooperative development contracts.

The condition of an efficient transaction system is critical in the applicability of the property rights approach. Some prominent economists are pessimistic about the applicability of the approach for environmental pollution problems whose transaction costs are high because of its characteristic of having a larger number of parties and/or being a bilateral monopoly.[6] They opt for relying upon governments or courts to assign optimal property rights through such property rights systems as emission standards, effluent fees, emission trading, zoning, eminent domain, and so on, whether to polluters, or to their victims or to both in order to guide environmental resource use efficiently. However, it may be very difficult for governments or courts to discover the optimal ones, given their high degree of uncertainty and the high information costs associated with them. Even if the rights are optimally assigned in the beginning, they may not be so when the economic values change. The rigidity of a government or court decision-making process precludes its smooth and quick response to the changes. Thus, the market mechanism of the property rights approach merits consideration, especially when the cost of pollution on the society as a whole becomes larger than its benefits as evidenced by the increasing number of NIMBY demonstrations staged and when the cost of transaction becomes smaller as the result of well-designed new institutions or of the development of new technologies.

In order to lower the transaction cost as much as possible, a well-designed institution requires that the environmental rights be collective in that the rights are regulated communal rights exercised by all who are affected by the use of the environmental resource rather than private property rights, since the high transaction costs associated with the private property rights do not allow for its development at present.[7] A single agent is authorized to act on behalf of the community with no directions as to the specific outcomes which may be forthcoming in his or her negotiation with the producer of pollution.[8] Buchanan (1973) believes that the new institution would result in efficient outcomes. However, the transferability of the right has been heavily criticized by the followers of the traditional environmental right since it is believed that environmental injustice may arise resulting from the sale of rights by the poor to generate personal income.

It seems there is a conflict as to the best way to define environmental rights, whether they are transferable and efficient or non-transferable and morally just. But, it is possible to eliminate this conflict by creating a New Environmental Right Theory. The New Environmental Right Theory divides property rights into two separate entities. One where the basic right to a healthy environment is protected and therefore non-transferable and one that is transferable and allows for various degrees of environmental quality so long as it stays within the limits which define a healthy environment. Environmental rights should be regulated communal rights exercised by the communities who are affected by the environmental resource whether it be the residents in an apartment building who are commonly affected by changes in their living environment or all the people who live on the earth who are commonly affected by problems such as global warming.[9] Thus, such concerns as justice, efficiency and transaction costs are all addressed in the New Environmental Right Theory.

The New Environmental Right Theory as outlined here is very useful in making facility-siting policies as well as environmental policies, since the NIMBY confrontations can be viewed as the efforts of victims to redefine the environmental rights when they are not satisfied with the present ones. If a firm or other entity wishes to use an environmental resource, it must first obtain a permit from the polity of the affected community. The permit may state both the regulatory approaches, e.g., the minimum emission standards, which represents the non-transferable part of the environmental rights, and the emission fees to be paid depending on the level of pollution so long as pollution is confined within the allowable range, which represents the transferable part. The polity of all communities where the environmental resource is located should take responsibility for managing the resource whether it be a fishermen's association, a mutual irrigation association, a tenants' association, a local government or the United Nations. The right does not have to be constitutional as such but can be written into laws, bylaws or regulations which establish organizations to manage the resource whether local, national or international. The laws can be revised when changes in transaction costs or in the values of the environmental resources call for a change from the recommended communal rights system to a private one.

2.2. Externality[10]

Since Baumol and Oates (1975) made the distinction between depletable and undepletable externalities and added two important taxation policies to their theory, it has been very interesting to watch the ongoing debate surrounding the issue. At present, the literature tells us that the basic policy prescription is the same in both the depletable and undepletable cases. The nature of undepletable externality is that of a public good (or bad), i.e., all residents of an area suffer from a negative externality, and one individual's consumption of the externality does not reduce that of any other individual. Thus, in a competitive setting, the optimal solution requires only a per unit tax on the generator of a negative externality but no compensation to the victims, since the nature of undepletable externalities is such that victims can use only defensive activities to combat negative externalities, which have no effect on the consumption of the externality by any other person.[11] If compensation for the damages caused by the negative externality was paid, then too many people would choose to live in the areas without giving any benefit to the others.[12] On the other hand, the nature of a depletable externality is that of a private good (or bad), i.e., one individual's consumption of the externality reduces that of the others. At first, Baumol and Oates (1975) thought that they had found an exception to the no-compensation rule and that the victims should be subsidized for their consumption of depletable externalities. However, as Freeman (1984) argues, if people can not choose the quantities of the externality they consume, the proper policy remains the same as that in the case of undepletable externality, since there is no need to apply a price incentive to change the people's behaviour. The optimal policy still holds even if it is extended to recognize the possibility of defensive activities by the victims, since such activities do not generate any external benefits or costs to others.

However, as Bird (1987) points out, the optimal policy would be different if it is extended to recognize the possibility of shifting activities by victims. An externality is shiftable if the victim can undertake activities to pass the externality along to other victims (e.g., they can transfer rubbish initially dumped on their property on to sites owned by others). Note that the undepletable externality must also be unshiftable since, by definition, one person's consumption or shifting of the undepletable externality leaves others unaffected. The required policy is that, in addition to the Pigouvian tax upon the generator of the externality, the victims must also be taxed on their shifting activities or be compensated for not shifting and accepting the externality, since shifting is also an externality-generating activity and accepting confers an external benefit to others. Bird (1987) argues that the two approaches, taxing or compensating the victims, are equivalent in that they both lead to the attainment of Pareto optimality. Baumol and Oates (1988) view Bird's policy of taxing victims on their shifting activities as an extension of the standard Pigouvian taxation policy.

They argue that the externality will be borne by victims to whom it does the least damage.

It seems that the debate has been concluded by Baumol and Oates (1988) once again. However, Shaw and Shaw (1991) point out that this conclusion is not perfect. This is because the possibility of resisting a shifted externality is not recognized. Whether an externality is shiftable or not depends not only upon the shifting activity of the original victim but also the resisting activity of his or her neighbours, e.g., guarding property or fencing fields. The Pigouvian tax upon the original victim is not sufficient to guarantee the attainment of Pareto optimality, since this tax is only appropriate when his or her neighbours can do nothing but accept the externality.[13] If his or her neighbours' resisting actions were not bound by laws, then they would still resist since there is still some externality being shifted by the original victim even if he or she is levied the Pigouvian tax on his or her shifting activity. Shaw and Shaw proved that a taxation policy upon both parties is required for the attainment of a Pareto-optimal solution when the success of the original victim's shifting activity depends upon his or her neighbours' resisting activities too. The shifters should be taxed and the recipients should be compensated at the rate per unit of externality shifted when the tax base is the output of the shifting and resisting activities. The rationale behind the policy is that the transference of the externality is viewed as an externality-generating activity and the acceptance of the externality as conferring a benefit on the rest of the economy. As such, the shifters should be penalized and the recipients should be rewarded explicitly.

The theory of externalities discussed above is very useful when looking at the NIMBY issue since a NIMBY activity is a perfect example of where such activity shifts a negative, depletable, shiftable and resistible externality. Usually externality generators are firms and the victims or recipients of the negative externality are the entire community. According to the theory, the firms should pay, i.e., be taxed. Within the community, the externality is undepletable, unshiftable and irresistible. On the other hand, the externality is depletable, shiftable and resistible between communities. Thus, according to the theory, it is the polity, not every resident, of a community which should pay (be taxed) or be compensated since it is the communities which shift or resist. The polity of a community may be a local government, a citizen group, a semi-public citizen association or the United Nations.

After taking into account both the theories of New Environmental Right and externality, the policy recommendation adopted in this chapter is first to recognize that local communities have environmental rights and then to allow decentralized negotiation between the developer and communities for cooperative development. The result of the negotiation would prompt the developer, in addition to compensating the community, to participate in the community's adjustment process in order to increase the potential gain from cooperation that can be shared between the developer and the community. The community which

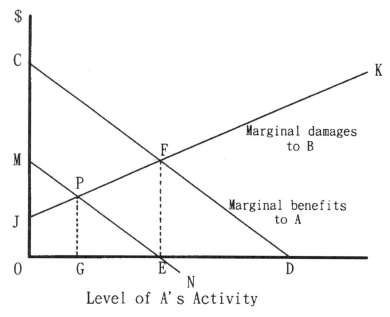

$

C

M

J

P

F

K

Marginal damages
to B

Marginal benefits
to A

0   G   E   D
          N

Level of A's Activity

Figure 10.1   Negotiation-taxation efficiency

does shift or resist could be discouraged by the government through various means.

2.3. Negotiation-Taxation Inefficiency

The concept of negotiation-taxation inefficiency proposes that a Pigouvian tax distorts resource allocation in the Coasian setting and, as is well known to all, was put forward by Coase (1960), Buchanan and Stubblebine (1962) and Turvey (1963). An excellent presentation of negotiation-taxation inefficiency can be found in the work of Baumol and Oates (1988, pp. 33–4).

In Figure 10.1, individual A imposes a diseconomy on individual B. Note the OE is the Pareto-optimal outcome where the marginal benefit to A is completely offset by the marginal damage to B. Note also that the Coasian equilibrium is represented by OE, which is also the socially optimal outcome. Suppose, however, that A is charged a Pigouvian tax equal to the marginal social damage EF at OE. Subtracting this from his or her marginal benefit gives us the dotted line MN, his or her marginal net benefits. It is clear that A will move to the socially efficient outcome OE in the absence of any negotiation. However, B will not be happy about the so-called socially efficient outcome since he or she is still suffering the total damage OJFE. Thus, he or she will stage a NIMBY protest. But suppose that Coasian negotiation and Pigouvian taxation coexist. It will then pay A and B to move back to point P and the associated output level OG. Although it is suboptimal, it maximizes the joint net gain to A and B together and B will not protest any more since he or she is fully compensated.

This negotiation-taxation inefficiency will not present in the setting of the proposed policy instrument when there are a lot of people involved. In this setting, A is a polluting firm, B is an affected and not-shifting community, whose polity is assumed to be well representative and efficiently functioning. According to the theory of environmental rights developed above, community B will exercise its communal environmental rights. In a Coasian world of negotiation, A would be prepared to pay B to be allowed to operate at a level of activity, represented by OE. The total payment would be OHFE if the negotiated tax rate is horizontal, EF; it would be OJFE if the marginal tax rate is variable and always equals the marginal damage to B.[14] Since B is the polity of the community, the compensation payment is a kind of public revenue and will be used for public facilities or expenditures which will avoid distorting the individual resident's behaviour. Thus, A is taxed and B is compensated in agreement with externality theory, when the externality is undepletable within the community and is depletable, shiftable and resistible between communities.

My proposed policy instrument actually consists of a Coasian negotiation between local polities and firms. The results of the negotiation would include a tax on firms and additional revenue to local governments. The only difference in the outcome is that the impost levied on A is paid to B in my setting, while it is not paid but rather absorbed by the government in the situation as presented by Coase. This difference will obviously result in the different behaviour of B, who resists under one set of circumstances, but under the other does not. Thus, negotiation-taxation inefficiency does not exist in my setting even if a lot of people are involved.

3. A REVIEW OF EXISTING POLLUTION-PREVENTION AGREEMENT PRACTICES AND RELATED LAWS IN TAIWAN AND JAPAN

In order to resolve the conflict between economic growth and environmental protection brought about by the NIMBY problem, several new approaches have been developed and utilized in addition to the traditional approaches of regulation and environmental impact assessment (EIA) in Taiwan and Japan. They give incentives to polluters to reduce emissions, or give incentives to residents not to shift the siting of the facility or to both in order to facilitate a reasonable, acceptable and socially optimal solution. Japan's cases will be reviewed first since Japan has faced up to the environmental problem earlier than Taiwan.

3.1. Japan

Legislated system of *ex ante* compensation without damage
Faced with strong public opposition to the siting of nuclear power plants and fossil-fuel power plants, and facing the possibility of an oil embargo or even an energy crisis, Japan enacted a three-part law in 1974 to facilitate the siting of the power plants: Law for Bettering the Public Facilities of Communities Neighbouring Electricity Facilities, Law for the Tax of Electricity Development and Law for the Special Accounting System for the Tax of Electricity Development. The purpose of the three-part law was to win the support of local residents in the siting of new power plants in order to establish a reliable supply of electricity. It simply places a tax on the amount of electricity generated by the power plant and then distributes the revenue raised by the tax through various grants to the host and neighbouring communities to construct and maintain public facilities, such as: roads; harbours; sewage systems; and recreation, education and public health facilities, based on a locally developed public facility plan. This approach is quite straightforward, and has functioned relatively well. There has not only been a limited amount of local opposition but even a good deal of competition among communities to try and attract the power plants to set up in their respective areas since the residents know that only a limited amount of pollution will result from the siting of the plant in their community because pollution levels are regulated by both national and local law and the facility-specific pollution-prevention agreement. In addition, the residents know that the siting of the plant in their community will also bring with it a better living environment as a result of an increase in funds, facilities and services. As a matter of fact, quite a few nuclear, hydro and other types of power plants have been put into operation as a result of this process.

However, the following shortcomings can be observed in the process. (1) The tax applied to the power plants is only in effect for 10 to 15 years as it is terminated in the fifth year of operation.[15] In addition, the tax revenue must be appropriated and used by the communities in the same year as it is generated, i.e., it can not be saved for later use. Thus, there is an incentive for local governments to promote the construction of too many public facilities in those tax years. When the tax is eliminated, the communities quite often do not have enough funds to maintain the new facilities. Some communities respond by inviting other polluting facilities to site in their area in order to maintain their high level of expenditure. (2) The tax base is the electricity generated, which is not a good indicator of pollution or the risk level. Consequently, the system cannot give correct incentives to the plants to reduce their emission levels. (3) Most importantly, local communities do not have the right to bargain on terms such as the tax rate, the revenue appropriation ratio, etc., with the power companies. However, this shortcoming is partly solved by the negotiated pollution-prevention agreements which will be discussed next.

Negotiated pollution-prevention agreements

Negotiated pollution-prevention agreements are agreements between polluters, and local governments and/or local organizations to supplement regulations that are imposed by law or ordinances with the aim of defining the essential duties of polluters in preventing pollution which results from the construction and operation of their facilities (Yamanouchi and Otsubo 1989). In most cases, one of the parties in the negotiations is the local government, i.e., the prefecture, city, town or village, which represents the interests of the residents affected by the pollution and, in rare instances, local organizations can be party to the negotiations. These local governments and local organizations may enter into agreements with the polluting entities either individually or jointly. By the end of 1988, more than 26,000 agreements had been entered into in Japan (Japan Environment Agency 1989). It has become such a regular practice that almost every local government has model agreements that have already been prepared.

The contents of each agreement differ. The most common obligations of polluters include pollution control measures, e.g., more stringent emission standards in terms of pollution concentration or total quantity of pollutants, the limit of sulphur content of the fuel, and specific types of pollution-prevention facilities and technology; emission monitoring and reporting (usually continuous and automatic systems); the establishment of a pollution-prevention committee; liability to compensate for damages (usually strict liability); enforcement provisions should a violation occur. An agreement usually does not require the polluter to obtain a permit for the construction or modification of its facilities from the local government and does not require *ex ante* compensation payments. From the viewpoint of the local government, the agreements are usually so comprehensive that they can succeed in filling the gaps inherent in the various pollution laws and ordinances. They can also best meet the differing needs and set of conditions of the various localities, which is impossible to do in laws and ordinances. On the other hand, polluters sign the agreements because of the benefits of building up a good-neighbour public image and the assurance that no further obligations will be imposed on them, even though they are obliged to adhere to more stringent controls than the law actually requires. Yamanouchi and Otsubo (1989) note that, in practice, the agreements are backed by the local governments' various administrative powers, and in theory, whether the agreements actually constitute a contract which is legally binding or simply a gentlemen's agreement (possessed simply of moral persuasion) is still under debate in Japan.

3.2. Taiwan

Taiwan power company's (Taipower) local contribution statute

As in other countries, publicly-owned Taipower, the only electricity power supplier in Taiwan, has been faced with strong public opposition to the siting of a nuclear power plant and a coal-fired power plant. Taipower imported the idea of the Japanese three-part law of electricity supply development and enacted the Local Contribution Statute in 1988. Although the two are similar, there are several differences between them. (1) The Japanese system is based on the three national laws. However, Taipower's Statute is only an internal regulation since its benefactor, the Ministry of Economic Affairs (MOEA), and the business community are still rather cool towards the idea of having it enacted as a law or even a MOEA ordinance. (2) Japanese power companies pay the tax to the central government which, in turn, allocates the tax revenue to local governments according to their public facility plan. However, Taipower gives the proceeds of the tax to the Local Development Foundation (LDF) which then distributes the funds to the various local governments for expenditures on expanding public facilities and services according to the plan contained in their application. (3) The tax on Japanese power plants is terminated at the end of the fifth year of operation. Taipower's continues to yield the proceeds of the tax to the LDF until the last year of operation. Thus Taipower's Statute has improved some short-comings of the Japanese system, although its non-binding legal status is a very important disadvantage. Both share the same problem of taxing or donating funds based on the amount of electricity generated. Both also share the same problem of an unequal distribution of bargaining power between the power company and local communities. However, Taipower's Statute is at a disadvantage when compared with the Japanese system because of the society's lack of tradition which has prevented well-developed negotiated pollution-prevention agreements from being reached.

Negotiated agreements
Negotiated agreements are very common in Taiwan. Among 108 NIMBY protests that took place between 1980 and 1989, 41 achieved their objectives and several agreements were reached between the local communities and the polluters (Hsiao and Milbrath 1989). Most protests sought compensation for damages and/or mitigation of pollution. Several protests, e.g., the Lin-Yuan incident, succeeded in gaining private compensation of equal amounts to every resident living in the community even if there was no private damage found. Some others insisted on mitigation of pollution and no compensation. The agreements reached usually are very simple and do not have detailed pollution-control measures as the Japanese ones do. The role played by local governments is usually that of a third party. This is different from the Japanese case where local governments usually represent the interests of the residents and are a party to the negotiations. Thus, the present status of negotiation breeds more NIMBY protests than necessary even though it has placed strong pressure on the government and polluters.

Negotiated environmental protection agreements

In addition to many negotiated agreements between the local communities and the polluters, there are only two cases of negotiated environmental protection agreements between local governments and developers of new facilities in Taiwan which follow the Japanese model of pollution-prevention agreements. The first agreement, between Kaohsiung county government and a new chemical plant, was reached in 1990. The second one, between Ilan county government and a new cement plant, was reached in 1992. The two agreements are the results of lengthy confrontation between the local communities and the polluters and the final involvement of local governments in the 1980s.

The contents of these two environmental protection agreements are very similar to Japanese pollution-prevention agreements. The only and very important difference is that Taiwan's agreements include an environment user fee which is very rare in Japanese agreements. In one case the environment user fee is based on the firm's output, and in the other case it is based on pollutant emissions. The revenue of the fee is used by the local government for public infrastructures and environmental protection.

There is another fundamental difference between Taiwan's environmental protection agreements and Japan's pollution-prevention agreements. In Taiwan, negotiated environmental protection agreements are the culmination of heated environmental disputes. Without disputes and conflict first, there would not be negotiation and agreement. In Japan there need not be conflicts in advance; pollution-prevention agreements have become a necessity that are negotiated before the construction or operation of a polluting facility begins. Thus, the transaction costs are usually higher in Taiwan than in Japan.

4. AN EVALUATION

In this section, we evaluate the above-mentioned approaches based on the following three criteria used by O'Hare et al. (1983): efficiency of process, efficiency of outcome, and fairness and equity.

4.1. Efficient Process

An efficient process entails as small an amount of consumption of resources and time as possible while at the same time producing an acceptable outcome. The approach of the EIA is obviously not process efficient. However, relatively speaking, the combination of the two Japanese approaches are more process efficient. Among the three negotiation approaches, all of which honour environmental rights, the Japanese one is more process efficient than Taiwan's two approaches since an agreement is signed before conflicts and disputes arise in

Japan. However, negotiated agreements are usually reached after a long process of bitter disputes and protests in Taiwan. Taipower's approach is not process efficient since non-negotiable compensation alone cannot reduce public opposition to the siting of power plants.

4.2. Efficient Outcome

Efficient outcomes include setting up a facility in the right location, and utilizing the right technology. In order to have an efficient outcome, the right amount of external cost that is a result of the pollution or hazardous risk must be revealed and felt by the developer; the right amount of public compensation must be given to the host community; the magnitude of the tax, fee and compensation should be proportional to the amount of pollution emitted; and the transaction cost must be lowered. The three approaches for negotiated agreements may produce more efficient outcomes than the two non-negotiable compensation approaches since the outcome of the negotiations may be more likely to reveal the true willingness of the parties to pay for or to accept the externality, given that both parties do not have monopoly power during negotiation. Among the three approaches for negotiated agreements, once again, the two approaches involving local governments are more efficient since the transaction costs are lowered by the participation of local governments, which are existing organizations, in the negotiation process while the other approach struggles to form new organizations to represent victims. Between these two negotiated agreement approaches involving local governments, Taiwan's environmental protection agreements would be more likely to result in efficient emissions than Japan's since environment user fees which are based on pollutant emissions or outputs are levied in Taiwan but not in Japan, although Taiwan's approach is still in its infant stage.

4.3. Fairness and Equity

A process is fair when it will not take something from anyone without justly compensating them for it. All the processes more or less consider victims' interests and include a scheme of fair compensation which is paid to the victims, assuming that adequate environmental standards are actually established and enforced.

5. CONCLUSION—A SITING PROCESS PROPOSAL

A call for the replacement of the current siting approaches, that is, regulation and EIA, is urgently needed. The current siting approaches breed rent-seeking, and local opposition, and waste resources and time, since they do not provide for fairness nor do they produce efficient outcomes. Although they were process efficient in the past, they may not be so now or in the future. Thus, the current siting approaches should be abolished and, in their place, a new law for the siting of polluting facilities should be legislated.[16] The proposed law mainly follows both the theory of New Environmental Right and that of externalities, and Japan's and Taiwan's laws and practices of reaching agreements with some revisions that make it more outcome and process efficient.

The proposed law defines the siting process that should be used in the case of polluting facilities. After the developer selects an optimal site based on his or her own criteria and following the local government's zoning regulations, the developer applies for a siting permit with the local government along with the required supporting documents such as a pollution-prevention plan and an EIA report. Then, the local government asks its Facility Siting Committee to review the application. The committee, which is composed of independent experts and government officials, is responsible only for the verification of the accuracy in the application materials. In the case of a non-significant polluting facility, if the review's result is positive then a siting permit will be issued. If it is a significant polluting facility, then the developer must follow the negotiation process outlined in the law in order to be granted a siting permit. According to the reviewed EIA report and criteria issued by the central government, the local governments that will enter into the negotiations are chosen. The result of the negotiation should be an environmental protection agreement whose contents are similar to those found in Japan and Taiwan, with an environment user fee whose revenue is used to compensate communities via increases in public facilities and services. No *ex ante* private compensation is allowed. The agreement will be open to discussion and a vote by the local assembly. If an agreement cannot be reached or approved then the case must go through an arbitration process headed by a committee of arbitrators. A siting permit will be issued if the arbitration committee approves. Therefore, there are two ways of having a siting permit issued either by having the agreement approved by the local assembly or having the agreement arbitrated by the arbitration committee. The result of the arbitration may be that no agreement is reached and the facility is not permitted to site. An agreement is not absolutely required by the proposed law.

The proposed law has the following features.

1. The law follows the theory of the New Environmental Right closely. It features a negotiated agreement, and pollution-prevention measures and environment user fees in the terms of the agreement. Furthermore, the theory calls for public participation and public monitoring.
2. Local autonomy of environmental resources is a principle that is also followed. The local government can negotiate the terms of the agreement and the local assembly can monitor negotiations through its right of approval. The local government can also use the revenue of the environment user fee to provide

better public facilities or services to its citizens.

3. The theory of externality is also followed. For example, the environment user fee is paid by the developer. It is also mandated in the law that private compensation is not allowed and the revenue of the fee can only be used in the form of increased public facilities and services since an individual's departure or entry will not affect another person's welfare. The social welfare of the community will be increased at least to the level without the polluting facility when the compensation takes the form of public goods rather than that of private goods. Thus, the two incentives to stage NIMBY protests are minimized.

4. The old EIA system is kept as a part of the siting process which, as a whole, provides a greater incentive for public participation and encourages negotiation and discourages confrontation.

5. The rate and base of the environment user fee is determined by the negotiations based on the information in EIA report on a case-by-case basis. The negotiated rate and base of the user fee may have a better chance to reflect the true willingness to pay for or to accept the externality in each case since usually neither party in the negotiation has monopolistic bargaining power. In order to reduce the agreement's enforcement cost, self-reporting of pollution emissions and a public monitoring system is mandated to be the responsibility of the developer by law.

The proposed law also has several appealing features. It is fair since the concentrated cost of the pollution borne by the local community is transferred to and borne by the developers, and ultimately transferred to consumers and the facility's owners. The community is also protected from excess pollution or risks because the facility has to meet the strict pollution-prevention measures set by the negotiated agreement. It is outcome efficient since developers have strong incentives to reduce pollution and associated risks in order to lower their user fee burden. To the extent that this fee increases the cost of production, those inefficient and highly polluting facilities with high production costs will not enter the market. Resources saved can be put to better use. The structure of the economy would be changed to be less polluting, less energy-intensive, high-tech, and produce higher value-added products. It is process efficient, too, since the community's incentive to be intransigent is minimized because it is compensated fairly, no *ex ante* private compensation is allowed, and a healthy and high quality environment is provided for the residents to live in. By adopting the proposal, it may be possible to hear fewer communities saying 'Not In My Back Yard'.

NOTES

1. Hamilton et al. (1989) propose a complicated setting which will reconcile the two approaches

without the inefficiency. However, the circumstances under which their proposal is workable is quite limited since the property rights holder must effectively imitate a socialist planner in choosing output levels where full information is required.

2. This is actually a restatement of the Demsetz Hypothesis which states: 'property rights develop to internalize environmental externalities when the gains of internalization become larger from changes in economic values, changes which stem from the development of new technology and the opening of new markets, changes to which old property rights are poorly attuned' (Demsetz 1967, p. 350).

3. Posner (1986, p. 41) and Livingston (1987) emphasize the critical confusion between property rights in the economic sense and legal sense. Inadequate attention to this distinction can lead to critical misunderstandings. In this chapter 'property rights' not only refer to ownership of physical goods in the legal sense but also to ownership of intangible goods and the institutions expressed in the rules of the game, laws, customs and mores of a society in the economic sense. The terms of 'physical property rights' and 'institutional property rights' will be used to represent the above two definitions. The former is a subset of the latter.

4. Except South Korea's constitution of 1980.

5. The relationship between property rights and environmental resources, and externalities has been studied very extensively since Coase's seminal paper (Coase 1960). Among the paper's many contributions is the Coase Theorem, which states that where there is costless bargaining between the generator and the victim of an externality, the optimal outcome will emerge so long as either party holds the pertinent physical property right. It does not matter which one holds the right. Furthermore, the above-mentioned Demsetz Hypothesis (Demsetz 1967) allows for the evolution and change of institutional property rights to accommodate an ever-changing world. Other important contributions include Demsetz (1964), Dales (1968) and Mitchell and Carson (1986).

6. E.g., Baumol and Oates (1988) and Posner (1986).

7. The private property right (PPR) is defined to be able to divide the environmental resources, e.g., air, water, into specific commodities, each of which is owned by an individual. Obviously, the transactions cost, including record-keeping costs associated with PPR regarding environmental resources, are prohibitive at present. A different PPR regime is defined in such a way as to require the agreement of everyone in a community before any inefficient low level of polluting activity could take place since it allows each person to be put in the strategy position of bargaining against all other persons who collectively own the public good, the environment.

8. Although usually a developer has to pay the holder of the environmental rights in order to use the environment, it is possible for the holder to subsidize the developer in order to have development and a better environment at the same time. Fu et al. (1993) have shown that the necessary ingredients to promote the latter case are a system of property rights and a Schumpeterian willingness to experiment.

9. This is actually the true meaning of local autonomy or self-governance in the case of environmental resources.

10. This section is drawn from my other paper (Shaw and Shaw 1991) where a formal analysis is provided.

11. The essence of the defensive activity is that it can only reduce the damage to the actor himself without any effect on others. One example is that of buckling up seat belts in cars to reduce the impact of car accidents.

12. This phenomenon is very obvious during the confrontation and negotiation process in the case of the Lin-Yuan incident mentioned above.

13. In addition to accepting the externality, the neighbours also have defensive activities at their disposal. As noted before, this defensive activity is not relevant to any policy which is required to attain optimality.

14. The variable tax rate is efficient both in the short run and long run. However, the horizontal tax rate is efficient in the short run only, since a firm's total tax paid is greater than its total external cost, even though its marginal tax rate is equal to its marginal external cost.

15. The 10 to 15 years include the five to ten years of construction and the five years of operation.

16. The proposed new law is developed in Shaw et al. (1990).

REFERENCES

Baumol, W. and W. Oates (1975), *The Theory of Environmental Policy*, Englewood Cliffs, New Jersey: Prentice-Hall.

Baumol, W. and W. Oates (1988), *The Theory of Environmental Policy*, 2nd edn, Cambridge: Cambridge University Press.

Bird, P. (1987), 'The Transferability and Depletability of Externalities', *Journal of Environmental Economics and Management*, 14: 54–7.

Buchanan, J.M. (1973), 'The Institutional Structure of Externality', *Public Choice*, 14: 69–82.

Buchanan, J.M. and W.C. Stubbebine (1962), 'Externality', *Economica*, 29: 371–84.

Coase, R.H. (1960), 'The Problem of Social Cost', *Journal of Law and Economics*, 3: 1–44.

Dales, J.H. (1968), *Pollution, Property, and Prices*, Toronto: University of Toronto Press.

Demsetz, H. (1964), 'The Exchange and Enforcement of Property Rights', *Journal of Law and Economics*, 7, 11–26.

Demsetz, H. (1967), 'Toward a Theory of Property Rights', *American Economic Review Proceedings*, 57, 347–59.

Environmental Protection Administration (1993), *The White Book of Environmental Conflicts Resolution*, (in Chinese), Taipei, ROC.

Freeman, A.M. III (1984), 'Depletable Externalities and Pigouvian Taxation', *Journal of Environmental Economics and Management,* 11: 173–9.

Fu, T.T., D. Shaw and B.T. Yu (1993), 'A Property Rights and Contractual Approach to Sustainable Development', Institute of Economics of Academia Sinica, Discussion Paper 9334.

Gresser, J., K. Fujikura and A. Morishima (1981), *Environmental Law in Japan*, Cambridge, Mass.: The MIT Press.

Hamilton, J.H., E. Sheshinski and S.M. Slutsky (1989), 'Production Externalities and Long-run Equilibria: Bargaining and Pigouvian Taxation', *Economic Inquiry*, 27 (3): 453–71.

Hsiao, H.H. and L.W. Milbrath, (1989), 'The Environmental Movement in Taiwan', paper presented at the Sino–US Binational Conference on Environmental Protection and Social Development, Taipei.

Japan Environment Agency (1989), *Annual White Paper*, Tokyo.

Livingston, M.L. (1987), 'Evaluating the Performance of Environmental Policy: Contributions of Neoclassical, Public Choice, and Institutional Models', *Journal of Economic Issues*, 21(1): 281–94.

Mitchell, R.C. and R.T. Carson (1986), 'Property Rights, Protest, and the Siting of Hazardous Waste Facilities', *American Economic Review*, 76: 285–90.

O'Hare, M., L. Bacow and D. Sanderson (1983), *Facility Siting and Public Opposition*, New York: Van Nostrand Reinhold.

Posner, R.N. (1986), *Economic Analysis of Law*, 3rd ed., Boston: Little, Brown & Company.

Shaw, D. and R.D. Shaw (1991), 'The Resistibility and Shiftability of Depletable Externalities', *Journal of Environmental Economics and Management*, 20: 224–33.

Shaw, D., C.H. Shu and Y.J. Huang (1990), 'Policies toward Siting of Polluting

Industries: A Multidisciplinary Approach', *National Taiwan University Journal of Social Science*, 38 (in Chinese).

Turvey, Ralph (1963), 'On Divergences Between Social Cost and Private Cost', *Economica*, 30: 309–13.

Yamanouchi, K. and K. Otsubo (1989), 'Agreements on Pollution Prevention: Overview and One Example', in S. Tsuru and H. Weidner (eds), *Environmental Policy in Japan*, Berlin: Ed. Sigma Bohn, 221–45.

11. The Green Movement in Korea and Its Impact in the Policy Debate

Hoi-Seong Jeong and Seong-Uh Lee

1. INTRODUCTION

Under government direction, the Korean economy has undergone remarkable growth during the thirty years since 1962, coming to be internationally recognized as the 'Han River Miracle'. Korean GNP was $2.3 billion in 1962, $8.1 billion in 1971, $60.5 billion in 1980 and $281 billion in 1991. Per capita GNP also has leaped from $87 in 1962 to $6,500 in 1991. This enormously rapid economic growth has, however, seriously polluted the land of the 'Silk River and Diamond Mountain' and diminished the quality of life in the 'Land of Morning Calm'.

The leading industrial nations' experiences prove that the public quickly becomes aware of, and cares deeply about, such quality of life issues. Therefore, it is time to begin an assessment of environmental degradation and its effects, and make a historical analysis of the Green movement in Korea in order to provide some plan to address them.

This chapter deals with the Korean citizens' Green organizations which, in our view, actually catalysed movement towards an environmentally friendly public policy. In order to obtain the best integration of public activism and government policy we should investigate and consider the basic Korean character and perspective. This chapter asks the following questions. What is the motivation of the civilian green movement, and from where comes its vitality? How have environmental activists influenced governmental policy? What are the real goals of the Korean civilian Green movement?

2. ANALYSIS OF THE CITIZENS' GREEN MOVEMENT

Under a capitalistic system, pollution is generally perceived as a result of market failure. It is also true that pollution is exacerbated by government failure. Most government failures in environmental policy area are enforcement problems, which come from lack of understanding and participation of those affected. An effective civilian Green movement is essential to address pollution problems, since a common understanding between the government and the public is necessary for the success of public policy.

Then what are the motivations for such activities in the interest of the general public among selfish individuals? As Mancur Olson suggests in his book *The Logic of Collective Action* (1965), the formation and maintenance of small groups can easily be understood even in the presence of a 'free-rider problem'. Individual members of existing small voluntary groups and some large voluntary organizations enjoy selective benefits. Under Olson's hypothesis, however, motivations for the formation and maintenance of large environmental voluntary organizations are hard to explain, since the organizations have nothing with which to provide their citizen members with economic benefits. None the less, in the US and other Western countries, large-scale voluntary environmental organizations are organized and growing.

Theoretical hypotheses suggested by American scholars explain the apparent illogic in the development of citizens' voluntary organizations. For example, there are express benefits that may come from the public interest activities of the organizations (Smith 1984). This suggests that while members of citizens' Green movements may act in the name of 'public interest' and 'the next generation', they actually find individual relief through the expression of their own concerns for the highest goals. For Walker (1983) and Hansen (1985), motivation for large public interest groups is supported by the patronage of external funding sources, either private or public. Motivation is thus fundamentally individual. An analytical model characterizing the Korean Green movement can be depicted as in Tables 11.1 and 11.2.

Table 11.1   Movement participants and their characteristics

Government	authoritarian/democratic
Polluter	specific minority/non-specific majority
Victim	specific minority/non-specific majority
Key members of organization	generalist/environmental specialist
Mass media and the public	unconcerned/concerned

Table 11.2   The Green movement and its policy impact

Sphere	local/regional/national/global
Objective	private interest/public interest
Counterpart	polluter/government/the public
Policy process	implementation/decision-making
Policy impact	*ex post/ex ante*

3. THE HISTORY OF KOREAN GREEN MOVEMENTS

The history of the Korean Green movement can be divided into four periods according to the model.

3.1. The First Period (1961–1980): Victims' Lonely Fight Against the Pollution Industry

Content and character
The first Korean Green movement was in 1966, an anti-air pollution drive against a thermoelectric plant in Pusan. By the end of 1970, while the industrial complex had grown rapidly, the Green movement was still just scattered groups of local residents suffering from industrial pollution. Government planning and policies at this period were to ignore calls for environmental protection in favour of economic growth.

The Korean government in this period favoured industry by prohibiting local residents' complaints, denying compensation awards, and the simple use of police power and blockades. Sometimes partial compensation or residence relocation was negotiated by the government, but always with very favourable consideration and results for big industry. Judicial satisfaction was possible, but the many difficult steps and hassles discouraged most local-level pollution victims.

The result was that industrial complexes recklessly spread air pollution, water contamination and industrial waste, ultimately to levels endangering the health and lives of both employees and residents. There was virtually no citizens' Green organization, only 'official' quarters. This was the 'Dark' period of the environmental movement, cowed by government and lacking broad social support.

Major Green movements and environmental organizations
Typical of the early Green movements of this period was a protest by farmers and fishermen living near the Ulsan industrial complex, who demonstrated against water and air contamination by a local chemical company and demanded financial compensation. At the time when the Ulsan industrial complex began start-ups in 1967–69, the local area was seriously hit by a variety of agricultural and orchard diseases. In 1971, greenfield farmers in Samsan plain, adjacent to the Ulsan industrial complex, demanded official countermeasures against the pollution and financial compensation through direct negotiation between victims and industrial abusers. Solutions and financial compensations were agreed upon. Again in 1974, groups of poor fishermen from Euichang county in Kyong Nam province demanded financial compensation from Jinhae Chemical Corporation. The first court decision took 10 years. During that time, three people had

committed suicide, and many fishermen had given up hope and left their home town in despair. Funds for attorneys were by then exhausted and there remained no representation for the victims. It was a lonely fight with little professional assistance.

The Korean government enacted the 'Environment Preservation Act' in 1977, which created sweeping new environment protection measures but overlooked the civilian Green movement itself. The government also announced the 'Charter of Environmental Protection' in 1978. The first civilian Green organization, the Institute for Pollution Studies, was founded by Mr Choi Yeol in 1977.

The impact on environmental policy

In early 1980, the Green movement was still suppressed by the government, and policy priorities were given to rapid economic growth. The Green movement was of little interest, and pollution victims still backed off under methodical pressure. In particular, pollution survey monitors compromised or abandoned their efforts, leaving environmental policy to evolve from the uncertain fortunes of victim groups. And only individuals, not groups, were allowed to negotiate with polluting industries for financial compensation and legal settlements.

3.2. The Second Period (1980–1987): The Green Movement as a Democratization Movement

Contents and character

A new era called the '1980 Spring of Seoul' began for the Green movement after the assassination of President Park in October 1979. In 1980 came the first constitutional guarantees of environmental preservation. Later that year came the establishment of the Administration of the Environment and further legal reforms. An officially reformed policy-making procedure began to address the accumulated environmental problems and to respect public needs, leading to an improved social atmosphere for the creation and activity of the Green movement. Between 1980 and 1987 the Green movement gained momentum and began functioning on an extensive scale. As urban residents were becoming aware of the value of a clean environment and awakening to the possibility of redress, the Green movement inspired citizens' participation among the general public.

The Green movement at this period is characterized by support from liberal social activists. But environmental organizations still could not transcend the immediate locality and each group's simple concern for its own interests. Local residents and Green activists often raised political issues, but their lack of technical expertise could not dovetail into rigid government protocol. Furthermore, established political opposition and press misinformation combined to weaken activist clout and stymie success. However, dogged persistence of the Green movement continued to invigorate citizens' Green activities.

Major Green movements and organizations

Typical of Green activism in this period was the local residents' movement in Onsan village near a non-ferrous metal industrial complex. Local farmers and fishermen banded together to extract financial compensation for environmental and health hazards. Their collective approach to negotiation was successful, and soon spread to other areas. Some residents of Onsan became sick in 1982 and 1983. By January 1985, following the establishment of this heavily polluting industry, about 500 farmers and fishermen were ill with a 'mystery' disease. The press made it a *cause célèbre*, with support from environmental organizations such as the Institute for Pollution Studies. But the 'mystery' disease, of unknown etiology, continued to be a problem and defied diagnosis. In the end, the mystery outlasted activist resources and resolution, and the government simply relocated residents away from the affected areas.

The Korean Institute for Pollution Studies, the first full-scale 'professional' Green environment organization, was established in 1982, and it paved the way for an anti-pollution campaign. During this period, famous dissident writer Kim Ji Ha organized the 'Hansalim (One Life–One Community) Movement' and led environmental protests based on oriental philosophy and humanism. His efforts failed to catch the national spotlight, but his persistence evoked sympathetic and continuing responses from the public.

The impact on environmental policy

The Korean government began to introduce full-scale environmental policy during this period. We do not claim that citizens' Green movements at this time had much effect on government policy, but there were some successful cases. The Ulsan and Onsan residents' Green movements had forced the government to involve itself in the investigation of polluted areas, and this resulted in population shifts. The 'Protect Youngsan River' campaign in 1983 was a partial success, and led to the abandonment of a plan for the Jin Ro Wine Company to establish itself there. But many Green activists turned out to be connected with anti-government activities, thus casting doubt on the sincerity of the movements' motives. With suspicion and enmity between the government and Green activists, there was little positive effect on public policy.

3.3. The Third Period (1987–1992): The Blooming of the Citizens' Green Movement

Content and character

Freedom of speech was bolstered in the June 1987 Success of Democratization Movement and further accelerated by the 1988 Seoul Olympic Games. The Green movement activists took full advantage to enhance public environmental awareness. This atmosphere of watershed democratization and openness allowed the Green movement to attract numerous professionals. Perhaps most important, many more civic-minded citizens joined the movement, and the government's negative suspicion of Green activism began to fade. Also, professional environmentalists and scientists brought new authority and credibility to Green activism, and the press increased its coverage of such activities.

During this period, the original thrust of the Green movement had evolved from mere local victim support to mass public education and calls for anti-pollution vigilance. The Korean Green movement was, however, still domestic at this time, with few international contacts. The government was in a wait-and-see mode, not actively involved in helping pollution victims, and citizens had to rely on the movement to monitor and correct industry abuses.

The Green movement had changed tremendously by the end of the 1980s. According to one survey (Whang and Kim 1993), 76 out of 132 (57.6 per cent) of surveyed Green organizations were founded after 1989, and focused solely on environmental issues, whereas previously founded organizations had other social activities as their original base. In 1989, water quality analysis showed heavy metal and water contamination in four large rivers. The year 1990 saw several incidents of drinking water contamination. The activities of Green organizations and the media on these very visible pollution incidents focused public awareness and brought nationwide attention and condemnation.

Major Green movements and environmental organizations

National conflict arose over the need for nuclear power plants and nuclear waste disposal sites during this period, since Korean natural resources and energy production could not keep pace with booming industrialization. The 1990 riot at Anmeon Island against a proposed nuclear waste disposal site gained nationwide attention and support, and resulted in the abandonment of the plan. More nationwide protests against nuclear facilities and hazardous waste disposal sites, and excessive use of chemicals at golf courses, succeeded in narrowing government policy options. Thereafter, the Green movement began to exert real force on public policy.

Youngkwang, Dalsung and Gori residents united in protests and strikes in 1988, and succeeded in reducing the scale of those facilities. Persistent conflict over nuclear power plants and radioactive waste disposal continued between the government and local residents. There were efforts to boycott chemically grown vegetable products in favour of those grown with environmentally friendly natural fertilizers. By the end of September 1990, the environmental complaints were responsible for over 20 per cent of the total complaints made to the Ministry of the Environment, mainly due to the increased professional expertise and growing public alliance in the Green movement.

Slowly the Green movement had evolved from fighting for victims' compensation after the fact to fighting for prevention of potential dangers. In Gunsan city, protest against the building of the TDI industrial complex in 1991 resulted in a 'Damage and Injury Assessment' by the Environment and Pollution Research Group. And that same year the Korea Eco-Club issued an environmental impact assessment (EIA) of the development of the Kum River Second Rest area, in support of local activists and residents.

Several Green organizations consolidated into the Korea Action Federation for Environment in 1988, and the Korea Institute for Pollution Studies changed its name to the Korean Alliance of Anti-Nuclear Peace Movements in 1989. The Environment and Pollution Research Group, at the forefront of pollution science research, was founded in 1989. It gave expert advice on pollution problems and lent its support to pollution victims. The group's real thrust was to identify potentially serious problems in advance and head them off. Green activism expanded throughout Pusan, Kwangju, Mokpo, Ulsan, Chun Nam and Inchon provinces, and many other professional Green organizations were established and led by college professors and environmental scientists. In 1991, the Korea Eco-Club started in Daejun, and combined with other groups to formulate a programme for nationwide environmental research. Many other civilian Green organizations were founded at this period. In the big cities, the Green movement had important religious components—Catholic, Buddhist, Presbyterian—as well as women's and consumer organizations, including the lower middle classes.

The impact on environmental policy
At the beginning of this period the government was only slowly responding to environmentalism, not offering support or even much attention. Since the government still viewed Green activism negatively, it just tried to ignore the movement. The mass media also tended to limit the scope of environmental exposés, reducing them to shocking but short-lived feature articles without productive in-depth analysis. But ever-stronger Green voices and ever-increasing media attention eventually led the government to respond to public opinion and alter its policies. Professionals worked to reduce dangers and guided public participation in policy-making. Thus numerous nuclear and solid waste disposal sites and golf course developments were postponed and some of them were cancelled. The Green movement at this period made the government realize the importance of citizens' participation in the environmental policy arena.

In 1988, victims received compensation from, and altered the operating plans of, the Sangbong-dong charcoal factory in Seoul. In that same year, the Young-kwang residents protested against the local nuclear power plant and received support from organizations like the Association of Physicians for Humanism, nurses, pharmacists and the Chun Nam branch of the Dentists for Health Society. Youngkwang residents also received medical screening at the local clinics. In 1989, there was renewed protest against the Youngkwang nuclear power plant, resulting in a government-imposed regional protection plan based on local resident input and needs.

In 1989, neighbours of the Hwasung industrial waste disposal site led a protest against noise, air and soil contamination with support from the Association of Physicians for Humanism and the Korean Lawyers' Association. A battle between government officials and area residents of Hwasung county in 1990 ended, following the appointment of a panel of investigators representing both sides who eventually hammered out a compromise that ushered in a new era. Finally, the Ministry of the Environment installed an air and water pollution monitoring system, and pledged 10 per cent of its yearly sales of the industrial waste disposal site to improve the residents' quality of life and develop the affected area. The Ministry also developed negotiation procedures between the government and local residents. Airport area protesters also received public attention which provided the momentum for government regulation of aircraft components and noise levels.

3.4. The Fourth Period (1992 UNCED in Rio to the Present): The Green Movement and Global Partnership

Contents and character
With the partial implementation of local autonomy in 1991 and the 1992 UNCED in Rio, the citizens' Green movement in Korea greatly expanded, united and reached out internationally. The early water pollution and nuclear waste disposal protests gave way to universal issues such as global warming and acid rain. Citizens' Green movements changed their focus to include these international and global issues, and began considering Green Capitalism. To solidify their membership bases, consumer groups and women's organizations all developed their own environmental agendas and programmes, and aligned their campaigns with religious organizations, well-known human activists and opposition politicians. Characteristic of this period was that Green activists involved themselves in government policy formulation and countermeasure planning. The government and Green organizations often collaborated to further the greater public interest.

Eventually the Korean government's intransigence and suspicion gave way to free exchange of information with an eye towards regulation, and in 1992 adopted an environmental policy-making process that was based on the opinions of its citizen stakeholders.

Major Green movements and organizations
The UNCED in Rio in 1992 had a great impact on the Korean Green movement. Green activism moved on a grander scale, no longer limited to Seoul, but expanding rapidly into a nationwide network of organizations. Name changes, expanded global interests and emphasis on public education all characterized this period. Korean Green organizations shared common interests in domestic problems as well as forging links with foreign environmental activists to address global issues.

Religious groups also dramatically changed their daily missions. In particular, Catholic, Buddhist and YMCA groups were actively involved in public environmental education, review of government policy and helping victims. In 1993, with the new view towards sustainable development rather than mere treatment and preservation, the YMCA and Sam Sung Electric Co. together led nationwide seminars for cleaner water reserves and a 'Han River Revival'. According to the report of the Ministry of the Environment in 1993, citizens' Green movement seminars had a total of 22 items on their agendas, 50 per cent of which urged regular environmental forums and meetings emphasizing public environmental education.

The impact on environmental policy
Effectively motivated by the 1992 UNCED in Rio, the Green movement gained public support for the mass release of environmental information and its use in blocking further business and government development plans that might endanger the environment. The loss of valuable natural resources caused by the destruction of the environment led people to band together with Green activists to form their own eco-plans, rejecting the government's technical, quick-fix solutions.

Again the Korean government's attitude shifted positively, embracing the citizens' Green movement. For example, in 1992 the Seoul Regional Office for Solid Waste Management requested the Korea Eco-Club to conduct an environmental impact study of the Kimpo solid waste disposal site and used the result of the study in negotiations with local residents. In 1993 the Presidential Committee for Administrative Reform consulted with the YWCA regarding the charge system for the improvement of the environment. The Ministry of the Environment also requested the Citizens' Environment Research Centre to study 'Ways of Strengthening the Civilian Green Movement'. The Ministry also consulted with civilian Green organizations regarding the effects of introducing a quantity-based charge system for solid waste in 1994.

4. EVALUATION OF THE KOREAN GREEN MOVEMENT

The Korean Green movement started under the infertile conditions of an authoritarian regime that gave its highest priority to rapid economic growth, and which only partially cared for pollution victims. In the early days, economic compensation was the only motivation for the victims' protest. During the second and third periods, the Korean Green organizations recruited heavily from democratization activists—the so-called 'political conscience group'. But many early Green activists used the movement to achieve their own political ambitions. Sometimes fights over hegemony, funds and membership among Green organizations were obstacles to mutual aid. These situations characterized the early Korean Green movement as the 'Anti-Regime Movement' or 'Dark Age of Environmentalism'.

Even though it has not been long since the Korean Green movement has awakened the public awareness and begun to alter government policy processes, it has gradually gained the public confidence and brought about the participation of environmental scientists, doctors and lawyers and their professional organizations in the movement. Since 1990, the Korean Green movement has considerably blocked and altered government planning, further bolstering a positive public attitude towards environmentalism.

Despite the many successes of the Korean Green movement, there still remain numerous shortfalls. For example, most of the Korean Green organizations are financially weak and headquartered in Seoul. One recent report (Whang and Kim 1993) indicates that 69.8 per cent of movement participants are based in the greater Seoul metropolitan area. The Greens have failed to mobilize massive public participation nationwide.

Now the Korean economy is strong and government control has been relaxed. An increasing economic power and expanding middle class have led to an increase in the membership of the Green movement. Even so, the Korean Green movement is still largely focused on domestic issues. There were approximately 166 citizens' Green organizations in Korea in 1994. These fall into two main groups: government-registered organizations, which number 87; and public/volunteer organizations, which number about 79.

The history of the Korean Green movement is summarized in Table 11.3.

Table 11.3   Characterization of the Korean Green movement

	1st period	2nd period	3rd period	4th period
Participants	victims	victims and 3rd parties	victims and 3rd parties	general public
Timing of Green movement	after incident	after incident	after/before incident	before/after incident
Sphere of activity	localized	localized	regional	national and global
Target of activity or resistance	polluter	polluter and government	government and polluter	public and government
Major activities	Ulsan area protest	Onsan area protest	anti-nuclear movement	education, monitoring and participation
Impact on government policy	none	little	a little on implementation	much on formulation and implementation

5. CONCLUSION

In all likelihood, the Korean Green movement will continue to expand its activities and mature in the process. In order to improve the present polluted environment, Korean citizens must speak out, participate actively in the public policy-making and implementation processes, and press for even more organizational activism. Full-scale participation of the Green movement must be an integral factor in Korean environmental politics in the future, as witnessed by the legacy of environmental devastation left by past rapid and under-regulated economic development. In order to influence government policies with the most inventive and workable solutions, the Korean Green organizations must continue to recruit professional members versed in the latest scientific techniques and political knowhow. Close connections with international Green organizations will build up the foundations of global environmental understanding and develop common interest strategies. And there must be a reemphasis of independent funds to ensure the stability of the Green movement.

The 1992 UNCED in Rio and the ensuing worldwide revitalization of Green movements have influenced the favourable evolution of Korean government policy. We are confident that the Korean Green movement will fall into line with the international mainstream, and with the strengthening of local autonomy in Korea scheduled for 1995.

REFERENCES

Environmental Pollution Research Group (1991), *Pollution Problems and Pollution Policy*, Seoul: Hangil-Sa.

Hansen, John Mark (1985), 'The Political Economy of Group Membership', *American Political Science Review,* 79(1): 79–96.

Ingram, Helen M. and Dean E. Mann (1989), 'Interest Groups and Environmental Policy', in James P. Lester (ed.), *Environmental Politics and Policy: Theories and Evidence*, Durham: Duke University Press, pp. 135–57.

Lee, Sang Hun (1993), 'A Study on the Ideology and Subject of Environmental Movements in Korea', Master's Thesis, Department of Environmental Planning, Graduate School of Environmental Studies, Seoul National University.

Ministry of the Environment (1994), *The White Book of the Environment*, Seoul, Korea.

Olson, Mancur (1965), *The Logic of Collective Action: Public Goods and the Theory of Groups,* Cambridge, Mass.: Harvard University Press.

Smith, V. Kerry (1984), 'A Theoretical Analysis of the Green Lobby', *Americal Political Science Review,* 70(1): 137–47.

Walker, Jack L. (1983), 'The Origin and Maintenance of Interest Group in America', *American Political Science Review,* 77(1): 390–406.

Whang, Myung Chan and Jong Soon Kim (1993), *A Study on the Korean Citizens' Green Organization*, Seoul, Korea: Institute for Public Affairs, Kunguk University.

12. Participatory Environmental Impact Assessment (EIA) for Energy Projects in the Philippines

Fulgencio S. Factoran and Rolando L. Metin

1. INTRODUCTION

In the Philippines, the people are generally hospitable. The Filipino host will not think twice about inviting a stranger to his home for a meal or a drink. But the Filipino is also protective of his or her personal space. A visitor who overstays his or her welcome, or abuses the host's hospitality, is bound to be asked to leave.

The Filipino is also aware of his or her rights and freedoms. After the 1986 revolution where the sheer force of people power drove away an entrenched dictator and installed a democratic regime, the Filipino people adopted a Constitution that put in place a representative democracy which affirms that sovereignty resides in the people and all government authority is derived from them. A Bill of Rights guarantees every Filipino the right to life, liberty, property, health and education, among others.

While Filipino hospitality and love for freedom have been lauded as positive traits, these have not always been respected by government and big business interests that come into our communities with development projects.

This chapter explores the relationship between local communities and development project proponents, and discusses positive developments in sustainable development. Taking off from the perspective of Filipino hospitality and the rules of engagement in Philippine society, the hospitable Filipino host is the community where a project is located; the visitors are the project proponents; and the Constitution and Bill of Rights, and the inherent hospitality of the people as well as its limits, prescribe the norms of the relationship between the visitor and the host. If a visitor intends to stay permanently, the host must be told about it. If the visitor wishes to tinker with the surroundings, the host must be consulted on why and how it should be done and its effects on the environment. If this results in something good, such benefit should be quantified *vis-à-vis* the adverse effects that such activity might cause the host. And if the visitor intends to make a fortune in the area where the host ekes out his livelihood, there should be an agreement on how to share the bounty between visitor and host.

2. A BRIEF OVERVIEW OF THE ENERGY SITUATION IN THE PHILIPPINES

The power outages from 1990 to 1993, which slowed down much of the economic activity in the country, dramatized the need for more energy-generating projects in the Philippines. Mindanao, in southern Philippines, for instance, was plagued with four- to five-hour power outages daily in 1992. Luzon, in the north, sweated though three to seven hours of brownouts resulting in a forced reduction of the labour force. Non-functioning traffic lights caused major traffic jams in Metro Manila, and tried the patience of commuters and motorists daily.

A 1993 study funded by the Asia Foundation cited a World Bank estimate that the loss to the economy due to the power crisis was as much as $600 million or P15 billion in 1992 (Abaya et al. 1993). Outlining the policy and structural reasons for the energy problem, the same study cited the delay in the issuance of Environmental Compliance Certificates (ECC) for the various energy-generating projects of the National Power Corporation as a major cause of the severe shortage in power supply. Delays in the issuance of ECC ranged from 27 to 54 months (Abaya et al. 1993). Often, these were caused by strong opposition to the projects from environmentalists and other concerned sectors, including local government officials. Clearly, many of these projects, in spite of their importance to an energy-deficient economy, did not pass the test of social acceptability.

The issue of the social acceptability of energy projects, as the study echoed some critics, is a political concern that is best left to the President, and not to the Department of Environment and Natural Resources (DENR), to decide. While there is logic in this proposal, such an idea negates one of the policy premises of the current as well as the immediate past Philippine government administrations: people empowerment.

How can a government preach and institutionalize popular participation in decision-making when official actions would deny such participation? When many of the citizenry and elected leaders voice their objections to an energy project consistently and vigorously because of their genuine concern for their livelihood and health, should not the bureaucracy show some sensitivity and respond accordingly? So difficult was the power situation in 1992 and 1993 that a group of politicians decided to cash in on the publicity offered by the subject by filing a case against the immediate past-President of the country in court.

3. ENVIRONMENTAL IMPACT ASSESSMENT

In 1978, Presidential Decree No. 1586 issued by the President of the Philippines, required that an environmental impact assessment (EIA) be conducted in areas where development projects are to be established. A related presidential proclamation (No. 2146 issued on 14 December 1981), classified *environmentally critical projects* which have high potential for negative environmental impact and *environmentally critical areas*. The former would require the submission of an environmental impact statement (EIS). The latter would initially require only a project description for evaluation by the DENR whether a full EIS would have to be made.

The Department of Environment and Natural Resources requires that an environmental impact statement or a project description be submitted before it issues an Environmental Compliance Certificate. DENR Administrative Order No. 21 issued on 5 June 1992 prescribes the revised guidelines for the implementation of the EIA.[1] In great detail, the Order provides the policy objectives and the scope and procedures that an environmental impact assessment must follow; the review of the proposed project by the Department and the public through a public hearing, if necessary; and the conditions under which an environmental compliance certificate may be issued.

The EIA establishes the past and current environmental conditions in an area (physical, biological, chemical, human) and determines the probable impacts of the proposed project. The EIA also aims to (a) guide the proponent in the planning and formulation of project activities so that environmental considerations are incorporated in the early stages of project development, and (b) involve, as much as possible, a wide spectrum of concerned sectors including the adjacent communities which will be affected by the project, in the exchange of views, information and concerns in order to effect projects that are beneficial to the majority and acceptable to the community.

The environmental impact statement (EIS) or project description is evaluated by an in-house review group of the DENR and an external Technical Review Committee, composed mostly of experts from academe and from among environmentalists. Some projects, particularly those in the energy sector, must undergo public hearing where multisectoral views are presented, recorded and evaluated before the DENR issues an Environmental Compliance Certificate.

4. PEOPLE'S PARTICIPATION IN PERSPECTIVE

A Filipino scholar describes people's participation as the active involvement of the community in the decision-making process. Active involvement exists when the purpose and content of any undertaking clearly originate from the people themselves and the people feel that they are acting as free agents and not under duress or pressure, or that they are being manipulated or deceived. People's participation implies that the people themselves determine their own needs, actions, institutions and social environment.[2]

Participation is characterized by consensual decision-making, appropriate sectoral representation, contribution of resources by participants to the overall efforts, and distribution of the benefits of the development process. It also requires involvement in the procedural and substantive aspects of planning, organization, implementation and evaluation of the project (Mayo 1983).

Dr Dioscoro Umali, former FAO Chief for Asia and the Pacific, described people's participation as both an instrument for self-reliant action and the fulfilment of basic needs. He said that it is an actual process in which people's initiatives are guided by their own thinking, using means and processes over which they have control, growing out of consciousness or critical awareness of institutionalized social injustices. To be authentic, people's participation should build on the people's capacity to redress these injustices, based on the democratic conviction that there exist extraordinary possibilities in ordinary people (Metin 1990).

People's participation in development projects is not only desirable and advantageous, it is also a basic right, especially when a people's lives and future are affected by a proposed project. One scholar even says that non-participation is a threat to freedom (Umali 1988, p. 36).

Studies indicate that people's participation facilitates rather than obstructs the implementation of projects. In fact, the lack of people's participation could result in apathy, project delays and additional costs. A case in point is a road-building project in Mt. Province in the Philippines which the local residents blocked, even though it would have created some comfort and benefits for them, because of a lack of local involvement and information. It proceeded after the people got involved, but also after the proposal had incurred expensive delays and overshot its budget (Carbonell 1976). In Nepal, a religious shrine restoration project in 1974 and a town-cleaning and beautification project in 1985 were able to proceed with some degree of success only after the population was informed, trained and enlisted in the projects' activities (Sokoken 1984). Similarly, government-initiated reforestation projects in Niger which did not enlist local participation were destroyed by the villagers because they were never involved in them (Felsenthal 1986).

Public involvement increases public confidence in the decision-making process of the government, and enhances the sustainability of projects by ensuring that the project interventions are relevant to the interests and concerns of the affected communities. People involvement also infuses local knowledge and information into the EIS process and subsequently into the project design, and assists in uncovering the social, economic and cultural issues and resources arising from the project. Furthermore, it provides local communities and socioeconomic interest groups with a foundatian for and an institutional role in project interventions that occur after the feasibility study has been completed, by allowing the community to have a voice in project planning, implementation, maintenance and operations (Noronha 1982).

Studies indicate that most communities would want to participate in development projects that will affect their lives. The local population has priceless indigenous knowledge and insights which should not be ignored in project planning and design.

It is important, therefore, that development projects include policies and mechanisms that promote people's participation. Project designs should deliberately accommodate people's involvement in project activities. This would not only increase the level of awareness and understanding of the local population about the project but also enable them to contribute their stock of knowledge on how best the project can be implemented with the minimum of disturbance or discomfort, and ensure a maximum level of benefits to all concerned.

5. PARTICIPATORY APPROACHES AND AREAS OF PARTICIPATION IN EIA

One question that is often asked is, 'Who are the people?'. Are they those who live in the direct impact areas of the project? Do they include the population located in indirect impact areas? Or do they encompass the larger society which depends on the environmental resources affected, such as forests and rivers, even if these resources are remote from their communities? What if only some segments of society are advocating a 'no-touch' policy as far as the environment is concerned?

There are no easy answers to these questions. However, policy makers and implementers must confront these questions even if the answers may seem arbitrary and unpopular. In the Philippine context, the people are the stakeholders. This means the people in the direct impact areas and the adjacent (although indirect impact) communities as well as their formal and institutional leaders. The people also means the larger society, other sectors that have strong opinions about a project and whose views should be heard. However, priority should be given to the wants and needs of the people who are likely to be affected directly when designing measures that would mitigate the impact of a project. After all, these are the people who will bear the immediate physical and emotional costs of a development project.

For it to be meaningful, participatory EIA should start with information: the people must know the purpose of an environmental impact assessment. They must realize the possible dangers to their environment and lifestyles and what should be done to correct the situation and contain the damage if such destruction occurs. This can be done to a considerable extent by involving the community in making the environmental impact assessment.

In the Philippines, the responsibility for the EIA has always been a function of the project proponent. In practice, however, environmental consultants or firms are hired by the project owners to do the actual assessment and preparation of the EIS. These consultants are mostly academics and university-based researchers who lend their credibility to the EIS.

The EIA involves several processes: from scoping or determination of parameters to be assessed, to data gathering, to the public hearing where environmental and even social and economic issues are raised by concerned sectors before representatives of the DENR. In all these stages of the EIA, which are summarized below, the people are encouraged to participate actively in the process.

5.1. Areas For People's Participation in the EIA Process

Scoping
Scoping is the process of identifying the aspects of the environment that must be studied *vis-à-vis* the project to determine its temporal and spatial dimensions. These dimensions refer to the time periods within which the effects of the project are to be assessed under various project scenarios, and the physical, hydrological, ecological and political boundaries of the project, including the development and selection of alternatives to the proposed project and other issues to be considered in the EIS. The areas and activities for public involvement in the EIA process can be identified during the scoping process.

Site visit and the walk-through
Besides developing a familiarity with the project site and the impact areas, a visit to the project site allows the EIA experts the opportunity to validate secondary data through a rapid assessment methodology. Most importantly, the site visit serves as an opportunity for identifying and relating with possible local partners for the succeeding EIA activities. The participatory process starts with consultations with the stakeholders: the local communities to be affected, people's organizations (POs), concerned NGOs, local government units and agencies, the religious sector and the academic institutions.

'Walking through' the site together, especially along areas which will be disturbed such as in civil works, gives the EIA experts and the residents some idea of the probable impact of the project. At this point, both consultants and residents can begin discussions and suggest to the project proponent, changes in activity location, such as the re-routing of roads to be constructed.

Consultation with the people during the site visit can be considered as the second scoping of the project EPA. It serves as a tool to refine and improve on the scoping guidelines provided by the DENY and the project owner.

Training

Meaningful participation in EIA is premised on an understanding of the project, and of the principles, objectives and mechanics of the EIA process. This can be achieved by giving instruction on the EIA to a portion of the affected population, including key village leaders, representatives of local NGOs and POs, and local government officials. The objective of the training is to generate a higher level of awareness and understanding of the project, the status of the environment, probable impacts of the project on the environment, appropriate mitigating measures and how these measures are formulated, and the development of an environmental monitoring plan. The training also discusses how the assessment is to be done, including the collection, analysis and interpretation of data. The role of the community, local government units and appropriate national government agencies in the approval of the environmental compliance certificate is also clarified.

Where possible, the EPA training should be conducted by linking with local academic institutions and interested community leaders and NGOs and POs. The EIA consultants form the core of the instructors. After the training, the EIA consultants work with the newly trained 'local and community EIA experts' in the actual conduct of the EIA in the field, in the analysis of data, and in consolidating the EIA report.

To facilitate learning, the instructors use the proposed project as a case study so that the training itself becomes a mechanism for providing key local leaders with an in-depth understanding of the project. The participants can then help refine and improve further the implementation of the EIA.

Data gathering

One of the most significant aspects of the EIA where people's participation finds more meaning is when the people supplement or complement the data-gathering efforts of the experts. Often, they are the principal resource persons of the experts, especially in giving information about the history, quality and uses of resources like rivers, streams and coastal areas as well as the local names and uses of certain plants, trees and marine life. They also provide historical data on the changes in land use, population growth, cropping systems, and the weather.

Validation of findings

To validate its findings, the EIA team returns to the project site and presents to the residents its preliminary findings on the assessment, and alternative options to mitigate, prevent or reduce the possible adverse impact of the project.

The provincial governor, city or municipal mayor and the *barangay* captain or village chief, the NGOs, POs and religious leaders such as the parish priest are invited to a formal validation meeting. To prepare for this meeting, the team seeks the services of volunteers to handle registration of participants; to help it find an appropriate venue; to prepare the programme; and to inform the residents about the objectives and schedule of the meeting.

People from all walks of life—farmers, housewives, fisherfolk, the youth, small traders, members of POs and NGOs, businessmen, landowners and entrepreneurs—attend these validation sessions, where they raise important questions on the probable effects of the project on their water supply, crops and health, among others. Among themselves, they debate the environmental and economic impacts of the project while the EIA consultants listen quietly, taking notes, careful not to take sides on any issue. It is important for the consultants to clarify issues from a scientific viewpoint, present their findings to the people as objectively as possible, and secure their comments and corrections which will be incorporated into the final EIS report.

The validation meetings are a prelude to the public hearing that may be held later, as required by the Department of Environment and Natural Resources.

Formulation of mitigation measures
While the formulation of mitigating measures is usually left to the individual EIA consultants or the EIA team, this can also be done preliminarily by consulting the residents in the direct impact area. There are two good reasons to do this: for the local residents to understand the impact of a project on themselves and their environment, and to allow them to participate in evolving measures that will mitigate or prevent any negative impact of the project.

Information dissemination
Information must be disseminated to the residents of the impact areas to increase their level of awareness and understanding of the project, to enable the residents to discuss intelligently among themselves what the project is all about so they can make an informed judgement about it, and to enable the residents to participate meaningfully in project activities.

Educating the public about a project is absolutely necessary to earn their support. But more than that, the public is entitled to information about any project that may affect their lives.

Field guides
If the consultants and even some of the local volunteers are not familiar with the project site, they must enlist the services of field guides who are knowledgeable about the place. While the field guides are paid, they, in effect, participate in the EIA by giving vital information to the experts.

Provision of services
The community participates in the EIA in other ways, such as providing services to the EIA team by renting out facilities like small boats for marine and oceanographic investigations, animal-driven sleds for transport of samples and portable electric generators, and by selling food to the consultants.

Recruitment, training and social surveys

For the social survey, the consultants often use the services of locally-based interviewers who are recruited from the village or recommended by the village chief. These locals are trained for two to three days on the objectives and mechanics of the survey. An initial briefing on the project and the EIA process precedes the actual training on how to conduct a social survey.

Socioeconomic survey

The conduct of the socioeconomic survey also needs substantive local participation. Local residents act both as survey enumerators and sources of valuable information. Their perceptions and opinions about the project are valuable inputs to decision-making and action planning by the project proponent and by the government.

Enumerators are recruited from the community as is being done by the Consolidated Asian Systems Development Inc. (CASDI) and GAIA South Inc. in their EIA activities in the Philippines. The locals are trained on the objectives and procedures of the EIA before they are coached on the techniques and mechanics of the demographic survey.

The survey instrument is translated into the local dialect and reviewed with the assistance of the enumerators and is pre-tested before it is finally administered.

Public hearing

The public hearing provides the public an opportunity to raise issues and air their feelings about the project and its environmental, health, social and economic impacts. It is, in effect, a collaborative dialogue between the government and the people. It is an occasion where a farmer, a local leader, a trader, a public official, a student, a priest, a member of a people's organization or an NGO, are provided equal opportunities in ventilating their ideas, opinions, comments, support, opposition, fears, apprehensions and expectations about the project. In this forum, the project proponent, sometimes with the assistance of the consultants, presents measures that will mitigate adverse impacts, a package of benefits that will accrue to the residents or their communities, and an environmental monitoring plan.

Preparation of the environmental monitoring plan

As far as possible, the environmental monitoring plan should incorporate suggestions from the leaders of the community and from the LGU. After all, the implementation of the monitoring plan will need the active participation of the community and its leaders and the LGU, as well as the DENR and the project proponent.

The participation of the community in environmental monitoring, both in the formulation and implementation stages, pre-supposes the earlier involvement of its members in the EIA process. Such involvement should have raised their level of awareness and knowledge about the project, its processes and environmental and social impacts.

The objective of all this is to ensure that there is always informed and responsible decision-making at the community level when issues arise. The residents, local government executives, people's organizations, non-governmental organizations and other influential groups in the area should serve as primary informants to the specialists who will conduct the study.

One way to promote participatory EIA is to recruit community and NGO leader volunteers to participate in key activities of the EIA, if not in the entire process. The idea is to identify highly respected community and local NGOs, including staff of the local government units and agencies, to undertake an intensive training in EIA and become part of the professional EIA team, of course, with appropriate support for their participation. The purpose is not to co-opt these leaders but to tap their knowledge and perspectives of local conditions in a systematic, well-thought-out and responsible manner. This way, a highly accurate and relevant EIA, especially with regard to the ameliorative and mitigative measures, can be developed.

The advantage of this approach is that local leaders are not only able to attest to the validity of the EIA. They also serve as a reservoir of responsible data who can share the knowledge they have gathered during the study. They should then be able to actively participate in other activities related to the project in the future, such as the Environmental Monitoring Programme.

5.2. Participatory EIA: The Case of the PNOC–EDC Northern Negros Geothermal Exploration Project

The EIA for the PNOC Energy Development Corporation's geothermal exploration project in Negros Occidental in the Philippines was deliberately designed to be participatory. The EIA for this project was conducted by the consortium of GAIA South and CASDI.

It was important for GAIA and CASDI that the EIA team be selected carefully, following two criteria. The first was the objectiveness, credibility and track record of the individual experts. They stipulated that the local population should be able to trust the competence of the team. The second criterion in selecting the experts was their belief and commitment to people's participation in the EIA process. In addition, it was important for the EIA team members to accept that the EIA investigation must be neutral, even if the proponent underwrote the expert group's expenses.

A complementary strategy was the employment of a community organizer and a communications specialist, who were locally based and respected, to join the EIA team. Their roles were to explain the PNOC geothermal exploration project and the EIA to the community, and to enlist and mobilize the participation of local NGOs, people's organizations, schools, church representatives, LGUs, the youth and women leaders in the EIA process, whether they were supportive or against the geothermal exploration project.

Protocols had to be observed. Senior members of the EIA team made courtesy calls on the Provincial Governor and other high-ranking local officials, as well as local officers of other government agencies, specially those that could provide data (meteorological, river stream flow, crop yield, etc.) on the project site, such as the Department of Agriculture, National Irrigation Administration and the DENR. These protocols and the coordination work not only helped the team access available data but also enlisted these key persons and offices in an environmental activity like the EIA.

The participatory process began with a two-day training on EIA of local volunteers drawn from the various sectoral groups, in the belief that the people would understand the project better if they knew the objectives and procedures of conducting environmental assessment. The training programme also served as a way of validating the proposed methodology for the EIA.

Local participation in the EIA was deemed important because of previous experiences of the principals of GAIA South and CASDI in earlier energy projects which were granted ECC only after protracted and emotional dialogues, as well as hostile confrontations with local residents and organizations. Among the projects that faced such difficulties were the Mt. Apo Geothermal Project of the PNOC-Energy Development Corporation, the coal-fired power plants of the National Power Corporation in Calaca, Batangas and Masinloc, Zambales, and more recently, the LNG-powered energy project in the Province of Cavite. Even as the environmental impact statements for these energy projects indicated that any adverse impact on the environment, people's livelihood and health could be prevented or mitigated, it was difficult for the proponents and even the DENR to get some of the more active environmentalists and stakeholders to agree to these projects. The difficulty in securing the support of the community persisted in spite of the daily occurrence of power outages in Mindanao and Luzon and some parts of the Visayas.

It may not be totally accurate to claim that the vehement opposition to these energy projects was due primarily to the lack of active participation by the stakeholders in the EIA process or in project planning for the power projects. But on hindsight, it would have been very helpful and instructive had the local population, their formal and informal leaders (political, civic and religious), local organizations (including NGOs) and the various sectoral stakeholders been enlisted to join the process of environmental assessment, the determination of both positive and negative impacts of the projects, the formulation of measures that would mitigate or even prevent adverse impacts, and the development of environmental monitoring and management plans for the area.

Going back to the PNOC Northern Negros Geothermal Exploration Project EIA, many of the EIA training participants as well as other *barangay* residents who did not attend the training joined the experts in data gathering and analysis, largely through the efforts of the team's community organizer and communications specialist. However, prior to the actual involvement in the EIA process, the EIA team and the local resident-volunteers had to agree on the scope and extent of local participation. This was essential because, at times, the process of doing the work was more important than the output itself.

The participatory process in data gathering was mutually reinforcing. As field data was gathered, the EIA experts explained to the volunteers what they were doing and why such procedures were being done. Simultaneously, the EIA scientists learned local names of terrestrial and aquatic plants and animals, farming practices, methods of gathering food and other products from the forest, livelihood activities and other social practices and beliefs from the people. For their part, the local population learned things about environmental use and protection from the EIA team. In the process, a working feedback mechanism between the EIA team and the community was put in place.

The social survey was another highlight in the local people's participation in the environmental impact assessment. The survey instrument was revised, translated into the local dialect, pre-tested by the enumerators, and finalized only after a group of NGOs made their own comments and suggestions. While the standard statistical design called for only a 10 per cent stratified sampling of the impact areas, upon the suggestion of the local NGO and concurred in by the project owner, the three villages or *barangay* were subjected to total survey. This way, all the residents of the project sites and immediate vicinities were given the chance to speak out and be heard.

As part of the assessment, a walk-through of the project site was done by CASDI staff, together with the PNOC–EDC staff, local residents and NGO members. This enabled the residents and the PNOC staff to see for themselves where the proposed road would pass and the areas that would be affected. The walk-through resulted in a decision to relocate the road in order to avoid touching at least ten houses, an upland fishpond, a mulberry plantation and other vegetation.

Before the EIA report was prepared for submission to the PNOC–EDC, the findings and proposed mitigating measures were presented to and validated with the people, right in their *barangay*. The validation sessions were actually informal public hearings because other than making comments on the tentative EIA findings, the local population started voicing their views on geothermal exploration itself. The validation process therefore became a mechanism for actual democratic participation in development project planning.

Something else was noteworthy in the validation meetings held in the two *barangay*: the local organization of NGOs, which was not known to be supportive of the geothermal exploration project, assisted in planning, facilitating and documenting the sessions. The validation sessions were attended by officials from the local governments, local residents and members of people's and non-governmental organizations, including the church.

Again, during the formal public hearings conducted by the DENR in Barangay Mailum, Bago City and in Barangay Minoyan, Murcia, where the geothermal explorations were to be located, the local NGOs and LGUs assisted in the preparations and in gathering the participants. Attendance was fairly sizeable. In Mailum, the venue for the hearing had to be relocated to the school grounds instead of holding it in a big classroom, as originally planned. There were placard-bearing groups, representing those who were for and against the project. While the discussions were lively and, at times, heated, it was inspiring to see the people discussing intelligently the effects of the geothermal exploration project on the environmental resources.

It is important to point out that prior to the public hearing, the EIA group sent a pair of senior experts to the project area to air the issues with top local government officials, NGO leaders and other sectoral representatives. This additional visit preceding the public hearing was deemed necessary to achieve a measure of understanding among the interested local sectors before they were brought together in a formal forum. This way, the locals were prepared to tackle the issues that were raised during the public hearing.

Four months after the public hearings, the Environmental Compliance Certificate for the exploration was issued by the DENR to the PNOC–EDC. It set a record for the processing of an ECC for an energy project in the Philippines.

The success of the participatory approach in the PNOC–EDC Geothermal Exploration Project was the result of the confluence of philosophy and attitude among three groups which favoured participation. CASEI/GAIN and the experts advocated for people participation. The community was more than willing to get involved in the EIA process. And more importantly, the PNOC–EDC willingly promoted and supported the involvement of the people and the interested sectors.

In February 1994, the PNOC–EDC decided to enter into the development phase of geothermal power generation in Northern Negros. Given its 1993 experience, the same group that conducted the EIA for the exploration phase was tapped to prepare the environmental impact statement. The 1993 EIA participatory processes were duplicated but this time a locally-based group, the Institute for Social Research and Development of the University of St. La Salle, was asked to handle the community organizing and mobilization work, the facilitation of the EIA training and the validation sessions. A significant feature of the EIA for the development phase is the inclusion in the EIA team of a young engineer who was a native of Bago City and who was just as interested and concerned as anyone else in protecting the environment in his community.

The validation sessions were held on 25 March at Barangay Mailum, in Bago City, the site of the geothermal project. More than 80 people, including the city mayor, a city councillor, *barangay* captains and the parish priest joined the farmers, housewives, the youth and plantation workers in hearing and discussing the initial EIA results. In Barangay Minoyan in the town of Murcia, another site of the project, more than 90 residents, led by the mayor and the *barangay* captains, attended the validation meeting on 26 March. Representatives of Pos and NGOs were present in both sessions, although some of them made it clear that they were attending in their personal capacity. As in the 1993 validation meetings and public hearings, issues and concerns about water, crops, animals, land, air, public health, livelihood activities, relocation and compensation, benefits to the community and even legal questions were raised. To the extent that they could, the EIA team responded to the issues. However, many of the concerns could be more competently addressed only by the PNOC–EDC.

The results of the validation sessions, including the questions that only the PNOC–EDC could answer, were submitted by the EIA team to PNOC. Some of the more specific questions focused on the effects of the geothermal project on the rivers, the residents and their farms within the project site, their crops, their health, and many more. So concerned was the PNOC–EDC that it sent its Environmental Management Division officials to the project site to validate the report of the EIA Team. After the trip, the PNOC decided to hold another validation session on 28 and 29 May 1994 where both the EIA team and the PNOC officials would discuss the EIA findings with the people. In effect, this decision of PNOC affirmed the impact of local participation in the company's decision-making processes concerning the geothermal development project.

The participatory approach which guided the EIA for the PNOC geothermal project, in a sense revolutionized the EIA concept. The process and results of the social survey became the core of the EIA, as it shifted the focus from the traditional emphasis on the biotechnical to the social costs of the project.

6. CONCLUSION

The PNOC–EDC experience in the EIA for the Northern Negros Geothermal Exploration and Development Project has influenced other similar projects. Project proponents in the Philippines have realized that the people must not only know what a project is, but they must also understand it. And since the EIA is a very visible and active process that occurs right in the community, people's involvement in the project should start with environmental investigation. For instance, very recently, the terms of reference for the EIA of a petrochemical industrial estate in the Philippines included a community organizer and a communications specialist in the EIA team who will specifically help in mobilizing local participation in the EIA activities. The developer of a cement company in the northern Philippines has agreed to include community organizing as one of the EIA activities. A hydroelectric project in Mindanao for which an EIA is scheduled to be conducted has also considered the participation of the local government and the community in the environmental investigation and in drawing up the environmental impact statement.

In the case of the PNOC Energy Development Corporation, it has adopted the participatory approach in doing EIA for its other geothermal exploration and development projects. It may not be long before official policy should require deliberate and active involvement of the local communities in conducting environmental impact assessments, whether programmatic or project-specific.

People's participation is time-consuming and costly, and it can discourage investors from proceeding with projects here. In fact, one foreign investor in the Philippines whose project had already been delayed for ten months because of the consultation process, asked why a country that needed investments so badly to effect an economic take-off, should bother to consult and seek the approval of the people for vital development projects. The investor was told that this was how democracy worked and that democracy and economic development were not incompatible. In the Philippines, many NGOs, POs and even some communities have achieved such a high level of organizational and procedural sophistication that they can forcefully and methodically articulate their views and opposition to a project. Furthermore, consultation is necessary in a country like the Philippines where the population is evident almost everywhere. Some areas, including what are classifed as forest land, are densely populated.

Taken in the larger context and in the long run, the people's support for a project enhances its sustainability and profitability. In more specific terms, recent experience has shown that non-participation could result in higher costs and in delays in implementation. It becomes a pragmatic investment, therefore, to invite genuine people's participation in the process. The more basic point, however, is that it is the people's inherent right to know about and to participate in activities that affect their lives. The people must have a significant and meaningful role in defining, charting and implementing development in their communities, which is sustainable and humane.

Participatory EIA is still a new concept. Ironically, it is growing roots in the energy sector, which has always had difficulty explaining to the affected populations that environmental protection and the exploration for and generation of power can peacefully co-exist. Needless to say, participatory approaches must be continually tested and improved. More avenues for participation have to be explored, regardless of sectoral economic activities that may be involved.

The people's capacity to participate in participatory approaches is another concern that environmental agencies, local governments and NGOs should strengthen through community organization and education for empowerment.

Finally, the government should continue giving more meaning to people empowerment if it truly believes in the inherent right of the people to pursue development. But even if it does not, there is no turning back for the Filipino people. The demand for participation in the processes that affect their lives can only grow, given the active involvement of NGOs in building viable and empowered communities and sectors. This empowerment ensures that the nation's collective misery under a dictator who imposed his greed on the people by way of development projects that disregarded their wants, their needs, their properties, their traditions, their history, and their environment will never happen again.

The participatory impact assessment process builds on the Filipinos' vaunted hospitality and love for freedom. It is a quintessentially Filipino contribution to genuine people empowerment.

NOTES

1. In the Philippines, most of the laws are not self-executory. Administrative bodies such as departments, bureaux or commissions have to issue implementing orders to carry out the mandate and objectives of the law.
2. Department of Environment and Natural Resources, Administrative Order No. 21, series of 1992.

REFERENCES

Abaya, Antonio C., Ely Anthony R. Oano and Ricardo B. Ramos (1993), *Energy Study: The Power Crisis in the Philippines*, Manila: Environmental Network Center, Inc.

Carbonell, Aurora (1976), '*Role of Citizen Participation in Development*', NSDB-UP Integrated Research Programme, Occasional Paper No. 5, June.

Felsenthal, Mark (1986), 'Sweeping Changes in Community Participation', *Development International*, Nov.–Dec., pp. 8–10.

Mayo, Geraldine C. (1983), 'Citizen Participation and the Delivery of Health Services', unpublished DPA dissertation, University of the Philippines, Diliman, Quezon City.

Metin, Rolando L. (1990), 'People's Participation in the Integrated Social Forestry Program: Implications for Development Program Management', unpublished DPA dissertation, University of the Philippines, Diliman, Quezon City.

Noronha, Raymo (1982), 'Seeing People for the Trees: Social Issues in Forestry', Conference in Forestry and Development in Asia, Bangalore, India, 19–23 April.

Sokoken, Darwin C. (1984), 'Community Participation and its Role in Rural Development; the Bontoc Case', *Philippine Journal of Public Administration*, Vol. 28, Jan.–Apr., pp. 135–67.

Umali, Dioscoro (1988), 'People Power and Upland Development', Report of the FAO Finland Workshop on People's Participation in Upland Communities, Bangkok, Thailand, 22–29 November.

PART IV

Industry: Partner or Culprit?

13. Risk Management Strategies for Environmental Exposures: Lessons from the United States

Paul Freeman

1. INTRODUCTION

Over the past 30 years, the United States has been evolving a societal conscience concerning the environment. It is an evolution marked by a significant shift in viewpoint. Instead of continuing to see the environment as a resource to be exploited for economic gain, Americans are increasingly coming to see the environment as a resource with economic and social value in its own right. Hundreds of Federal, state, and local statutes have been enacted in a relatively short period of time to protect that value by assigning liability for environmental contamination of the air, water and soil resources of the United States—and to stipulate who will pay for the cleanup of this contamination. The burden of this liability is falling largely on the shoulders of the private sector and, more specifically, on property owners.

The financial implications of this liability are enormous. It is estimated that accrued liability for environmental risks on real property total approximately US$2 trillion, which is 16 to 20 per cent of the total estimated US$10 to $12 trillion value of all property in the United States.[1] As a result, corporate risk management has evolved to include environmental issues, as well as the more traditional elements of health and safety. Environmental risk management, in fact, has become an important component of corporate responsibility in the United States today.

But environmental issues are no longer solely a concern in the United States. They now also strongly impact Canadian and European business. It is highly likely that Asian businesses will soon need to address their exposure to risks posed by environmental issues. For example, the chairman of China's national legislature's environmental committee was recently quoted as saying that economic loss from pollution in China totals US$11.5 billion, or three per cent of China's gross national product.[2]

What lessons can Asian businesses learn from the United States about environmental exposure that will better prepare them to handle that exposure? The next section of the chapter provides a perspective on the history of environmental legislation in the United States to indicate the challenges that businesses face in developing risk-management strategies. Section 3 outlines the different phases of the risk-management process followed by a discussion of the role that insurance can play in the management of environmental risks (Section 4). Finally, Section 5 summarizes the challenges facing industrial firms in managing environmental exposures.

2. ENVIRONMENTAL LEGISLATION IN THE UNITED STATES

The seriousness with which a society views particular issues is best reflected in the tools it is willing to give its government to deal with those issues. Where the environment is concerned, extraordinary powers have been given to the US government—powers that can affect virtually every US business, not just those involved in pollution-causing activities.

The environment, in fact, is subject to more government direction about acceptable standards of behaviour than any other area of potential catastrophe. Additionally, that direction is frequently revised. While the definition of accep-Table behaviour is being created by regulation, the legal structure upon which liability is to be imposed is also being dramatically transformed through court interpretation. As a result, the process of identifying and evaluating potential environmental risks is a difficult task.

2.1. The Early Environmental Movement and the Environmental Protection Agency

The post-World War II years gave rise to a new political constituency in the US—one that was younger, more secure financially and better educated. As this generation grew in wealth, leisure time and knowledge of the world around them, they became more interested in the natural world and in the effects of development, particularly suburban sprawl, on that world. They were the first American generation to have the opportunity to concern themselves with 'quality of life' as well as with 'bread and butter' issues.[3] This generation brought concern for the environment into the public arena and supported legislation to protect the environment.

In response to the rise of this new constituency, Congress began to implement significant water and air quality statutes in the 1960s. In 1970, President Nixon created the Environmental Protection Agency (EPA) by Executive Order. For the first time in US history, a separate agency, reporting directly to the President of the United States, would focus on environmental protection. Initially, the EPA assumed the role of enforcer of environmental regulations. In the mid-1970s, however, the EPA recast its role, shifting from one of enforcer of rules for a pure environment to one of protector of public health by assuring a clean environment.[4]

2.2. Clean Water

The Clean Water Act (CWA) was the first significant piece of environmental regulation enacted in the US. Adopted in 1972, and amended a dozen times since then, CWA is designed to protect the quality of surface water primarily by implementing a permit system to govern the amount of contaminants that may be discharged into the nation's waterways. Businesses are required to comply with discharge limits based on the 'Best Practicable Control Technology Currently Available'. Basically, then, the purpose of this act is to keep water clean, and, if water has already been polluted, to give it a chance to become clean by reducing the amount of discharge. It is a technology-driven regulation based on an underlying assumption that pollution does not remain in water at toxic exposure levels indefinitely.

2.3. Clean Air

US air pollution control legislation dates as far back as 1955, but the most significant clean air legislation, the Clean Air Act, was enacted in 1977. Some of the findings that this act were based on include:

- the biggest part of the nation's population is located in rapidly expanding metropolitan areas that generally cross the boundary lines of local jurisdictions and even states;
- growth and amount of air pollution brought about by urbanization, industrial development and increasing use of motor vehicles, resulted in mounting dangers to the public health, agriculture and property;
- prevention and control of air pollution at its source is the primary responsibility of state and local government; and
- Federal financial assistance and leadership is essential for the development of cooperative Federal, state, regional and local programmes to prevent and control air pollution. In other words, ensuring clean air was a proper responsibility of the Federal government.

The 1977 Clean Air Act set air quality standards for specific types of pollutants based on scientific and technical criteria. Like the Clean Water Act, this environmental protection strategy is technology-driven, sets specific limits on amounts of discharge, requires permitting, and is geared to making air cleaner and keeping it clean. The assumption is also present that pollution does not stay in the air, but dissipates over time.[5]

2.4. Clean Soil

Environmental regulations concerning toxic substances in the soil are based on an entirely different set of assumptions and goals than are regulations concerning air- and water-polluting substances. First of all, soil retains pollution. To clean up the soil, the contaminants must be physically removed. Someone has to pay for that removal. Who is liable for that cost? Three major pieces of US regulation assign that liability.

Resource Conservation and Recovery Act (RCRA)

Enacted in 1976, RCRA was designed to protect the environment, conserve natural resources, and provide 'cradle to grave' legislation governing the handling of hazardous waste. Its provisions also prevented open dumping and facilitated the conversion of existing open dumps to facilities that pose no danger to the environment or to public health. The liability imposed by RCRA applies primarily to companies that deal with hazardous materials in the normal course of their business.

Comprehensive Environmental Response, Compensation and Liability Act (CERCLA)

Four years later, in 1980, the United States Congress passed this act to address the environmental problems they felt RCRA did not adequately address, specifically problems created by hazardous waste produced and abandoned in the past. CERCLA gives the government, through the EPA, authorization to undertake emergency cleanup measures if a threat from hazardous substances presents 'an imminent and substantial danger to the public health or welfare'.

CERCLA is often referred to, incorrectly, as 'Superfund'. Superfund is actually the name of a hazardous substance trust fund created under the legislation that enables the EPA to finance the immediate cleanup of abandoned hazardous waste dump sites where the liable parties are unable to pay the costs of cleanup or where they cannot be found.

CERCLA mandates a strong liability scheme that dictates that those responsible for environmental contamination will, to the extent possible, pay the costs of cleanup. The courts have interpreted CERCLA as imposing a system of broad liability of three types:

1. *Joint and several liability* Imposes liability without respect to proportioning liability among parties. If a business is liable for any portion of a contamination, it may have liability imposed for the full cost of the contamination

cleanup.
2. *Retroactive liability* Imposes on current owners of a property liability for all environmental cleanups now required, even for prior activities that may have been done by prior owners and which may have been perfectly legal at the time the activity was carried out.
3. *Strict liability* Imposes liability without requiring a showing of criminal intent or contribution. A business can be liable for a current environmental cleanup solely because contamination now exists at unacceptable levels, even if the current owner had always complied with prior standards of behaviour.

CERCLA specifies that four classes of people can be held liable for cleanup costs:

1. Current owners/operators of hazardous waste facilities.
2. Any person who formerly owned or operated a facility at the time of disposal of any hazardous substance.
3. Any person who arranged for disposal or treatment of a hazardous substance at any facility owned or operated by another person (a 'generator').
4. Any transporter of hazardous waste to a facility.

In addition, the US courts have interpreted CERCLA to include lenders on a property as liable parties for cleanup, if the lender could exercise control over environmental matters, whether or not such control was actually exercised.

The bottom line of CERCLA for every American business is this: *property owners are liable for all cleanup on their property, regardless of whether they created or contributed to the contamination.* Including CERCLA, some 200 Federal, state and local statutes impose this liability. In fact, a full 80 per cent of all environmental liability is imposed at the state and local level. It is virtually impossible for a business to avoid this liability.

Underground storage tanks (UST)
A 1986 EPA survey estimated that 18 to 35 per cent of the approximately 1.6 million underground storage tanks in the US were leaking. The agency also estimated that a leak of one gallon of gasoline can contaminate the water supply of a city of 50,000 people. Since one-half of the US population depends on groundwater for drinking water, regulations for these tanks were considered critical. Rules for tanks include requirements for leak detection or inventory control and tank testing; recordkeeping and reporting; corrective action; closure; and financial responsibility for corrective action and third party liability. New tank performance standards include requirements for design, construction, installation, release detection and compatibility.[6]

A complicating factor in the assessment of environmental risk is the fact that, often, public perception of an environmental risk may drive public policy or governmental activity as much as, or more so than actual harm. Liabilities for cancerphobia, imagined health effects without any scientific support, and 'NIMBY' (Not In My Back Yard) are all examples of perception intruding into risk analysis. The actual risk of non-environmental catastrophes can often be easily measured. In the environmental area, the risk-assessment process must not only evaluate the real harm, but also the perceived harm. Often the costs of the perceived harm are as expensive as the actual damage caused.

3. THE RISK-MANAGEMENT PROCESS

Risk management is the process of identifying and reducing the costs of risks. Effective risk management involves three steps: assessment, control and financing.[7] The interrelationship among all three must be carefully balanced. After exploring each of these stages I will suggest how insurance can play a role in risk management. After exploring each of these steps, I will suggest appropriate roles for insurance to play in the overall risk-management process. Let us explore each of these steps.

3.1. Assessment

In this step, risk managers seek to identify and evaluate specific risks associated with a business enterprise. Initially, they inventory potential sources of risk from *all* sectors of a business's activities. But risk managers will then begin to narrow their focus and attend more closely to the task of identifying risks that could have a potentially catastrophic impact on the business. Catastrophic events are defined as those that have a low probability of occurrence, but, if they occur, will have a highly adverse affect on the business's operation, both in terms of dollars and in public perception of that business. Some generic examples of these risks are damages from natural disasters, environmental and technological events such as the oil spill from *Exxon Valdez* and the release of toxic chemicals from the plant in Bhopal, India. Once these risks have been identified, they are evaluated in terms of their potential to impair the business. Evaluation methods include scenario testing ('What if?') and probabilistic risk analysis.

3.2. Control

In the second step of the risk-management process, risk managers focus on techniques that can be employed to 'control' identified risks by avoiding them altogether or mitigating their impact. A key consideration is the adoption of cost-effective loss-prevention or loss-control measures that can reduce risks that could affect the business.

3.3. Financing

Even after reasonable control efforts have been undertaken, there always remains a residual risk which needs to be financed. Three of the most common ways are through the budgeting process, adopting cost-containment strategies and purchasing insurance.

4. UTILIZING INSURANCE FOR MANAGING ENVIRONMENTAL RISKS

As a separately identifiable area of risk in the United States, environmental risk is of recent origin, dating back to the 1960s. As a result, environmental risk has proved to be the area with the most significant increase in exposure for US businesses during the past twenty years. Multiplying the EPA's estimated $25 million average site cleanup cost by the 1993 number of National Priority List (NPL) sites yields a $29 million cleanup estimate.[8] A 1991 University of Tennessee study gave an estimate between $105.5 billion and $301.5 billion,[9] and the US Congressional Budget Office gave a 1994 estimate between $106 billion and $462.9 billion,[10] to clean up all current and future, non-federal, NPL sites.

These numbers indicate that environmental liability will remain at the forefront of major concerns for business during the foreseeable future. Three unique aspects of environmental issues make them particularly troublesome for risk managers to assess, control and finance. These are:

1. the government plays the major role in establishing liability;
2. the perception of harm may have as serious a consequence as actual harm;
3. there are limited databases of information upon which to base risk-financing decisions.

Utilizing the techniques being employed by the insurance industry is highly valuable for the risk-management process. For insurance use to be an effective policy, there is a need to develop premiums based on risk-assessment techniques, to encourage firms to control their risks by encouraging loss-prevention measures and finance any losses should an accident occur. Like risk managers, insurers must assess, control and finance risks. For them, the task is to develop premium structures which will yield profitable results on exposures for which the insurance is developed. In order for insurance to assess, control and finance risks, however, the risks must be insurable.

4.1. Conditions of Insurability

Insurance is a mechanism to contractually shift risk. Insurance operates because, on the one hand, insurers are able to find safety in insuring a large number of risks, and on the other hand, insureds want and need protection from the loss fluctuations a single risk may have on them. Not every risk is insurable. In some situations, the amount of potential loss cannot be quantified or the coverage may violate laws or public policy. In many cases, a premium level that satisfies both the buyer and the seller cannot be reached.

The conditions of insurability are widely discussed in insurance textbooks, formalized in a book by Berliner (1982),[11] and applied to issues of environmental risk by Kunreuther (1987).[12]

Two fundamental problems arise when environmentally-related insurance concepts are tested against the basic criteria of insurability. First, the courts have required insurers to pay damages for losses insurers never intended to cover. This is a direct result of policy coverage interpretation problems, which have intensified on account of changing definitions of liability. Because of changing policy language interpretation, the determination of loss and loss limits has been arduous and the setting of rates extremely difficult.

The second fundamental problem is that many environmental problems lack the historical information necessary for traditional actuarial modelling. Statistically valid information regarding the probability of loss and magnitude of loss simply does not exist in the environmental arena. Companies, therefore, cannot calculate the cost or claims component of their product. Faced with these problems, most traditional insurers have chosen not to explore the environmental market.

In order for environmental risks to be insurable, two tasks must be completed. First of all, there is a need to specify the maximum possible loss as well as the frequency of losses of different magnitudes so that an appropriate premium structure can be constructed. Insurance companies offering conventional coverages use historical data as the basis for their insurance rates. Since most environmental risks are a result of governmental policy and have developed only recently, little historical loss data exists on these exposures and other methods of loss assessment must be found.

The second formidable task is to maintain the integrity of the policy language. Every insurance policy defines the contractual limits of coverage, establishes the maximum possible loss (MPL), and describes precisely what risks are insured. If the policy language is interpreted differently from that intended by the insurer, the original MPL may be drastically affected and the insurer has different exposure than anticipated, in an amount that the premium may not cover.

4.2. Assessing Environmental Risks

The role of science is critical to the assessment of environmental risk. Scientific models have been used by environmental insurance providers as replacements for historical standard actuarial models to define the maximum possible loss, average loss and the frequency of loss.

The scientific modelling process is based on a thorough examination of the insurance opportunity. Each risk characteristic is analysed in detail. The pressure points relating to randomness, causes of loss, limitations of loss and customer selection are uncovered. These are used to identify insurable situations that exist within the market. The key components of the scientific approach are:

1. The environmental risk must have a generally accepted scientific or engineering standard for assessing the environmental factors associated with the risk. Without a measurable baseline standard of behaviour that is accepted by all potential insureds, it is impossible for the insurer to generate enough uniformity for the formulation of appropriate insurance coverage and underwriting of insureds. The uniform standard can arise from government regulation, from industry, from financial institutions or from other areas of influence.
2. A well-defined protocol, incorporating the uniform engineering standard, based on sound scientific principles and backed by scientific data must be developed to reduce the risk. This requires the insurance company to develop close associations with members of the scientific world.
3. Underwriting standards must be developed based on the integration of the existing objective standard and the scientifically-based model.
4. Rates must be based on the scientific models, with pricing set to reflect the use of non-traditional models.
5. Underwriting must select insureds who conform to the scientific model. This step differs slightly from standard insurance underwriting criteria. Usually, underwriting selects insureds who match standard statistical norms.
6. Insureds must be closely monitored to ensure that their behaviour conforms to the prescribed standard.
7. The original model must be adjusted as additional scientific and statistical information becomes available over time.

Governing insureds' behaviour is essential to the development of any environmental insurance product. The insurance company, however, cannot be the party to impose the standard on the market. Generally, insureds are unwilling to both change behaviour to conform to a standard and purchase insurance for the same risk that the standard is addressing.

4.3. Controlling the Risk

One of the important ways that insurance can help control risks is by being linked to a performance standard. More specifically, if a firm does not meet a specific performance standard it will not be provided with coverage. For example, insurers will not provide contractors with coverage against liability to third parties for property damage and bodily injury as a result of a release of asbestos fibres, unless the contractor adhered to standards set by the Occupational Health and Safety Agency (OSHA).[13]

From a marketing standpoint, the performance standard must be widely accepted in the market as a precondition for the successful sale of the insurance coverage. If it is not accepted, the insurance will not sell. The market will assume that the adoption of a performance standard is sufficient to control its exposure. Since the performance standards for environmental coverages are often newly developed, it takes time for the standard to become routinely accepted.

The case of underground storage tanks illustrates this process. One effective methodology for early detection of leaks in underground storage tanks and hence controlling the risks of groundwater contamination, is the regular measurement of fluid levels in the tanks. An unexpected drop in fluid level indicates a leak. Monitoring fluid levels could be one performance standard for insurance coverage providing protection against leaks. Insurance that protects against the impact of a potential leak can be designed based on the monitoring. The insurance will not be marketable, however, if customers do not adopt reasonable fluid monitoring requirements.

4.4. Financing Risk Exposure

The basis of insurance depends upon an insurer being able to attract enough customers so that a risk can be spread among a large number of insureds. In specialty markets such as environmental insurance, the law of large numbers requires that a statistically significant number of insureds be included in the defined risk pool. Further, the creation of a product is of little value if it is not accepted by the market. The role that insurance can play in monitoring behaviour is limited by the number of insureds purchasing the insurance product. Marketing presents unique challenges in the environmental insurance arena.

Environmental insurance is purchased for other business reasons as frequently as it is for protection against the impact of an environmental incident. Sometimes the purchase of environmental insurance is mandatory. Government regulations regarding underground storage tanks, for example, require that owners demonstrate that they have the financial capacity to pay for potential cleanup from tank leakage. Insurance is one method to meet this requirement. In some states, insurance is the only method smaller owners of tanks can use to meet it.

In other instances, customers purchase environmental insurance in order to free the company to proceed with its core business activity, unimpeded by environmental risk. For example, a commercial property owner may be unable to lease commercial space because asbestos exists on the premises. The owner may rightfully have little concern about health risks arising from the asbestos, but he or she needs insurance for asbestos exposure to allay potential tenants' concerns and lease the property.

Similarly, an asbestos abatement contractor may *not* be concerned about the health impacts of an asbestos release during abatement activity. However, property owners will require insurance coverage for exposure as a prerequisite for starting the job. The insurance is purchased to meet short-term business reasons, not to provide protection against asbestos-related risks.

A securitized mortgage manager may purchase environmental insurance on properties in the portfolio in hopes of earning a higher rating on the securities, not because of environmental concerns. A real-estate developer saddled with a potentially contaminated property may be willing to pay for environmental insurance, even at a premium price, in order to sell a property the market perceives as environmentally tainted.

Finally, the purchase of environmental insurance may be driven by a business's low tolerance for risk. It will purchase insurance to assuage concerns about the impact of an environmental incident or discovery upon the financial viability of the business. If there is significant ambiguity as to whether an environmental risk will threaten a company's business, insurance is likely to be viewed as a valuable protective mechanism.

5. SUMMARY

The risk management of environmental exposures will be an increasing concern throughout the world. The process of assessment, control and financing of these exposures will be more complicated than the historical risks managed by industrial firms. New techniques in evaluating the risks must be employed which confront the changing nature of governmental concern. Governments will respond to society's decreasing tolerance for environmental impairment as a necessary cost for economic development. Insurance coupled with well-specified standards offers an opportunity to address this and other challenges associated with the risk-management process for environmental exposures. Asian businesses can learn from the US experience what types of policy tools they may utilize for managing environmental risks in both an equitable and efficient manner.

NOTES

1. Wilson 1991, p. vii.
2. Associated Press, 5 June 1994.
3. Landy et al. 1990, p. 22.
4. Ibid., p. 42.
5. Rothenberg and Telego 1991, pp. 5–10.
6. Ibid., pp. 151, 154.
7. For a further understanding of these concepts, refer to the work of H. Felix Kloman, and especially his publication 'Risk Management Reports: A monthly commentary on strategic risk management'.
8. US Environmental Protection Agency. *4th Quarter FY 1993 Superfund Management Report*, pp. I–1, I–2, I–6, V–4.
9. Colglazier et al. 1991, p. 65.
10. US Congressional Budget Office, *The Total Cost of Cleaning Up Nonfederal Superfund Sites*, 1994, p. 16.
11. Berliner 1982.
12. Kunreuther 1987, pp. 180–97.
13. Freeman and Kunreuther 1996.

REFERENCES

Associated Press (1994), 'Development push begets "black rain"', wire story, 5 June.
Berliner, Baruch (1982), *Limits of Insurability of Risks*, Englewood Cliffs, NJ: Prentice Hall.
Colglazier, E.W. , T. Cox and K. Davis (1991), *Estimating Resource Requirements for NPL Sites*, University of Tennessee, Waste Management Research and Education Institute.
Freeman, Paul and Howard Kunreuther (1996), 'The Role of Insurance and Regulations in Dealing with Environmental Risks', forthcoming in *Managerial and Decision Economics*.
Kloman, H. Felix (1974–1994), 'Risk Management reports: A monthly commentary on strategic risk management', Lyme, CT: Seawrack Press, Inc.
Kunreuther, Howard (1987), 'Problems and Issues of Environmental Liability Insurance', *The Geneva Papers on Risk and Insurance*, 12:180–97.
Landy, Marc K., Marc J. Roberts and Stephen R. Thomas (1990), *The Environmental Protection Agency: Asking The Wrong Questions*, New York: Oxford University Press.
Rothenberg, Eric B. and Dean Jeffery Telego (1991), *Environmental Risk Management: A Desk Reference*, Alexandria, VA: RTM Communications, Inc.
US Congressional Budget Office (1994), *The Total Cost of Cleaning Up Nonfederal Superfund Sites*, Washington, DC: US Government Printing Office.
US Environmental Protection Agency, (1993), *4th Quarter FY 1993 Superfund Management Report*, Washington, DC: US Government Printing Office, pp. I–1, I–2, I–6, V–4.
Wilson, Albert R. (1991), *Environmental Risk: Identification and Management*, Chelsea, MI: Lewis Publishers.

14. Pollution Control and the Challenge of Industrial Efficiency in Indonesia

Ismid Hadad

1. INTRODUCTION

Issues of 'sustainable development' have become increasingly important for Indonesia over the last decade. While Indonesia's past development performance has been remarkably successful in stimulating economic growth and reducing widespread poverty, however, the pace and pattern of that development have led to growing concern about the sustainable use of natural resources (land, forests, water and energy) and the social and economic costs of urban and industrial pollution.

If the country's past success story has been based primarily on natural resource intensive growth strategy of developing oil and gas, agriculture and rural development, the future of Indonesia's development will be fundamentally different from the past. It is a transition from a dependence on oil and agriculture to reliance on rapid industrialization based upon a development strategy that emphasizes the increasing efficiency and competitiveness of domestic manufacturing production, higher productivity and value-added for the vastly growing labour force. This industrialization process will have even greater implications for the environment and the sustainability of critical ecosystems throughout the country.

Indonesia's development strategy for the Second Long-Term Development Plan (1994 to 2019) will rely heavily on the growth of manufacturing industry for the creation of higher productivity jobs and non-oil export revenue. Growing urban congestion and industrial pollution in Indonesia's main urban centres, however, will erode the efficiency of public and private investments, reduce Indonesia's ability to attract foreign investment, and eventually lead to strong community resistance to industrial expansions, with serious implications for the growth rate of the economy as a whole. Increasing efficiency of the manufacturing industries is therefore required not only for improving the domestic environment, but also because it will be the main factor for Indonesia's exporting producers to have a competitive advantage in the international market which is increasingly dominated by 'the green consumers' demanding imported products with 'eco-labelling'.

The following discussion will focus on the issue of industrial efficiency and the challenge of pollution control in Indonesia in the above-mentioned context. It will start with the story of industrial growth and structural changes in the Indonesian economy, then the growing threat of urban and industrial pollution especially in Java where most development and people are concentrated, followed by discussion on environmental legislation and standards, government policies to control industrial pollution and industry's response to such policies and programmes.

2. GROWTH OF THE INDUSTRIAL SECTOR

The industrial sector of Indonesia has experienced rapid and sustained growth since 1985 stemming from effective deregulations and macroeconomic policies and industry's use of Indonesia's comparative advantages of reasonably priced labour, energy and raw materials. The pace and pattern of this economic growth, however, have brought with it several inherent problems of structural changes, and also the socioeconomic problems of equity and the environment.

Throughout the oil boom years of the 1970s and early 1980s, Indonesia relied heavily on public investment to stimulate growth and employment, with oil providing the necessary fiscal revenues and foreign exchange earnings to support a relatively inward-looking growth strategy. The private sector, including foreign investment, was highly regulated and the incentive structure was oriented towards supplying the domestic market through an import substitution strategy. During the 1970s the economy grew at nearly 8 per cent per annum, and government revenues increased dramatically because of the rising world oil market price; however, this pattern of development resulted also in a 'high-cost' and globally uncompetitive economy.

The sharp drops in oil prices in the 1980s and associated changes in the economy altered the economic environment for Indonesia. The weakening oil market in 1982, coupled with a worldwide recession, and the decline in the prices of several important primary commodity exports caused serious problems in the Indonesian economy. In 1986, Indonesia suffered a second set of external shocks when oil prices fell by almost one-half and non-oil commodity prices weakened further and Indonesia's debt service payment rose sharply. These events have driven the government of Indonesia to adopt more austere macroeconomic policies and stabilization programmes.

The government also changed its 'import substitution' policy into 'export-oriented' strategy and embarked upon a major programme to restructure the economy so as to reduce the dependence on oil and gas as a source of foreign exchange and budget revenues. These new economic reforms and deregulation policies adopted since 1985 are meant to change the sources of growth from oil and gas to non-oil manufacturing industries, from domestic to international markets, through a more outward-looking, private-sector-oriented development strategy.

As a result of these economic policy reforms, despite the external shocks, which together accounted for 8–9 per cent of GDP, Indonesia still managed to achieve an average growth rate 5.4 per cent per annum during the 1980s, with the non-oil export sector leading the way. Non-oil exports between 1986 and 1989 have doubled, exceeding the value of oil-related exports for the first time since 1973. In 1982 oil accounted for about 70 per cent of government revenues and 72 per cent of total exports; by 1992 oil accounted for only 36 per cent of government revenues and 30 per cent of total exports. These structural adjustments in the Indonesian economy greatly improved the competitiveness of domestic industry, with manufactured goods now becoming the fastest growing non-oil export, increasing at an average of 27 per cent a year for the past five years.

3. THE GROWING THREAT OF URBAN AND INDUSTRIAL POLLUTION

The industrial pollution issues faced by Indonesia are directly related to the pace and pattern of past industrial sector growth, and likely future trends. Although the potential level of industrial pollution rises with industrial growth, the characteristics of the pollution load depend on the sectoral composition of manufacturing output: the costs and consequences of this pollution depend on the concentration and location of industrial production. More highly concentrated industrialization imposes a greater burden on local ecosystems, and higher levels of pollution in urban areas increase human exposure and the corresponding health costs.

It is important to begin the assessment of pollution from industrial sources, therefore, with a review of basic trends in the manufacturing sector itself. The sectoral composition of industrial development in Indonesia has been based on manufacturing census data for the period 1975–89, and projected into the future based on an analysis of the pattern of industrialized and industrializing countries.

During the 1970s and 1980s, Indonesian manufacturing output doubled in volume every six to seven years. Thus, by 1990, manufacturing value-added was approximately eight times its 1970 level in real terms. According to World Bank estimates, it is likely to expand another 13-fold by the year 2020. This rate of growth exceeds that of the economy as a whole. Manufacturing, which contributed only about 13 per cent of total GDP growth in the 1970s, and 23 per cent in the 1980s, is expected to contribute more than 33 per cent in the 1990s and nearly 45 per cent in the following decade. Industrial growth is expected to be faster in the outer islands than on Java, and the off-Java share of production is projected to increase from 25 per cent in 1990 to about 35 per cent by 2020.

The continued growth in manufacturing output will be accompanied by a gradual shift in sectoral composition. For the purpose of analysing pollution from industrial sources, it is useful to make a distinction between the materials-processing sectors, and those primarily engaged in assembly. The pollution characteristics of these two broadly defined categories differ significantly, with processing sectors generally being more pollution-intensive.

According to some projections, the share of basic processing industries in total industrial output will fall from today's figure of 72 per cent to about 65 per cent in 2010 and 60 per cent in 2020. The pattern of structural change, however, will be quite different between Java and the outer islands. On Java, assembly industries will grow faster than the processing sectors, and may overtake processing in value of total output by the year 2020. In contrast, processing industries off-Java are projected to grow almost as fast as the assembly sectors. From an initial share of 85 per cent in 1980, they are still expected to account for about 80 per cent of off-Java industrial output by the year 2010. The expected concentration of new assembly industries on Java would be consistent with a number of factors, including the need for a more highly-trained, factory-experienced labour force, and greater availability and reliability of supportive infrastructure.

The different sectoral composition of industrial growth on Java compared to the outer islands is reflected in the urban/rural distribution of production. The rapid expansion of assembly operations on Java has led to an increasing concentration in and around Java's main urban centres, in part because many of these industries require a factory-trained labour force which is more readily available in urban areas. In the early 1970s, for example, about 55 per cent of industry on Java was located in urban areas. Since then, the urban share has risen to 60 per cent. Four cities alone (Jakarta, Surabaya, Bandung and Semarang) account for 36 per cent of Java's—and 27 per cent of Indonesia's—total industrial output. The urban concentration of industry on Java is likely to intensify. The urban share of industrial production on Java rising to more than 70 per cent by 2010.

Off-Java, the projections indicate that the urban share of production is likely to fall continuously from processing industries in the outer islands, most of which need to be close to the supply of the relevant commodities, rather than urban areas.

4. THE NATURE OF INDUSTRIAL POLLUTION

Indonesia's recent development has been led by rapid growth of manufacturing output. However, much of the industrial expansion has taken place without due regard to the environment and has led to serious environmental degradation, particularly in Java where 75 per cent of industry is located. As described below, this degradation has become increasingly evident in the form of contaminated water, air and land, adverse health impacts, and damage to both 'downstream' activities, and coastal and marine ecosystems. In broad terms, these impacts can be traced back to industrial pollutants of three major types: traditional water pollutants (e.g., biochemical oxygen demand (BOD) and suspended solids); traditional air pollutants (e.g., particulate, sulphur and nitrogen oxides, and carbon monoxide), and toxic and hazardous waste (e.g., bioaccumulative metals).

4.1. Water Quality and Pollutants

Water is a critical element in the environment. By the year 2000 it is projected that there will be a demand for about 150 billion cubic metres per year, the majority (61 per cent) of which will come from rivers. The overall demand for water in Java will increase by 52 per cent between 1990 and 2000, but water consumption in industries will increase by more than 75 per cent. Most people use water directly from natural sources which are susceptible to human, industrial and agricultural waste. Available data show that the quality of fresh and surface water is deteriorating in the more densely populated regions and industrial areas. Eight major rivers in Java's north coast are significantly polluted. The biochemical oxygen demand (BOD) is increasing 2.7 mg/litre per year in the Citarum river of West Java, while in the Banjir Canal, which provides drinking water for Jakarta, the BOD is increasing by 1.06 mg/l per year while the heavy metal content is also growing. Major pollutants or contaminants include organics, inorganic solids, floating materials and micro-organisms coming from industrial, domestic and agricultural waste sources.

Results of recent monitoring of the discharge of large industries reveal that industrial pollution constitutes from 25 per cent to 50 per cent of the total pollution load in different rivers in Java. Monitoring results vary widely, but a 1989 survey in Surabaya estimated that industrial effluents accounted for 38 tons per day (tpd) of BOD in the Brantas River, out of a total load of 120 tpd. Monitoring in the Jabotabek area indicates that industries account for 84 tpd of BOD out of a total of 171 tpd.

Groundwater provides a significant amount of the total water supply in many areas of the country. About 60 per cent of water for domestic uses in rural areas is from wells; and about 30 to 80 per cent of the domestic water supplies for urban households in Java comes from groundwater. Although groundwater is of major importance as a water supply source, however, little attention has been given to the monitoring and protection of groundwater quality. So the total amount of groundwater pollution attributable to industrial discharges is also unknown. However, the presence of typical industrial effluents, such as phenol, detergents and nitrate has been observed in shallow aquifers in the Jabotabek area. Pollution of groundwater is also caused by mismanagement in the storage of hazardous material, such as the reported incident involving a fertilizer firm in Lumajang, East Java. In this case, the chemicals of the fertilizer plant, which were stored carelessly, infused the soil and polluted the surrounding wells. Other incidents where groundwater on Java is no longer potable because of industrial wastes are anecdotal, but the number of cases reported seems to be rising.

4.2. Air Pollution

Vehicle emissions constitute the most important source of air pollution in urban areas, but the industrial sector is also a major contributor. Annual average concentrations of total suspended particulate (TSP, dust) in three locations of Jakarta are between 200 and 400 microgram/m^3, which is up to 4.4 times the newly proposed annual standard of 90 microgram/m^3. Monitoring of sulphur dioxide (SO_2) and nitrogen dioxide (NO_2) has shown very high 24-hour concentrations. Recent emission inventories prepared by BAPEDAL indicate that in Jakarta, industrial sector emissions account for about 15 per cent of total SPM, 16 per cent of NO_x and 63 per cent of SO_x loading. In Surabaya, the industrial sector shares are about 28 per cent, 43 per cent and 88 per cent, respectively. As noted below, the health costs of air pollution are already high in Jakarta and probably in other large cities. In the absence of effective measures to reduce such emissions from industry and other sources, these costs will rise substantially in the coming years.

4.3. Hazardous and Toxic Wastes

Hazardous wastes are defined as having one or more of the following characteristics: flammability, corrosivity, reactivity or capability to produce a hazardous leachate. Toxic wastes cause poisoning of humans and the environment, leading to death or serious illness. A further example is the 'land-filling' of thousands of tons per year of plastic waste from paper factories and other industries. Another example is depositing of sludge containing a high content of toxic metals. These non-biodegradable wastes are today being spread out on agricultural land and rivers. Most of Java's rivers undoubtedly contain a variety of hazardous and toxic substances, but the precise levels are difficult to establish. The monitoring that is carried out on a regular basis, for example, does not measure concentrations of mercury, copper or chromium.

What is evident is that substantial quantities of toxic and hazardous waste are now increasingly deposited in uncontrolled landfills, dumped in rivers along with other industrial wastes, and in some cases, spread to agricultural areas by irrigation water and wind. The discovery in the early 1980s of significant mercury contamination in sediments and marine biota of Jakarta Bay first brought the issue to public attention. Overall, while little reliable information is available, it is clear that a continuation of present practices can only mean that the problems will worsen.

A recent study of hazardous waste estimated that about 2.2 million tons per year of such waste are currently being generated in West Java and DEI Jakarta. Toxic materials represent a particularly dangerous threat to human health, most especially the bio-accumulative metals that may build up in the sediments of inland and coastal waterways, and the food chain. These can be prohibitively expensive to remove, which places a very high premium on minimizing their use in production processes wherever possible and ensuring proper treatment of contaminated waste wherever that is not possible.

4.4. The Concentration of Industrial Pollution

The costs and risks of industrial pollution are heightened by the fact that they are concentrated in urban areas and in those provinces with the highest population densities. While Java's share in the total load of traditional water and air pollutants, for example, will decline from 60 per cent to under 45 per cent between 1990 and 2020, in absolute terms these pollutants will expand about eightfold from the current relatively high levels. Java's share of toxic pollutants will remain roughly constant—about two-thirds of the total, and more than 75 per cent of the bio-accumulative metals—and 85 per cent of these will be concentrated in its urban centres. While the share of industrial pollution in urban areas will decline from 70 per cent today to 60 per cent in 2020, the absolute level of industrial pollutants in Indonesia's cities will expand nearly tenfold from their current levels.

5. ENVIRONMENTAL LEGISLATION, STRUCTURE AND POLICIES

Indonesia is among the first of the few Asian countries which have made serious efforts to adopt national policies and set up institutions to cope with the growing pollution and environmental problems. After the Stockholm Conference on Human Settlement in 1972, a national environmental policy was first formulated in the 1973 Guidelines of State Policies (GBHN 1973), and in 1978 the appointment of a Minister of State for the Environment and Development Supervision in the Cabinet, followed by the establishment of local Bureaux of Population and the Environment (BKLH) at the provincial and district levels of regional government in 1980.

But the really important breakthrough in the overall management of the environment in Indonesia was in fact made in 1982 with the promulgation of the Act of the Republic of Indonesia No. 4 of 1982 concerning the Basic Provisions for the Management of Living Environment. This environmental legislation (EMA 4/1982) strongly advocates the development approach of Indonesia to be based upon sustainable use of natural resources and environmental considerations; recognizing the rights and important roles of the NGOs and local communities in pursuing sustainable growth and the well-being of present and future generations.

Thus on the basis of EMA 4/1982 and a series of other legislation, government regulations and development policies have been adopted to include 'sustainable environment' and 'polluter pays' principles built into the provision of its articles and implementing guidelines: Government Regulation No. 29 year 1986 was issued to regulate the process of environmental impact assessment (EIA) for every development project; Government Regulation No. 20 year 1990 was issued to regulate water pollution control; and so on.

The Office of the State Minister for Population and the Environment which was created in 1978, has a mandate to make policy and conduct national coordination on environmental issues. The operational authority for implementing those environmental policies, however, is not in the hands of the Environment Ministry but rests with the sectoral ministries at the central government level, and with the Governors at the regional/provincial government levels.

In order to counter the increasing pressures of development on the environment, the government of Indonesia in 1990 established the Environmental Impact Management Agency (BAPEDAL) with the goal of 'better environment through compliance'. In brief, BAPEDAL's primary task and mandate are to prevent environmental degradation, manage environmental impacts and restore environmental quality. At the same time, BAPEDAL's task also includes building institutions and capacity for Indonesia's environmental management implementation at the central and regional levels, and to develop people's awareness and public participation in environmental impact management.

The Head of BAPEDAL is concurrently the Minister of State for the Environment, who has two deputies, one responsible for the Environmental Pollution Control Division and the other for the Environmental Development Division. The establishment of the BAPEDAL Central Office will soon be followed by the creation of BAPEDAL regional offices at the provincial and perhaps later at the district levels, so that implementation of policies and law enforcement will be assured nationwide.

Faced with the complex problems and gigantic tasks of pollution control against a background of relatively low public awareness and weak institutional capacity, BAPEDAL cannot simply copy the environmental regulatory systems used in Western countries. Therefore BAPEDAL is utilizing various methods and instruments, termed 'mixed policy tools', to achieve its goals. The regulatory system is continuing and is developing rapidly. But BAPEDAL is new and understaffed while government capacity for environmental law enforcement is still weak. Licensing and permit systems are only recently being developed. Market-based instruments and other incentive/disincentive systems are in fact much needed, but they are still at a very early stage of development.

And so the Ministry of Environment and BAPEDAL have been and still are embarking on public awareness campaigns by pursuing popular action-oriented programmes related to environmental control, which could attract voluntary participation of other government agencies for compliance through a more active involvement of the mass media, NGOs and local communities. In this case BAPEDAL has successfully implemented PROKASIH (Clean Rivers Programme) and ADIPURA (Clean Cities Programme) and has formulated the LANGIT BIRU (Blue Sky Programme). These programmes not only encourage participatory compliance but significantly increase public, local government and corporate environmental awareness.

The previously cumbersome process of AMDAL (environmental impact assessment/EIA) is now streamlined and made more effective for BAPEDAL to enforce, following the revisions in Government Regulation No. 51 year 1993 on AMDAL. Programmes to encourage developers to use environmental audits are now starting. BAPEDAL has submitted a proposal to UNEP to establish a National Cleaner Production Centre in Indonesia and is embarking on programmes to encourage industry to use clean production technologies. In short, the appropriate mix of policy tools for managing environmental and pollution problems in Indonesia is between a Westernized litigious/punitive process and a more coercive approach, such as used in Japan. These policy and management tools as currently applied by BAPEDAL include administrative sanctions, criminal/court sanctions; consultation, mediation and alternative dispute resolution; incentive and market-based instruments; public education, disclosure and consumer pressures; and self-regulation.

6. ENVIRONMENTAL STANDARDS AND PERMIT SYSTEMS

In order to evaluate environmental performance it is necessary to establish a clear criteria and standard to measure compliance by project developers and users. The government of Indonesia, through the State Ministry of Population and the Environment (and later BAPEDAL), issued several Ministerial decrees for setting environmental standards and permit systems to assess environmental performance in some sectors. This standard system is important, because the cost of pollution control depends strongly on the standard. If the standard is high or tightened, the cost will normally increase exponentially.

6.1. Ambient Environmental Standards

Water pollution control has the highest priority for environmental management, and so water pollution is the only parameter which is quantitatively regulated in Indonesia today. Through Government Regulation No. 20 of 1990 on Water Pollution Control, the government adopted receiving-water standards which apply to four categories of receiving water. Category A is water quality considered adequate for domestic drinking water and most other uses including the biota. Category B water would require treatment prior to domestic use, but would be adequate for industrial and irrigation purposes. Category D water would be useful for irrigation of salt-tolerant crops, and for some industrial uses. The regulation requires that the Governors categorize surface waters according to uses, thereby establishing ambient standards for these waters. Most rivers in the PROKASIH programme have now been categorized according this regulation, but other rivers have not.

The ambient standards now serve two purposes, target levels for water quality, and an interpretation of pollution for enforcement such as for the two recently held court cases concerning pollution of water. However, ambient standards would be much more effective if implemented with a wastewater discharge permit system.

6.2. Industrial Effluent Standards

Through Ministerial Decree No. KEP–03/MenKLH/11/1991 in February 1991, the Minister of the Environment stipulated effluent quality standards for existing operations in 14 industrial sectors. These industries include: caustic soda, metal plating, leather tanning, oil refining, palm oil, pulp and paper, rubber, sugar, tapioca, textiles, urea fertilizer, ethanol, monosodiumglutamate and plywood.

The standards for pollution load are 'never-to-be-exceeded' values. The standards deal with the maximum concentration of controlled parameters, the maximum waste flow rate, and the maximum pollution load. The industry is required to sample and analyse the effluent once a month and submit a report to the relevant authorities. Effluent sampling and testing are to be done by a laboratory appointed by the Governor at least once a month at the expense of the discharger. These results are to be sent to the 'Agency responsible for environmental monitoring' which one must assume is BAPEDAL or regional BAPEDALs. If all parameters are to be monitored, this may be very costly. Water flows will be monitored daily.

The Decree states that effluent standards for other categories of industries can be stipulated (in the future). The Governor can also stipulate a stricter standard than contained in the Decree. The Decree only applies to existing (ongoing) activities (industries), but another draft Decree is being prepared by BAPEDAL that would apply effluent standards stricter than the above standards to new industries, and to both existing and new industries in 1995. The industrial effluent standards are found to be adequate for the moment and the plan for further standards development is sensible. However, further assistance in the development of revised standards for new or expanded projects under current industrial and environmental requirements may be needed.

6.3. Air Quality Standards

Ministerial Decree No. KEP–02/1988 prescribes standards for ambient concentrations of nine air pollutants (air quality standards). While some standards are equal (TSP, HC) to World Bank Environmental Guidelines, some are different and difficult to compare because of different methods of measurement. The air pollutants of major concern to the industries, such as TSP, SO_2, NO_x, however, are comparable.

The Decree KEP–02/1988 also lists emission standards (standards for discharge to the atmosphere) for 19 pollutants. The standards are given for three control categories: strict, medium and light. The Ministry and BAPEDAL themselves acknowledge that the KEP–02/1988 standards are outdated and generally considered too high, therefore it needs to be revised. But presently this review on air quality standards has low priority.

6.4. Discharge License/Agreements

Licences (permits) for waste discharge have not been issued to individual dischargers. Instead, such as in PROKASIH areas, written agreements concerning the discharge quality/quantity have been reached between the discharger and government. Some of these agreements are due to expire. While some dischargers attempted or succeeded in meeting the terms of the agreements, others did not. Agreements not met are being followed with warnings from Governors; extension of the time limits; and finally, court action.

Although agreements have provided some measure of interim control, they should not be considered to be a satisfactory substitute for a discharge permit, which would carry effluent standard stipulations to individual dischargers and thus allow for timely enforcement actions against individual dischargers who have violated permit terms.

6.5. Monitoring and Resource Inventories

Except for PROKASIH areas, monitoring for water quality has been mostly spontaneous with little attention given to programmes for acquisition of long-term data on quality trends in fresh water, marine water and groundwater. Monitoring programmes and data collected by individual government agencies for their own programme purposes have not been coordinated with other agencies. Data quality is largely unacceptable for making environmental management decisions. Monitoring information is particularly scant in the areas of groundwater and seawater quality.

Standardized air monitoring has occurred, as described earlier, in Jakarta and at locations included in the Ministry of Communications network. However, these data on air quality do not include some parameters that are important to public health. Additional stations are needed in key airsheds along with additional monitoring parameters and sampling frequency. Also, air sampling and analytical procedures should be standardized with quality assurance and control built into the sampling programme.

6.6. Laboratory Resources

Although there is a modest array of government and private laboratories throughout most of the country, many are not equipped to serve the emerging BAPEDAL pollution control programmes. Laboratory capability for air and water analyses needs significant improvement. For water, the PROKASIH programs found that laboratory results are often inconsistent, inaccurate and inconclusive.

Necessary equipment is not always present, and there is a continuing problem with equipment maintenance, i.e. investigation indicates substantive 'downtime' for key equipment in poor shape, and after-sales service by suppliers is cited as a problem in maintaining equipment.

Many of the laboratory deficiencies can be overcome by the construction/operation of a central reference laboratory recently built by BAPEDAL as a modern complex Environmental Management Centre (EMC) in the Serpong area near Jakarta, with technical assistance from the OECF fund of the Japanese government.

The laboratory situation highlights the need for: (a) central guidance concerning standardized procedures for sample transport, preparation, analyses and reporting, and (b) an accreditation (certification) programme to certify laboratories which produce acceptable analytical results.

7. THE STATE OF INDUSTRIAL POLLUTION IN SEVEN SUBSECTORS

A study in 1991 commissioned by the World Bank in cooperation with the Indonesian Ministry of Industry and State Ministry for Population and the Environment provided an overview of the Indonesian industrial sector, assessed briefly the environmental impact from industry and estimated the potential financial requirements if seven selected industrial subsectors should comply with Indonesian environmental standards.

The seven polluting industrial subsectors surveyed in 1991 were: pulp and paper, textile, leather-tanning, chemicals, cement, food and metal industries. The data collection study was then continued with an investment study in 1992 to review the requirements in four industrial subsectors which have been identified as high priority because of the magnitude and/or the toxicity of their pollution, i.e. the cement industry, the iron and steel industry, the leather-tanning industry, and the pulp and paper industry.

The following is a brief description of the seven industrial subsectors and will serve to illustrate the characteristics of pollutant load and its magnitude relative to permissible load, the production process technology and machinery currently used by those industries, and the necessary capital investment required to reduce the pollution load to an acceptable level.

7.1. Characteristics of Pollutant Load

The impact of an industrial enterprise on the environment is often quite complex. Different pollutants are discharged to water, air or soil in various quantities. Some pollutants are toxic, while others deplete the oxygen level in the river, add to the dust pollution in the area or contribute to the acidification of the rainfall in the region. The study identified one or a few pollutants which are characteristic to the industrial subsector and which may be used for ranking procedure. Table 14.1 lists the characteristic pollutant(s) used in the ranking. The table also lists other pollutants which are important in an environmental assessment of the subsector. Generation of solid or hazardous waste was not selected as a characteristic parameter, partly because permissible standards are not available, and partly because data collected does not allow ranking on that basis. Noise has also not been selected for the same reason: there were no available standards.

The total quantity of pollution discharged from the industrial subsectors is very complex. For the purpose of ranking the total discharge to the environment (water or air) of the characteristic pollutant(s) has been estimated in Table 14.2. The table lists the estimated total load quantity $L1$ of the characteristic pollutants discharged to the environment. The unit is tons per year. The table further lists the permissible discharge $L2$ for each subsector, which was estimated on the assumption that the enterprises comply with the relevant standards for discharge of wastewater or emission of air pollution to the atmosphere. The difference $(L1 - L2)$ is the total quantity which must be removed through industrial efficiency and pollution-abatement measures at the individual enterprises. The last column in Table 14.2 lists the percentage quantity $100 (L1/L2)$, which is an indication of the present load of pollution relative to the permissible load. The total load and the relative load are used in the ranking of the subsectors.

Table 14.1   Characteristic pollutants and other typical pollution parameters in seven industrial subsectors

	Subsector	Recipient	Characteristic Pollutant	Other Typical Pollutants
A	Pulp and Paper	Water	BOD	TSS Metals, AOX
		Air		SO_2 Dust, Noise,
		Soil		Waste, Metals
B	Textiles	Water	BOD	COD, TSS, Cr
		Air		SO_2, Dust, Noise
		Soil		Waste, Metals
C	Leather Tanning	Water	BOD, Cr*	Sulphide,
		Air		Odour, VOC,
		Soil		Waste, Cr
D	Chemical etc.	Water	NA	BOD, COD, etc.
		Air	NA	VOC, SO_2, etc.
	Chlor-Alkali	Soil	NA	Waste
	Alcohol	Water	Hg*	
		Water	BOD	
E	Cement	Water		TSS
		Air	TSP	SO_2, NO_x, Noise
		Soil		Waste
F	Food	Water	BOD	TSS, SO_2
		Air		Dust, Odour, Noise
		Soil		Waste
G	Metal	Water	Metals*	CN, Waste Oil
		Air	TSP	SO_2, NO_x, VOC
	Batteries	Soil		Waste, Metal
		Air	Pb*	

Key:
BOD   Biological Oxygen Demand (in water)
AOX   Absorbable Organic Halogenes
TSS   Total Suspended Solid (in water)
TSP   Total Suspended Particulates (dust, in air)
Metals Heavy metals (Cu, Cr, Ni, Cd etc.)
Cr   Chromium
Hg   Mercury
Pb   Lead
SO_2 Sulphur Dioxide (in air)
NO_x Nitrogen Oxides (in air)
VOC   Volatile Organic Compounds
*   Hazardous and toxic pollutants
NA   Not applicable
CN   Cyanide

Table 14.2 Estimated annual characteristic pollution load in seven industrial subsectors in Indonesia

Industrial Subsector	Recipient	Charac-teristic Pollutant	Total Load L1 tons/year	Permissible Load L1 tons/year	Load Reduction L1 – L2 tons/year	Relative Load 100 L1/L2 %
A Pulp and Paper	Water	BOD	25,200	9,000	16,200	280
B Textiles	Water	BOD	5,500	1,200	4,300	460
C Leather	Water	BOD	7,000	1,300	5,700	540
Tanning	Water	Cr*	660	150	510	440
D Chemical-Chlor-Alkali	Water	Hg*	6	0.08	5.92	7,500
Chemical-Alcohol	Water	BOD	48,600	1,620	46,980	3,000
E Cement	Air	TSP	164,000	42,000	122,000	134
F Food	Water	BOD	133,000	8,000	125,000	1,660
G Metal	Air	TSP	35,000	3,700	31,300	950
Water	Metal*	2,000	100	1,900	2,000	
Lead Smelting	Air	Pb*	12,000	1,000	11,000	1,200

Key: * Hazardous and toxic pollutants.

7.2. Location

The typical location of the enterprises in the seven industrial subsectors is mainly in the urban and residential areas, mostly in the densely populated island of Java, and much of it is surrounded by houses—planned or illegal. So many industries discharge pollutants which can affect residential communities, horticultural or agricultural crops (e.g. chromium in wastewater, airborne mercury or lead).The majority of the establishments are medium and large enterprises, and only in two subsectors are small-scale industries clustered in residential urban and rural areas. For example, pulp and paper, chemical and cement industries are medium- and large-scale enterprises located mainly in industrial areas, some of which are located next to urban residential areas. Textile industries are also medium and large enterprises located in industrial areas as well as in residential rural and urban areas. Some leather-tanning industries are medium-scale enterprises located in industrial areas, but many of the smaller-scale industries are clustered in urban/rural areas. The majority of medium and small food-processing industries are dispersed in urban areas.

7.3. Technology

An assessment of the average age profile of the technology and the machinery used in the enterprises of the seven subsectors gives a rough indication about old equipment that has probably been written off financially, but is technically still in full operation, and about the old and outdated equipment and its relation to a high level of pollution in that area. The following is an overview of factories and their technology in the seven industrial subsectors surveyed, and its relation to both the level and nature of pollution divided into three age categories:

- *Very old technology* (more than 20–30 years old). These include some factories in the food, fermentation, textile, tannery and cement subsectors. The equipment is outdated, and poorly maintained. The pollution is often extreme in quantity, but mostly non-toxic (wastewater with high BOD, dust pollution, etc.). Some factories in the metal subsector emit toxic metal fumes and SO_2 and some old tanneries discharge toxic chromium.
- *Medium-age technology* (5–20 years). These include the majority of industries from *all* sectors. The equipment is often outdated, not well maintained and the pollution normally exceeds standards. The pollutants include non-hazardous substances such as BOD, suspended solids in wastewater and dust in the air, but they include also a wide variety of toxic and hazardous substances such as mercury, chromium, lead, chlorinated organics, and so on.
- *Modern technology* (less than 5 years). These include a number of well-designed plants, e.g. in the chemical subsector, which are usually up to international standards. The pollutants are complex chemical substances, often hazardous, toxic or carcinogenic. The pollution level, is however, usually below standards. New factories are of course subject to AMDAL or EIS approval and therefore are supposed to comply with the Indonesian environmental standards.

7.4. Investment Requirement

In order to reduce the pollution from the seven industrial subsectors to the permissible levels, it is considered necessary to make investments in industrial efficiency and pollution abatement. The estimated investments directly related to reduction of the characteristic pollutants are summarized in Table 14.3, together with the pollution load L1–L2 to be removed. The table also shows the cost effectiveness measured in tons of characteristic pollution removed per million US dollars over an assumed lifetime of 10 years of all new investments.

Table 14.3   Estimated IEPA investments in seven industrial subsectors in Indonesia

	Industrial Subsector	Recipient	Characteristic Pollutant	Load Reduction (L1 – L2) tons/year	Investment A Million $US	Cost Effectiveness C t/mill.$US
A	Pulp and Paper	Water	BOD	16,200	9	18,000
B	Textiles	Water	BOD	4,300	57	750
C	Leather	Water	BOD	5,700	29	2,000
	Tanning	Water	Cr*	510	7.5	680
D	Chemical-Chlor-Alkali	Water	Hg*	5.92	55	1.1
	Alcohol	Water	BOD	46,980	6.4	73,400
E	Cement	Air	TSP	122,000	220	5,600
F	Food	Water	BOD	125,000	226	5,500
G	Metal	Air	TSP	31,300	27	11,600
		Water	Metal*	1,900	10	1,900
	Lead Smelting	Air	Pb*	11,000	8	13,800

Key: *Hazardous and toxic pollutants.
Note: Assuming a ten-year lifetime of all new investments.

8. STRATEGY OF CONTROLLING INDUSTRIAL POLLUTION

As Indonesia moves into its Second Long-Term (25 years) Development Plan, it is well on its way to newly industrialized country (NIC) status. Future development of Indonesia will bring less reliance on petroleum and agriculture, and more on manufacturing and industrialization. Although government's role will still be there providing the roadmap, recent foreign investment policies emphasize that the private sector will be the 'engine of growth'. Thus industrial growth and the urbanization process are an economic necessity for national progress, however, they are also affecting the health of the millions, especially the poor who are unable to avoid the dangers of industrial pollution. Rapid industrial development is also putting severe pressures on Indonesia's abundant but finite natural resources. With the past pattern of development and current inefficiencies and rates of ecosystem degradation, development sustainability becomes questionable.

The most critical environmental issues of industrial sector growth involve the rapidly increasing social and economic costs of industrial waste, especially in urban areas where most of industry is located. These costs could, in fact, represent the potential benefits to Indonesia in terms of industrial pollution control. However, to obtain these benefits, it will be necessary for the government to influence the behaviour of polluting firms who, according to the 'polluter pays' principle, should bear the costs of pollution control and clean-up.

And here lies the dilemma. Industrial pollution itself is a recent phenomenon not only for Indonesia, but even for Western industrialized countries. Their response to growing industrial pollution has followed a fairly common pattern of regulatory measures. On the other hand, government mandate for pollution control remains diffused, while political support is generally weak and, in the absence of enforcement, there is relatively little response from the private sector. Serious attention to environmental protection has come only after a catastrophic event galvanized government action, and popular support—often based on the fear of toxic and hazardous waste—was finally able to overcome the resistance of the business community and the political bias in favour of jobs and economic growth. A similar pattern of development seems to be happening in Indonesia, except that while the constraints for enforcing regulations are greater, the opportunities for making a short-cut strategy of improving the policy and incentives framework for both efficient industrial growth *and* environmental improvement are equally great, perhaps even greater.

From the above-mentioned studies of seven industrial subsectors in Indonesia it is clear that the existence and growth of those polluting industries have been the product of past development strategy in the pre-environmental era of Indonesia. They used old equipment and outdated technology which have no waste treatment facilities, and many plants operated with little or no attention paid to water or air pollution control and noise abatement. The regulatory standards and policies of the government have also focused almost exclusively on 'end-of-pipe' treatment and abatement investments that add nothing of value to the production process. As a result of this regulatory approach of the West focusing primarily on 'end-of-pipe' pollution abatement, the prospects for preventing pollution or significantly reducing waste at the source remain largely untapped. The industries are inefficient ecologically, but also economically they become even more inefficient and less competitive.

Over the past two years the rate of increase in the value of Indonesia's exports and of foreign investment in manufacturing have both levelled off. Although the Asia–Pacific economy continues to grow rapidly, the competition among low-income Asian countries to satisfy the markets is becoming more intense. Consumers of personal and business products throughout the world are increasingly linking their buying to 'Green technologies'. Even Indonesian consumers are beginning to be aware of environmental and Green issues, and some are insisting on a cleaner and healthier environment.

All of the above developments necessitate the need for Indonesia to apply a new approach in the development strategy as well as in the strategy for industrial pollution control, which should move away from the conventional 'command and control' methods and use more 'incentives and market-based' policy instruments. The following is a brief example of two important programmes recently launched by the Indonesian State Ministry for the Environment and BAPEDAL to illustrate the new approach of 'management for sustainable development', which is basically applying a mixed policy comprised of regulation with market-based instruments and other incentive/disincentive policies.

9. POLLUTION ABATEMENT AND THE BUSINESS PERFORMANCE RATING PROGRAMMES

The challenge of the Ministry of State for the Environment and BAPEDAL will be to integrate environmental issues into the development process, and to make environmental policies an integral part of the national development policy. The recent reorganization of the Ministry and BAPEDAL has already led to the adoption of policies to encourage the use of clean technology, management and immunization of wastes, minimizing environmental impacts, and compliance to regulations through the application of mixed policy tools, including: consultation with impact generators, social and consumer pressure, administrative sanctions, criminal sanctions, import duty exemptions and market mechanisms.

After launching a number of popular action-oriented programmes such as PROKASIH (clean rivers), ADIPURA (clean cities), AMDAL (EIS) and JA-GATIRTA, there is now an urgent need for BAPEDAL to strengthen mechanisms that not only build awareness, but as well, encourage compliance through self-regulation. Three such systems are briefly described here: the credit scheme for pollution-abatement equipment (PAE) programme, environmental audits, and the Business Performance Rating (BPR) programme

Through a soft loan from the OECF of Japan, BAPEDAL and the Bank of Indonesia have recently provided funds to be lent as soft credit in Rupiah currency to small and medium-sized enterprises in Indonesia to finance investments in equipment and/or related technical assistance for preventing industrial pollution and protecting the environment. The loans are intended to be used by the national enterprises in Indonesia to control or reduce pollution, by minimizing waste through technical modification to 'in-plant process' as well as by treating its waste through 'end-of-pipe-treatment'. This low-interest credit is provided through a number of selected public and private handling banks, with priority given to small/medium-scale industries with potentially serious pollution problems, and for improvement of existing pollution sources. The programme is also focused on controlling water pollution with priority to support the Clean River (PROKASIH) Programme. The PAE soft loan funds can only be used to finance investments in pollution-prevention and pollution-control equipment and not to finance operation and maintenance expenses. Among eligible items for investment financing under this credit scheme are: pollution-control equipment, waste treatment facilities/infrastructure, civil construction works for waste treatment, production process modification for pollution prevention, consulting services for designing pollution-control or pollution-prevention equipment, and so on. Although the OECF loan agreement with the government of Indonesia was signed in November 1992, this programme only started to operate at the beginning of January 1994.

The second system instituted recently by BAPEDAL is policy on environmental audits as management tools for business which should be voluntary, but the government will reserve the right to 'order' regulatory audits for controversial or problem industries. Guidelines for environmental audit systems and procedures are currently being drafted in the form of a Ministerial Decree, with the consultation and discussion at a series of workshops involving various government agencies, private business, NGOs and professional associations.

The third system is the Business Performance Rating (BPR) programme which was also started by BAPEDAL in 1994 with the intention of changing companies' behaviour patterns and reducing environmental pollution. The concept is to encourage industry self-regulation by rewarding companies that exemplify sound environmental management practices and by identifying and publicizing those companies that pollute. The programme will enable Indonesian business to move more directly to cleaner production technologies. Thus the BPR programme is expected to generate public and corporate environmental awareness at the same time as encouraging compliance and reducing the level

Table 14.4   Performance rating criteria

Rating Level	Performance Level	Criteria
Gold	Excellent	Zero discharge of pollutants, uses best available clean technology, corporate policy exemplary and clearly enunciated, regular complete environmental and energy audits, leaders in community development, and in occupational health and safety.
Green	Good	Uses best practicable clean technologies to minimize losses of polluting substances, practises recycling and energy conservation, corporate policy includes regular compliance audits, above-average levels of emergency response, community development and occupation health and safety.
Blue	Inadequate	Utilizes best practicable technologies to achieve, verified compliance with all regulations and standards, and practises acceptable, emergency response, community programmes and occupational health systems.
Red	Not adequate	Does not achieve compliance with allowable discharge levels, and does not adequately monitor or work towards sound management of wastes.
Black	Poor	Discharging dangerous levels of pollutants, causing pollution of the environment dumping hazardous wastes, causing community health problems.

of pollution. This will be done by making an assessment of the environmental performance of business enterprises against compliance with standards and regulatory requirements where quantitative information is available, and against qualitative criteria for general management performance. In order for BPR to be successful, the rating system must be transparent and understandable, and the data used must be reliable and credible.

The BPR defined five easily identifiable categories for the business's environmental performance, represented by colours as shown in Table 14.4.

The BPR programme has been evolving since its inception in December 1993, and now a pilot programme is being undertaken in order to test the practicality of design alternatives. The ratings are based primarily on effluent quality, which then are modified in steps according to a quantified assessment of the other environmental factors. From the 1,400 industries in the PROKASIH (clean rivers) programme, 130 industries were selected for rating in Phase I.

In addition, businesses were invited to volunteer, on the understanding that the effluent quality would be assessed against BAPEDAL draft effluent quality standards. A total of 31 companies have volunteered to come into the programme. To date, a total of 71 factories (including eight of the volunteers) have been rated. These ratings are still to be verified.

REFERENCES

BAPEDAL and REDECON (1991), *BAPEDAL Development Plan*, Final Main Report of a Five Year Development Plan for the Environmental Impact Management Agency (BAPEDAL), prepared by REDECON (Resource Development Consultants), under the Japanese Trust Fund of the World Bank's 'Environmental Management Technical Assistance Grant', Jakarta, December.

BAPEDAL and IEA, Labat-Anderson and REDECON (1994), *Inception Report and PAE Program Manual of the Technical Assistance Unit of the Pollution Abatement Equipment (PAE) Program for BAPEDAL and the Bank of Indonesia*, Submitted to Badan Pengendalian Dampak Lingkungan (BAPEDAL) by International Environmental Associates Ltd, Labat-Anderson Ltd and PT REDECON, Jakarta, July.

BAPEDAL and Lembaga Penelitian IPB (1994), *Penyllsunan Repelita VI Lingkungan Hidup. Laporan Akhir*, Badan Pengendalian Dampak Lingkungan (BAPEDAL) bekerjasama dengan Lembaga Penelitian Institut Pertanian Bogor, Bogor, July.

BAPPENAS-Ministry of Forestry and US-AID (1993), *Final Report on Environment and Development in Indonesia: An Input–Output Analysis of Natural Resource Issues;* prepared by Associates in Rural Development and Institute for Economic Analysis, New York University for USAID, Jakarta, June.

Hadad, Ismid (1992), 'Environmental situation in Indonesia:, A Review, of Problems and *management issues*', Paper prepared for Second Indonesia–Canada Conference, organized by Asia-Pacific Foundation of Canada (Toronto) and Center for Strategic and International Studies (Jakarta), at Toronto Prince Hotel, Toronto, Canada, 27–29 September.

Indonesia (1991a), *Data Collection Study for Industrial Efficiency and Pollution Abatement Project*, prepared by COWIconsult, Consulting Engineers and Planners of Denmark, for the World Bank and the Indonesian Ministry of Industry, Jakarta, March.

Indonesia (1991b), Keputusan Menteri Negara Kependudukan dan Lingkungan Hidup No.: KEP-03/MENKLH/II/1991 tentang *Baku Mutu Limbah Cair bagi Kegiatan yang sudah beroperasi*, Jakarta, February.

Indonesia (1992), *Industrial Efficiencv and Pollution Abatement (IEPA: Project Preparation Studies. Study of the Potential IEPA Investments in Selected Industries*, COWIconsult in cooperation with Chemcontrol A/S, Danish Technological Institute, PT Ciriajasa and Balai Besar Selulosa, Indonesian Ministry of Industry, A Project of the World Bank and the Ministry of Industry, Jakarta, January.

Indonesia (1993), *Environment and Development: Challenges for the Future*, World Bank Report No. 12083-IND; Environment Unit, Country Department III, East Asia and Pacific Region, Washington DC, August.

Makarim, Nabiel cs.(1994), 'Business Performance Rating: A Link to Clean Products for Indonesia', paper presented for Seminar on Organizing for Environmental *Management*, organized by ECO-LINK Center for Business and Environment, IPMI Campus, Jakarta, 14 June.

Potter, Clifton (1994), 'Environmental Audits and Business Performance Rating: Tools for Business and Management', paper presented for Seminar on Organizing for *Environmental Management*, organized by ECO-LINK Center for Business and Environment, IPMI Campus, Jakarta, 14 June.

Sarwono Kusumaatmadja (1994), *Kebijaksanaan Bagi Pengembangan Industri Pulp dan Kertas Yane Berwawasan Lingkungan*, Makalah Menteri Negara Lingkungan Hidup/Kepala BAPEDAL pada Seminar Sehari tentang 'Teknologi Pemutihan dengan ECF (Elemental Chlorine Free) dalam Industri Pulp dan Kertas di Indonesia', diselenggarakan oleh Departemen Perindustrian bekerjasama dengan PT REDECON dan Balai Besar Selulosa, Hotel Papandayan, Bandung, 21 July.

15. User Charge for Wastewater Management in Industrial Province

Qwanruedee Limvorapitak and
Dhira Phantumvanit

1. INTRODUCTION

Samut Prakan is located 25 kilometres east of the Bangkok Metropolitan Area (BMA). It is the second most industrial province in Thailand next to Bangkok. The per capita gross provincial product (GPP) of this province is approximately four times the national per capita gross domestic product (GDP).[1]

Environmental degradation is not so much a consequence of industrial growth as the result of the failure to manage land conversions and infrastructure provisions. Conventional efforts to manage the spatial character of industrial growth in Samut Prakan have clearly proved inadequate. Where growth is driven by industrialization, sustainable development must depend on integrating environmental knowledge with policies relating to industrialization.

2. INDUSTRIAL WASTEWATER IN SAMUT PRAKAN PROVINCE

Our results show that from a total of 4,021 factories in Samut Prakan, 1,603 of them produced 22,590 tons of biochemical oxygen demand (BOD) load in 1991, or 61,880 kg/d. This wastewater load is about 1.3 million persons equivalent (1 PE = 0.048 kg BOD/d).[2] In comparison, industries caused more water pollution in Samut Prakan than households. Industries produced 22,590 tons/year of BOD load (or 58 per cent) whereas households released 16,240 tons/year (or 42 per cent). Only about 421 factories treated their wastewater themselves. These factories were located both within and outside the two industrial estates. Approximately 9,030 tons/year of BOD were treated and 13,560 tons/year were discharged into the water resources.

Household[3] and small-scale[4] industries outnumbered other types of industries in this province. Because of their small scale, inadequate funds, and outdated technology, most of them neither treated nor controlled their waste. It is yet to be investigated whether their low output and poor technologies might even have caused them to generate more pollution per unit of output than large-scale industries.

3. RATE OF CHARGE

In order to arrive at the rate of pollution charge for Samut Prakan Province the average costs for different items on treatment plant investment in various zones in the BMA are used. The costs for the BMA public treatment plants are from engineering and these are likely to be not so different for Prakan, which is considered to be a part of the BMA. Assuming a continuous investment of the plants, the average capital cost per cubic metre of wastewater treatment for the BMA[5] is close to 1.88 baht.[6] Per cubic metre cost of pipeline is 1.25 baht while that of land is about 2.5 baht. Operation and maintenance (O&M) costs follow the equation of the Industrial Estate Authority of Thailand (IEAT) because they have the same assumption. O&M cost is about 10.47 baht/kg BOD. The equation used to calculate capital cost is not the same as that of the IEAT's since the wastewater treatment facility is designed to serve small industrial areas in IEAT. The IEAT's construction cost of wastewater treatment facilities and the collection system costs are high. Based on the above estimation, the initial formula for pollution charge was as shown below:

$$
\begin{aligned}
\text{Charge(baht/month)} &= [(\text{investment charge} \times \text{effluent quantity}) \\
&\quad + (\text{operation charge} \times \text{BOD load of discharge})] \\
&= (WC + C + LC) \times V_f + OC \times B \\
&= 5.63 \times V_f + 10.47 \times (X - 0.02) \times V_f
\end{aligned}
$$

where

WC = construction of wastewater treatment facility per unit of wastewater volume, 1.88 baht/m^3

PC = piping or collection system cost per unit of wastewater volume, 1.25 baht/m^3

LC = land cost for central treatment plant per unit of wastewater volume, 2.5 baht/m^3

V_f = effluent quantity, m^3/month

OC = operation charge, baht/kg

B = BOD load of discharge, kg/month

X = BOD concentration at discharge point, kg/m^3

To ensure equity in administering pollution charges, the strength or the quality of wastewater treated must be considered. The high BOD loading is associated with the high operation and maintenance costs or increased biological or other advanced wastewater treatment. As far as BOD load of discharge is concerned, the amount of BOD discharged from each factory can be determined from the result derived from monitors by measuring only BOD or its estimation. The amount of BOD to be discharged in theory should be the excess of the required effluent standard. Based on the existing 20 mgA standard, the amount of excess discharged should be $X - 0.02$ kg/m^3. The load should be that of the factory's normal operation. (Unusual discharges should be priced strictly according to damages; the above formula is only for normal operations.) *Note that discharges with less than 20 mg/l will automatically receive the compensation for the above standard performance resulting in lower charges.* This is an incentive for factories to improve effluent quality. As long as cost per unit of BOD concentration is lower, firms would treat the waste before discharges. This is an important contribution to the efficiency management of the whole system.

In addition to the monthly fees, the government should impose an industrial waste surcharge for industries that contribute wastewater which exceeds certain norms accepted in the treatment field.[7] This addresses the fact that plants will need additional funds to accommodate these particular uses that regular customers would not otherwise demand. In addition, a pre-treatment process is required so that factory owners will reduce the strength of the discharge into the sewerage system.

4. THE AMOUNT OF POLLUTION FEE

4.1. For Factories

Factories producing 5 kg BOD/day or above

The estimation shows that approximately 600 factories not located in Bang Poo and Bang Phli industrial estates produce 5 kg BOD/d or more, of which 117 have installed their own wastewater treatment facilities. Factories which do not have their own wastewater treatment facilities should be required to pay the full cost. The amount of the pollution fee depends on the quality or the intensity of wastewater discharged.

$$\text{Pollution Fee} = 5.63 \times V_f + 10.47 \times (X - 0.02) \times V_f$$

Revenue: A pollution fee of about 767,000 baht/d can be collected from the factories. About 57 per cent of revenue comes from food and textiles manufacturers or 34 per cent of the total 480 factories.

Factories producing less than 5 kg BOD/day

About 2,990 factories produce less than 5 kg BOD/d, but only 24 out of that total have their own wastewater treatment facilities. Because those which do not have their own wastewater treatment facilities cannot afford to pay the whole pollution fee rate on account of their limited revenue, the fee charged is therefore based on the estimation of the collection system, construction and land costs. The operation and maintenance costs are not included in the fee. On the other hand, the reasons why these factories must pay more than households are: first, they discharge higher BOD loading than households: only one factory producing 5 kg BOD is equivalent to BOD discharged from 100 human beings; second, because of the distribution of their locations which make their investment cost in constructing a collection system high. In short, the amount of pollution fee being collected from these factories depends on the volume of flow.

$$\text{Pollution Fee} = 5.63 \times V_f$$

Revenue: Approximately 1.1 million baht/d or 403 million baht/y can be collected from their factories.

Factories located in industrial estates with installation of their own wastewater treatment facilities

In 1991, there were 429 industrial firms located in Bang Poo and Bang Phli industrial estates. Both these estates have central wastewater treatment facilities. Normally these factories pay the pollution fee to the IEAT every month. In this case, if the quality of wastewater discharged from both industrial estates is lower than the standard, IEAT must be responsible for paying the daily penalty, set at four times the normal operating expenses of its waste treatment facility.

Similarly, for factories that have installed their own wastewater treatment facilities—if they discharge effluent of lower quality than the standard, they must pay the penalty the same as IEAT.

4.2. For Households

A pollution fee applied to households should be collected from areas which receive their water supply from the Metropolitan Waterworks Authority. For this study, it is assumed that these areas are urban areas. Households would pay a pollution fee of at least 3.8 baht/m^3 of the total volume of wastewater discharged (considering that wastewater is equal to 80 per cent of water used). Approximately 23,150 kg BOD/d would be generated from about 438,100 people.[8] The pollution fee can be estimated roughly at about 591,000 baht/d or 215.7 million baht/y.

Table 15.1   Source of pollution fee revenue in Samut Prakan province

Activity	Amount of fee (mill. baht/y)
Factory	
1. Producing 5 kg BOD/d or more	280
2. Producing less than 5 kg BOD/d	403
Household	216
Total	899

$$\text{Pollution Fee} = (WC + C)V_f = 4.38 \times V_f \, \text{baht/m}^3$$

The total fee which could be collected from both industrial and household activities would total about 899 million baht/y (Table 15.1). In the first year, this revenue could be used to update wastewater collection/treatment systems. Revenue in the later years could be used to maintain the system, expand its distribution network, install new wastewater treatment facilities in new areas and protect its watershed areas.

4.3. Inspection and Monitoring

Different intensities of inspection and monitoring should be applied to different discharge intensities. For *small dischargers* (below 5 kg BOD/d), inspection should be minimal and be applied whenever there is a specific element of doubt about the existing estimates. Monitoring by third parties where possible is unnecessary, but if applied, the costs should be incurred by the public sector.

For *medium polluters* (5.1–25 kg BOD/d), the inspection should be carried out randomly according to the size and type of industry. Considering that there are about 360 factories located in Samut Prakan (Table 15.2), approximately 700 inspections would be needed (or twice a year per factory). Conservatively assuming that the inspection capacity would cover four factories per day, this task would require one man-year of inspection. Monitoring on the other hand, should be conducted at least once for each quarter. If this is put into practice, factories would be subjected to discharge monitoring four times a year at a cost of about 3,000 to 4,000 baht per year per factory. The resulting estimates of

Table 15.2   Estimation of the number of inspections and monitorings

Factory	No. of factories	No. of inspections	No. of monitorings
Large polluters (≥ 25 kg BOD/d)	240	$240 \times 2 = 480$	$240 \times 6 = 1440$
Medium polluters (5.1–25 kg BOD/d)	360	$360 \times 2 = 720$	$360 \times 4 = 1440$
Small factories (≤ 5 kg BOD/d)	3,420		

concentration and flow in each quarter would be used to calculate the charges for that quarter.

For *large polluters* (more than 25 kg BOD/d), inspections could be carried out more frequently. Considering that there are approximately 240 factories, then each should be inspected at least twice a year (480 times). This probably requires 1 man-year of inspection. Monitoring could be conducted at least 6 times per year (1,440 times).

Particular attention should be paid to public management under the pollution charge system. Since the polluters have already paid for the pollution they produced, it is the public sector which needs to comprehensively monitor for the desired ambient standards and to impose appropriate effluent standards corresponding to the former. The standards will have to be adjusted accordingly and the rates of charges will have to be more stringent, based on the standard level.

5. COLLECTION OF WASTEWATER TREATMENT SERVICES FEE

Local administration should provide and manage the central wastewater treatment system. The collection of the wastewater treatment service fee at the rate fixed by Samut Prakan municipality should be assigned to the Metropolitan Waterworks Authority to be collected together with the water bills. Samut Prakan municipality will in turn remunerate and compensate the Metropolitan Waterworks Authority for expenses incurred for fee collection.

6. CAPACITY OF FACTORIES TO PAY FOR THEIR WASTEWATER TREATMENT

Assuming that the product cost is 80 per cent of the revenue, or the profit margin is 20 per cent of the product cost, then it is clearly shown that 77 per cent of 483 factories producing more than 5 kg BOD/d would be charged less than 1 per cent of their profits for polluting, as shown in Table 15.3.

7. CONCLUSIONS

The proposed user-charge system would provide the local government with a source of revenue of about US$36 million per year to support its pollution control programme. It can also be used to finance and enhance enforcement activities, including investment in wastewater treatment facilities, operation and maintenance and replacement of the treatment system. Moreover, the user-

Table 15.3   *Percentage reduction of profits from pollution charge on factories with five or more kg/d BOD*

Cost in % of factory profile	Number of Factories						
	≤ 1	> 1–2	> 2–3	> 3–4	> 4–5	> 5	Total
TSIC Code 311–312	64	4	2	3	4	4	81
313							
321	40	15	10	2	3	13	83
322	45		1		1		47
324	30						30
331	1						1
332							
341	1						1
342	2					1	3
351							
352	10			1			11
354	11	6	2	2	1	1	23
355							
356	1						1
361	9	7	4	3		10	33
362							
369	2						2
371	4						4
372							
381	57	6	1				64
382	32						32
383	18						19
384	30			1		1	35
385						4	
390–391	13						13
Total	370	38	20	12	8	35	483

Note: Assumes 20 per cent profit margin over production costs.

charge approach imposes significantly lower compliance costs on industry because it allows polluters the freedom to choose their own ways to minimize the cost of compliance: they can pay the charges, reduce or treat their waste, change their input combination, reduce their output, change their production technology or move to a different location.

NOTES

1. Bank of Thailand, 1991.

2. Pansawad 1987.
3. I.e. 10 or less employees.
4. I.e. 10 to 50 employees.
5. Suwannarat 1991.
6. 25 baht = US$1.
7. Oldham 1992.
8. Population equivalent value after passing through septic tank is 48 g/c/d.

REFERENCES

Oldham, Richard D., III (1992), 'Impact Fees: The Experience of Orlando, Florida (USA)', paper presented in the Workshop on the Role of the City in Environmental Management, Bangkok.

Pansawad, T. (1987), *Domestic Wastewater and Water Pollution Problems in Bangkok and Its Vicinity*, Report submitted to the Office of the National Environment Board, Bangkok (in Thai).

Suwannarat, K. (1991), 'Policy and Investment of Wastewater Treatment in BMA', paper presented at the Seminar on Environmental Management in the Next Decade (in Thai).

16. Regulating the Philippine Energy Industry: Efficiency, Equity and Environmental Sustainability

Manuel S. Gaspay

1. INTRODUCTION

The chapter explores the regulatory state of the Philippine energy industry and subjects it to the criteria of economic efficiency, social equity and environmental sustainability. These criteria embody the operational definition of sustainable development.

The segments of the energy industry are energy resource development, power generation, transmission and distribution.[1] Private participation is encouraged in the development of the country's energy resources, but the government through the PNOC (Philippine National Oil Company) is heavily involved in it also. In the 1970s, as a result of a policy to bring the industry under increased government control, power generation and transmission in the whole country became a monopoly of the NPC (National Power Corporation), a government corporation. Distribution continues to be under private enterprise, but with increased government participation through the rural electric cooperatives that it organized and financed. Electricity distribution utilities continue to be state-granted monopolies that lack competitive pressures but subject to substantial regulation through terms in their franchise agreements.

Regulation is exercised through separate agencies that use distinct sets of regulatory instruments. Among them are: the various bureaus of the Department of Energy (DOE),[2] the Energy Regulatory Board (ERB), the National Electrification Administration (NEA), and the Environment Management Bureau (EMB) of the Department of Environment and Natural Resources (DENR).

The four bureaus of the DOE are tasked with various regulatory activities. The Energy Resource Development Bureau of the DOE is in charge of the country's energy resource development plan. The government, through other agencies such as the Department of Trade and Industry (DTI), may also provide incentives to private enterprise to support this plan. Clearly, the policy is to stimulate the development of the indigenous energy resources, given the country's net deficit in energy supplies.

The Energy Industry Administration Bureau regulates downstream energy industries. It oversees activities such as allocation of oil and coal importation licences/quotas, approval of additional gas service station applications, and setting technical standards for the power industry with the Bureau of Product Standards.

The Energy Utilization and Management Bureau deals with demand-side management and the development of non-conventional energy sources. The Energy Planning and Monitoring Bureau, on the other hand, manages the Oil Price Stabilization Fund (OPSF) and assesses current energy policies plans, and programmes.

Perhaps the most prominent energy regulatory agency is the ERB, because it regulates energy prices (e.g., oil, gasoline, diesel and electricity prices). The prices of energy products are subject to intense political interest in the Philippines. The ERB is also tasked with the non-price regulation of the private power distribution utilities. It monitors their performance with respect to the terms in their awarded franchise. Congress, however, wields the authority for awarding these franchise agreements.[3]

NEA regulates all electricity distribution cooperatives. It approves the tariffs charged by the cooperatives, as well as their technical and financial operating standards. The extent of NEA's regulation and involvement in the management of these cooperatives is much more than the ERB's control over the private utilities. NEA also funded the establishment of these cooperatives.

Environmental standards for the whole energy industry, however, are set by the EMB. It also monitors and ensures compliance through the DENR's regional offices. DOE assists the EMB in these tasks.

Energy policy is currently being liberalized. Private participation in power generation has already been allowed under schemes such as the Build–Operate–-Transfer (BOT).[4] The whole industry is slowly being deregulated. Privatization and deregulation are not equivalent. Privatization refers to the return of state-owned and operated enterprises to private ownership. Deregulation, on the other hand, is the easing of government restrictions on the activities of private enterprises. An enterprise may be privatized but remain heavily regulated. Deregulation need not lead to the complete elimination of regulatory controls, but only to the decrease of their incidence.

What controls must be retained? Price control is crucial in the light of public resistance to recent attempts at price deregulation. The need to protect our environment and conserve natural resources has also assumed the same magnitude of importance as the other traditional considerations of energy policies. Economic growth, efficiency, social equity and public safety must now compete with the new concerns in the design and conduct of these policies. The question is all the more relevant because protecting the environment requires more regulation, in contrast to the liberalist thrust towards deregulation for economic efficiency.

2. UNDERSTANDING THE REGULATORY FRAMEWORK

2.1. Resource Development

The power industry is heavily regulated in the Philippines. Government inter-venes right from the energy resource development point. The DOE identifies and plans the exploitation of the nation's potential energy resources. Among these are hydro, geothermal, coal, limited quantities of oil deposits, and natural gas. Currently, hydro and geothermal are being exploited. Local coal will soon be utilized, while natural gas is being eyed for utilization at the turn of the century. From the Power Development Programme (1993–2005) of NPC in 1993, local oil and nuclear power are not yet considered as sources for electric power generation.

Only very limited supplies of non-conventional energy from indigenous sources such as wind, solar, mini-hydro, and biomass are being exploited or planned. There is a policy of developing these resources to reduce the country's dependence on imported energy sources such as oil and coal. But the possibility of economically using these resources in significant amounts is dim. Table 16.1 summarizes the country's energy resources.

Table 16.1   Energy resources inventory

	Hydro	Geothermal	Coal	Nat. Gas
Utilized:				
Sites	23	4		
Capacity (MW)	2,214	887		
Potential:				
Sites	270	27	15	1
Capacity (MW)	12,153	3,405	1,820	1,760

Source: Data from NPC's Power Development Program (1993–2005).

The table indicates that most of the known potential is in hydro and geother-mal. Currently, only a quarter of geothermal and a sixth of hydro resources are being used. Used capacity is serving less than half of current peak demand requirement. However, total potential of 19,000 MW is barely above the peak demand capacity (18,000 MW) projected for the year 2005.

Given the considerable buffer between installed capacity and peak demand required for reliable system performance, and the long leadtimes to develop energy resources (over ten years), the country will continue to be a net energy importer.

Government has relied on NPC to develop hydro resources. For geothermal, it depends on PNOC and the Philippine Volcanology Office. Private enterprise, in the form of PGI (Philippine Geothermal Inc.) a subsidiary of a Californian energy development company, was invited in the 1970s to develop the first commercial geothermal fields in the country. Currently, other foreign-owned ventures are being solicited for geothermal energy development, but without success. One hindrance cited is the 60 per cent royalty payment required (inclusive of the 35 per cent income tax) under PD 1442.[5]

Private enterprise is engaged in the exploration and development of domestic coal mines, oil wells and natural gas fields.[6] While developers are awarded attractive exploration franchises to entice them into these risky ventures, they are also subjected to restrictions in terms of regulations on rules of entry, and environmental impact assessments and standards.

The rules of entry include: limitation of foreign participation to firms which must have at least 40 per cent Filipino ownership (1987 Constitution and RA 4072), and adequate financial and technical capability to undertake the resource development. The SEC (Securities and Exchange Commission) checks and implements the ownership provision. The DOE examines the technical and financial requirements.

Another agency that affects private participation is the BOI (Board of Investments). It approves eligibility for financial incentives following the investment priorities guidelines of the country.

2.2. Power Generation

The country has electric power plants generating a total capacity of 7,900 MW.[7] All these plants, except six recently completed under BOT schemes, are owned and operated by NPC.[8]

NPC monopolization

NPC used to be limited to hydropower generation. Private utilities like MERALCO (the electric franchise in Metro Manila) operated their own power plants (e.g., oil-fired). PD 40 in 1972, however, made NPC responsible for power generation in the country, a policy reversed only in 1987 by EO 215. The rationale for nationalization was to ensure that the power industry supported the economic growth plans of the country. It was argued that private enterprise was unresponsive to the growing power needs of the country. Neither were they capable of responding, because of the huge amounts of capital required, especially for rural electrification. The general policy regime at that time (Martial Law years) was also biased towards *dirigisme* or state controls.

State monopolization of power generation allowed it to plan and execute a national power development programme, which not only supported the government's economic development thrust, but also raised system efficiencies. One problem before state monopolization, for example, was MERALCO's refusal to guarantee power purchases from NPC's hydro plants. This made it difficult to commit long-term investments for more efficient hydro plant expansions. Moreover, an electric distribution utility also engaged in power generation can unduly favour its more expensive self-generated power, because it can pass on this extra cost to captive consumers.

Return of private participation
President Aquino's election in 1986 ushered in a new mindset for regulating the energy industry. It was realized that power generation is not a natural monopoly. Thus, there can be private competition.

Government also saw other advantages in privat-sector participation in power generation. Among these were: widening of the capital base for capacity expansions; lowering of prices in the long run due to competition; and, acceleration of the transfer of technology from the installation to the operation phase.

Government began this private power programme approach through BOT (Build–Operate–Transfer) schemes. Republic Act 6957 (1990), permits BOT participants to engage in power generation, distribution, electrification and related functions for operating a utility franchise. However, several perceived restrictions to privatization remain.[9]

Since NPC still owns the transmission grids, through which the privately generated power will have to pass before distribution to end-consumers, private power generators effectively face a monopsonist. Terms of the power supply contracts have to be negotiated with NPC, and power-generation investors complain that the method through which NPC computes the 'avoided cost' is neither fair nor transparent.

'Avoided cost' is the benchmark price for negotiating power purchases between independent power producers and the NPC (or the private electric utility as the case may be).[10] It is not the NPC grid price. It is based on the least-cost power expansion plan, and would be the representative cost of the various types of power plants needed to meet the increased market demand, if NPC undertook the expansion itself. Hence, if the independent power producer's price is less than the 'avoided cost', it justifies NPC's purchase from an independent producer. To be a fair basis for comparison, 'avoided cost' must be calculated using consistent assumptions under a level 'playing field'. In other words, costs that NPC is not incurring because of some special privilege (e.g., tax exemptions, ODA interest rates) must be accounted and thrown into the computation.

Thus, although EO 215 already mandates NPC to submit its 'avoided costs' computations to the DOE, there are still clamours for ways of dealing with the 'avoided cost' controversy. One suggestion is to require NPC to regularly submit and update their calculations and assumptions for 'avoided costs' to reflect changes in their power expansion programme. Another suggestion is for NPC and DOE to arrive at a standard calculation methodology.

One more provision of EO 215 which the private sector perceives to be restrictive is the size limitation on the private generating facility — e.g., largest generating unit size, or 10 per cent of the coincident NPC grid demand. EO 215 also restricts the independent power producer from directly connecting to the electric distribution utility, without interconnecting with NPC. Thus, the independent producers are relegated to the role of peaking power suppliers instead of being encouraged to provide viable baseload supply alternatives. There are recent moves, however, which indicate the government's positive response to these criticisms. The Pagbilao coal thermal plant is intended to be a baseload plant.

Government as strategic grid planner

The current regulatory mood effectively retains government's role (e.g., NPC) as the strategic planner for the national power grids. Thus, government reaffirms its legitimate lead role in expanding power supply for supporting its economic development plans. NPC also leads the country's private power programme. It identifies additional plant requirements, drafts a power development plan and communicates this to independent power producers.

The power development plan in 1993 identified the least-cost energy mix that meets the power demand projected until the year 2005 (Table 16.2). There are a number of points to note in this development plan:

Table 16.2   Generating capacity mix (in MW)

	Oil-Fired	Hydro	Geothermal	Coal	Total
1992	3,226	2,177	885	405	6,693
Cap.%	(48%)	(33%)	(13%)	(6%)	
Gen.%	(54%)	(17%)	(22%)	(7%)	
1994*	4,895	2,217	1,238	405	8,755
Cap.%	(56%)	(25%)	(13%)	(5%)	
Gen.%	(52%)	(16%)	(25%)	(8%)	
1998*	3,838	2,217	2,558	2,605	11,218
Cap.%	(34%)	(20%)	(23%)	(23%)	
Gen.%	(23%)	(10%)	(36%)	(31%)	
2005*	5,541	4,049	2,558	12,805	24,953
Cap.%	(22%)	(15%)	(10%)	(51%)	
Gen.%	(6%)	(10%)	(16%)	(68%)	

Notes
* Projected. Data from Power Development Programme (1993–2005), 1993.
** Assumes undetermined base-load (4 per cent for 1998, 51 per cent in 2005) is going to be from coal, which appears likely in the PDP plans. Generating mix is based on gigawatt-hours of baseload.

1. Energy from indigenous sources, though expected to rise from 43 per cent in 1992 to 52 per cent in 1998, will again drop to 29 per cent by 2005.
2. Oil use is expected to drop from an annual average of 23 mil. barrels in 1993 to about 15 mil. by 2005. Coal, however, will rise from 3.1 mil. MT annually to 19.5 MT.
3. Geothermal is going to be more important in the near-future, but hydro sources are going to play a lesser role. Fossil fuel, will remain the dominant source as oil-fired merely shifts to coal-fired.
4. The energy mix is going to be costly in the short run as the fast-track projects use diesel and other oil distillates.
5. These projections do not include the possibility of local natural gas being developed. Experts say that the country's gas reserves may not be developed until after the turn of the century. Projections also do not include future acceptability of nuclear power in the country.

The strategic importance of power in the country's development, and the complexities of planning in the energy industry, make government hesitant to fully privatize this industry. The projected deficit in indigenous energy resources makes it even more critical. The planned shift to coal is clearly being driven by such deficit. Coal, apart from being cheaper than oil, also is less subject to international political instability.

Privatization will likely proceed further. But the deregulation of the power-generation side of the industry may be limited.

Price control
All energy prices are set by the ERB. It approves adjustments in NPC's grid price, as well as the purchase price agreements between NPC and the independent power producer. This is a highly political process, involving public hearings, which must consider equity objectives apart from the recovery of costs.

NPC prices are different for each grid because of differences in grid-generating costs. But a uniform schedule of rates applies to all customers in the same classification in an interconnected system. In theory, the rate structure should also allow NPC to recover costs plus a 10 per cent return on the base value of assets. In practice, NPC has not even been able to achieve the 8 per cent rate of return mandated by its major lenders such as the World Bank.

Environmental regulation
Power plants must comply with environmental standards set by the EMB. Prior to construction and operation, plants must acquire an Environmental Compliance Certificate (ECC) based on a prior EIA (environmental impact assessment) study and consultations with the project host community. The EMB may also require an Environmental Guarantee Fund (e.g., Calaca II project) to answer for any eventual claims for environmentally-related damages. The operational

power plant is also subject to periodic inspection and monitoring to ensure that emission and effluent standards are being met.

The ECC system forces the internalization of environmental costs in the overall project costs. But it is always difficult to accurately anticipate and completely account for all the possible impacts of a project. A guarantee fund addresses this weakness.

One issue is the weak ability of government to implement its rules and regulations. This is more so in environmental protection. Quintos and Intal (1994) claim Philippine environmental standards to be the most stringent in the developing countries of Asia. But these standards are not effectively implemented. Only 35 per cent of the large and medium-sized firms, and none among the small firms, comply. The electric power deficit from 1990–93, for example, forced government to resort to a fast-track mode of adding new power capacities. Under this scheme, environmental clearances were suspended.

In power generation, most of the environmental risks are faced by the host community. However, the community may share only marginally in the benefits of the project. Therefore, there is an inherent social inequity issue. In the past, host community welfare was usually discounted in favour of the national interest. While the EIA–ECC system and the emission/effluent standards serve to correct this flaw, there remains a tendency to override the interest of the host community because of the weak implementing capability and the need for cheap power.

The major off-site environmental problems (i.e., outside of the host community) from power generation are the release of so-called greenhouse gases (e.g., carbon dioxide). Developing countries, however, contribute very little to this problem as their electricity consumption per capita is low compared to that of developed countries.[11] As a result, Philippine emission standards are limited to abating pollution at the periphery of the project site, e.g., there are no emission standards for CO_2.

2.3. Transmission

Transmission lines and services are monopolized by the government (NPC). Transmission is a natural monopoly that justifies regulation but not necessarily nationalization. Hence, the privatization of NPC (power generation and transmission) is under study.[12] The best option is to sell NPC transmission assets to the power distributors, along with the BOT and power purchase contracts. Only planning, control, dispatching and power-generation contracting would remain centralized. The second-best option is to create vertically integrated regional utilities.

Another policy initiative is to interconnect the island grids to increase overall system efficiency. Interconnection also lowers installed capacity as standby capacity can be drawn from a larger pool. Furthermore, interconnection maximizes the use of indigenous energy sources that are located in low-demand areas. Interconnection, however, strengthens the argument for a national monopoly on transmission. But a model where planning, control, dispatching and power generation contracting remain centralized achieves the same purposes.

Power transmission does not entail major environmental problems. Nevertheless, a transmission project must also secure an ECC to ensure protection of the environment. Problems associated with transmission projects are the clearing of trees in areas passed by the transmission lines, disturbing endangered or fragile ecosystems, and inadequate compensation for land occupied by the transmission lines.

2.4. Distribution

Electric power distribution remained in the private sector despite the shift to state-control policies during the 1970s. Government, however, increased its regulatory role and encouraged the establishment of rural electric cooperatives (RECs) to promote rural electrification.

The theory of power utility regulation assumes that distribution utilities are natural monopolies. Their cost curves are such that marginal costs are falling as supply volumes increase (Kahn 1991). Hence, without intervention a monopoly will arise, and the level of supply will be restricted below the socially optimal level as the firm maximizes its profits. State intervenes by awarding a state-sponsored monopoly, through a franchise contract, in return for certain restrictions such as pricing controls and obligation to service customers inside the franchise.

There are 27 distribution utilities in the country, 16 of which are owned by private companies, and 11 by municipalities. In addition, there are over a hundred electric cooperatives serving some 3 million people. They are all small in terms of megawatts of load served, but their characteristics vary widely according to the territory served. Some are isolated systems served by a diesel generator, but most are supplied from the NPC grid. MERALCO, the private utility serving the national capital region, dwarfs all other utilities. It purchases 65 per cent of NPC's total power.

The main issues in the regulation of power distributors (Nuqui 1992) are: institutional arrangements for service coverage; mode of distribution and pricing; and the availability and reliability of power supply.

Service coverage
A major issue in service coverage is the provision that allows some industrial users to connect directly to the NPC transmission grid, thus bypassing the distribution utility. This violates the service coverage integrity of the utility's franchise. The practice is especially widespread for the Mindanao grid where 41 per cent of NPC energy sales in 1991 went to directly connected industries.

Direct connection is harmful to the utility. Industries that directly connect, because of their large loads, often are the most profitable customers of the utility. The practice of subsidizing households at the expense of industrial users, further aggravates the problem. Direct connections, however, are argued on the basis of making more industries competitive by lowering power costs.

Direct connection started as an incentive for industries to relocate from Luzon following the development of hydroelectric resources by NPC in Mindanao. At that time, electric utilities in Mindanao were in no position to service relocating industries. In 1974, PD 395 allowed NPC to sell directly to some industrial users subject to certain qualifications. The policy was approved as a BOI (Board of Investments) industry incentive. Eligibility for direct connection rested on the inability of the local utility to provide reasonably priced power, its inability to provide power reliably and the poor health of its finances.

From a total system view, direct connections are more efficient for providing power to some industrial users. But the cross-subsidization practice complicates the problem, since direct connection allows the beneficiary to escape the burden of the cross-subsidy at the expense of the utility. Currently, there is a moratorium on further direct connections. But existing arrangements have been 'grandfathered'.

Pricing and operating standards

Private utilities are supervised by the ERB while the RECs are supervised by NEA. The most important aspect of supervision is the approval of rate structures and petitions for rate increases. As illustrated in Table 16.3, the most significant part of the electric utility's price structure is its power cost. Often the latter is the NPC grid price. Hence, ERB approval of electric rate adjustments is made in tandem with decisions on NPC grid prices and the fuel price.

The next most significant costs are due to system losses. These are really a problem of theft rather than of technical inefficiencies. Costs of system losses are in fact more than twice that of the cost of transmission and distribution, and more than the combined costs of transmission/distribution and interest payments.

RECs tend to have higher costs (e.g., less efficient) than private utilities. This is because: RECs serve less profitable markets (e.g., lower customer density per area and fewer industrial customers); RECs generally have inferior management and technical capabilities; and RECs are subject to local political meddling.

The high system losses and cost of distribution tend to increase the markup over the cost of generated power. As it is, the price regulation system through RORB (rate of return on base) targets does not encourage efficiency. Regulators have tried to correct this problem by establishing allowable standards on system losses and other technical operating criteria. Only those within the standards may be justifiably claimed as recoverable costs from the electric tariff rate adjustments.

Unlike privately owned utilities, RECs are not subject to rate-of-return criteria as they are supposed to be non-profit-making. They are allowed, however, to recover full costs plus a 25 per cent system loss allowance and provision for reinvestments.

NPC's power supply reliability
Power shortages from 1990–93 caused substantial actual and opportunity losses to electric distributors. As a result utilities want to be given the authority to generate their own power, independent of NPC. Given well-known theoretical arguments against allowing electricity distributors to generate their own power, such policy change must be studied carefully.

Appropriate regulation is also necessary in case vertical integration is allowed in the power industry. NPC's inability to provide adequate power was not entirely of its own making, nor an inherent flaw in the system of separating power generation from distribution. It was caused more by a failure to plan adequately for the economy's growth, and approve price adjustments that should have provided NPC with the financial resources to undertake expansion.

Environmental concerns
Environmental issues are not prominent in the distribution part of the electricity industry. Environmental clearances for the distribution lines, however, must also be secured.

2.5. Price Control and Demand-side Management

Prices not only allow build-up of financial resources to expand power supply. They also provide signals to consumers to properly conserve their use of electricity. A traditional cheap electricity policy, however, has undermined the former price functions. The result is a perception that households and industries are inefficiently using electricity.

That prices are not efficient is caused by cross-subsidization (between regions and from industries to households) and the failure to price according to the principle of long-run marginal cost (LRMC). Cross-subsidization does not promote efficient use of electricity by the households. It also creates production distortions in altering the competitiveness of affected industries.

Table 16.3   RCG/Hagler, Bailly study results

	Present Rate	LRMC Rate	Recommended Interim Rates
Average Luzon Grid	P 1.84	P 1.84	P 1.84
MERALCO	1.84	1.64	1.80
Small Utilities	1.79	1.84	1.80
Other Utilities	1.79	2.24	1.80
Non-Utilities	1.84	2.09	2.22

The RCG/Hagler, Bailly study in 1990 (Table 16.3), for example, claimed that MERALCO was being charged by NPC a margin 12 per cent higher than the strict LRMC price equivalent. Other utilities, meanwhile, were being charged at a subsidy of 12 per cent.

Anderson (1993) reports that use of electricity is highly inefficient in most developing countries. Appliances and industrial plants are technically antiquated, and electricity prices too low, to offer any incentive to save energy. To these reasons might be added the argument that electricity consumption levels in these countries are too low for savings to be worthwhile.

In the Philippines, households account for 23.2 per cent of end-use of electricity, with industry (including commercial) accounting for the rest. But electricity expenses account for only 1.2 per cent of total household expenditures, far lower than the 13.1 per cent spent for rice consumption alone.

Electricity expenses account for only 3.2 per cent of total input expenditures, and only 1.5 per cent of each peso of sales received, of industry. There are only a few industries where the cost of electricity is a major expenditure item, such as in ice-making and the cement industry. Table 16.4 lists the top thirteen industries in terms of their electricity-intensiveness. Note that except for ice-making and cement, all sectors spend less than 10 per cent of their total costs on electricity.

Since the misalignment in energy prices suggested in reports such as that of RCG/Hagler, Bailly, Inc. (1990) are not in the order of magnitude sufficient to significantly alter these expenditure share estimates, correct pricing alone will not be adequate to elicit significant energy conservation efforts. Moreover, low-income families may have a disproportionately high discount rate per cent) on energy-efficient durable goods, compared to high-income families. Therefore, what will probably be needed are incentives of the type used by Angus

Table 16.4   Electricity-intensiveness

Sector	Percent of Total Costs
Ice-Making	36
Cement	11
Social Services	8
Educational Services	6
Watch/Jewellery Making	6
Telecommunications	5
Hotels/Restaurants	5
Personal Services	5
Glass Products	5
Basic Chemicals/Plastics	5
Bakery/Confections	5
Sugar Milling	4
Rubber/Footwear	4

Note: Most manufacturing classifications register only a 2–3 per cent energy use intensity. Steel and Foundries, for example, register only 2 per cent, similar to that of commercial offices in general.

King in 1989 in Maine, US.[13]

King contracted to sell power to the utility by inducing his customers to save on current consumption. He offered to pay for two-thirds of the cost of installing more efficient appliances and equipment. The user paid for the remaining third of the cost, but he also kept the resulting savings on his electricity bill. This reportedly cut back the customer's payback period for the energy-saving investment from 5 years to 18 months.

Demand-side management has not been effectively pushed in the Philippines. Efforts have been limited to the labelling of appliances as to their energy-efficiency and other informational campaigns. These efforts will not be effective given the high implied discount rate and the low share of electricity expenditures.

Simply stated, the conservation of electricity on a per user perspective may not be that worthwhile, even if power prices are right. However, from a total system perspective it is worthwhile. Hence, the gap must be addressed through carefully designed instruments.

3. SUSTAINABILITY ASSESSMENT

Government's involvement in the energy industry was motivated by the belief that energy is essential for sustaining national economic development. Historically, that vision of development has been a unimodal expansion of the national production base for the sake of increased abilities to consume. Increased consumption leads to increased social welfare, and energy availability could be a critical bottleneck if the private sector did not respond on time to the future needs of expansion.

Shifts in the development paradigm, to what is defined as sustainable development (SD), have occurred. SD, as defined in Agenda 21 of the Rio Conference, calls for environmental sustainability, social sustainability or equity, and economic sustainability. Note that there has been no consensus on the vision of the quality of development that must be pursued, only an agreement on three criteria of sustainability.

There have been strong representations, at one extreme, to supplant the expansionist model with a conservationist model that puts 'strong' limits to growth based on 'hard' levels of environmental carrying capacities. At the other extreme is an optimistic vision that believes in the regenerating capabilities of nature and the technical ingenuity of mankind to overcome practical limits to growth. The mainstream view is that there are 'weak' limits. This latter view recognizes that there are various types of natural capital with varying substitutability possibilities. Some are practically impossible to replace within conceivable periods of time.

The latter SD point of view is adopted in making an evaluation of the Philippine energy regulatory framework. The premise of the existing framework that government must ensure the availability of power in line with economic growth targets is accepted, but reconciled to the SD paradigm of sustainability.

3.1. A Snapshot of the Policy Framework

Figure 16.1 is a snapshot of the energy policy and strategy framework. Government is the strategic planner. Its primary objective is to sustain economic growth. The main instrument components are the PDP (Power Development Plan), policies for increased private sector participation and resource mobilization, and policies for deregulation, increased competition and increased public accountability. The operational concerns are environmental sustainability, social sustainability equity and economic sustainability (efficiency).

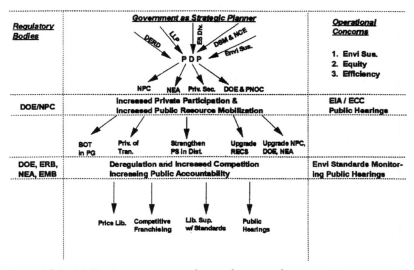

Figure 16.1   Philippine energy regulatory framework

The PDP articulates strategies of domestic energy resource development, energy source diversification, demand-side management and non-conventional energy source development, environmental sustainability and least-cost planning.

Increased private participation and mobilization of resources are reflected in the BOT schemes of power generation, plans for privatization of the transmission grids, upgrading of the DOE, NPC, NEA, and the RECs. Deregulation, increased competition and increased public accountability are reflected in plans for price liberalization, competitive franchising, liberal franchise supervision with stringent standards, and more transparent public hearings.

This basic energy policy framework must answer whether it is environmentally sustainable, fair, and efficient.

3.2. Environmental Sustainability

In principle, the strategy is environmentally sustainable. The EIA/ECC is mandated for all energy resource development, power generation, transmission and distribution projects. It is simple and effective if completely enforced. There may be complaints as to the transparency in arriving at the standards and their rationality, but in general, these standards are appropriate and quite high for a developing country (e.g., Quintos and Intal 1994). If strictly implemented, they will fully internalize the costs of environmental degradation and natural resource depletion that the project may incur, and therefore, lead the project planners to a more socially efficient decision. The problem is in implementation.

So the question becomes, are privatization and deregulation going to worsen or improve the implementation of environmental regulations and the firms' compliance?

Privatization will likely improve implementation. Government regulation itself has some credibility problems. Moreover, in many countries, the government is a major polluter, second only to the natural-resource-based industries. In the domestic oil industry in the Philippines, for example, the government firm (Petron) has no oil-spill emergency equipment of the calibre that Caltex and Shell have. NPC, for that matter, had to borrow the equipment of these private firms when it suffered a spill in its Laguna Lake-based power plant recently.

Deregulation is not a clearcut matter, however. Price deregulation will probably improve compliance, especially in the industries with a monopolistic structure. Investments in environmental abatement and improvement equipment raise the asset base of firms, thereby, improving their profit margins under RORB rules (e.g., the A–J–W effect). Deregulation also frees government resources, now committed to implementing the regulations to be liberalized, to more effectively pursue other functions such as implementation of environmental rules. Deregulation that eases the rules of entry, however, threatens the margins of a firm and fragments the industry into smaller firms. This may create a negative impact on environmental compliance.

From a global perspective, the Philippine energy strategy poses problems as it shifts to the use of coal without an adequate policy towards carbon dioxide emissions. Global warming, though a legitimate global concern, is more of an OECD priority than a developing country (DC) priority. Opportunity costs for the Philippines in reducing GHG (greenhouse gas) emissions in its power projects are much higher than the value of the benefits that may accrue to itself. The OECD countries, on the other hand, have higher marginal benefits from reducing GHG compared to developing countries. In addition, their marginal costs of reducing GHG may be higher than the marginal costs of the developing country's corresponding efforts to reduce them. Therefore, there is some validity to the argument that the OECD country must compensate the LDC country for the latter to reduce its GHG. Unless there are compensatory schemes, the Philippine approach may be to pay attention only to preventing the host community impacts of energy projects, which it had just begun to properly address.

3.3. Social Sustainability

There is a tendency to discount the burden on host communities and heavily favour the need of urban communities for cheap power, especially in hydroelectric projects. Will privatization and deregulation worsen the problem?

There are no inherent reasons for their privatization or deregulation to worsen the discrimination against host communities. Government energy bureaucrats and private entrepreneurs equally share an incentive to complete a project despite host community opposition. The government's relative inefficiency over private enterprise, however, provides the host communities a better chance of solidifying their opposition and articulating their demands. But it really depends on how the implementation of government policies to protect the interest of host communities will be affected by privatization. There are no clear indications for this.

The worst atrocities against host communities for the sake of energy supply were perpetuated during the time of the Martial Law regime when state control was supreme. Profit-seeking objectives, however, can equally be harsh against community resistance.

Host communities suffer from the insatiable demand for energy that modernization in urban communities creates. The greater political clout possessed by urban interests tends to overwhelm the host community resistance.

Ironically, the government's greater reliance on imported energy alleviates the burden for host communities and their local environment. But it exports the burden to foreign host communities. If all countries, however, were appropriately internalizing these local environmental impacts, then world prices should be optimal.

Another equity issue is the disparate ability of people to participate in power project investments. The large sums of money required make it likely that only the rich and landed can benefit from the privatization opportunities. The lack of competitive capital markets in the Philippines worsens prospects of public participation. Deregulation, in so far as it 'levels the playing field' will be a direction towards equitability. However, these are empirical questions that may not depend on the policies themselves but on how they interphase with the existing economic and political structure of the country.

Deregulation of energy prices will take away the cross-subsidization of households by industries. How this is going to impact the overall distribution of income is unclear. Lifeline rates already ensure that basic needs are met. But electricity prices cheaper than their true costs only subsidize large users of power who are the richer households. In that sense, price deregulation can lead to a more equitable situation.

3.4. Economic Sustainability

The regulatory reform initiatives heavily address the economic sustainability issue. This is justified, given that it is where a lot of improvements are needed. Energy efficiency can be consistent with environmental sustainability and, to a certain extent, with social equity.

A lot of studies have investigated this issue. Privatization is recommended, not only because it taps a much larger pool of finance for power projects, but also because it promotes efficiency. The failure of government, exposed in the 'power crisis' of the country, has lessened the faith in state-led approaches. However, the government still has a legitimate role as the strategic planner and the source of signals for long-term investments in the energy sector.

Privatization and deregulation allow the government to concentrate on those more important tasks of governance. Power generation was ideal for starting these reforms. In theory, there are no natural monopolies when the same power requirement can be provided by different types of resources from different points. That argument assumes the existence of a unified transmission system which the competing power suppliers can hook up to, and then convey power to any point of use or demand without substantial spatial efficiency losses.

But the privatization of transmission grids is also being considered. Distributors are also being given flexibility to use their own generated power. In the absence of clear policies here, government appears to be heading for a pragmatic approach of adopting what seems to be most efficient on a case-to-case basis.

One glaring gap in the government's strategy for efficiency is the insufficient attention paid to demand-side management. This was inherited from years of regulation addressed only at the supply side. With the new DOE, this will probably change. But the DOE's efforts must move beyond promotional, informational and educational campaigns. The latter measures can have only minor impacts since the expenditure share of electricity is low for most users. But the cost of investment to increase the efficiency of electricity use is substantial. A better approach to overcome the 'lumpiness' issue is needed. The gains will be large, as efficiency avoids more costly, as well as more environmentally harmful, new projects.

NOTES

1. The energy industry as discussed in the chapter does not include power for the transportation sector.
2. The Ministry of Energy, abolished by the Aquino administration in 1987, had its functions

replaced by two agencies (Energy Coordinating Council and Office of Energy Affairs) under the Office of the President. The Ramos administration, however, revived energy affairs as a ministerial concern with the recreation of the Department of Energy in 1992.

3. Since 1975, the extension of the franchises of private electric utilities has been handled by NEA (Aboitiz 1993).

4. Hopewell and Enron, two foreign-owned firms, completed power plants last year under the BOT scheme.

5. The royalty paid to government (computed as a percentage of net revenue) artificially raises the price of geothermal fuel to levels which make it uncompetitive with competing fuel sources like imported oil. PD 1442 superseded RA 5092 which only required a 1.5 per cent royalty plus the 35 per cent income tax.

6. While oil off the Palawan shores has been discovered and is being exploited, it is not for electric power generation.

7. National Power Corporation 1993.

8. These are: Hopewell gas turbine in Navotas; Enron's diesel plant in Pinamucan, Batangas; Enron's diesel plant in Subic; the two Alson and Tomen diesel plants in Iligan; and the diesel power barges of Far East Levingston in Calaca, Batangas. See Viray 1993.

9. These concerns were raised in a public forum between the private sector and the policy makers at the Powertech Conference, at Mandaluyong, in November 1993.

10. See RMI–CRC study (1994) for a full treatment of 'avoided cost' as used in the BOT contracts.

11. Worldwide CO_2 emissions from energy consumption in 1987 was 22.7 billion tons, 6.6 billion of which were due to electricity generation. Developing countries account for only 0.9 billion tons or 14 per cent of total. Moreover, their per capita CO_2 emission rate (0.3 ton) is only 1/15th that of the developed countries' 4.4 tons/capita average. The Philippines has a much lower emission rate than the developing country average (Winje 1991).

12. Pricer Waterhouse was commissioned in 1992 to study the privatization options for NPC.

13. See Cairncross 1993.

REFERENCES

Aboitiz, Alfonso (1993), 'Davao Light and Power Co.: A Corporate Strategy', Masters Thesis, Asian Institute of Management, Makati.

Anderson, Dennis (1993), *Energy Efficiency and the Economics of Pollution Abatement*, Washington, DC: The World Bank.

Cairncross, Frances (1993), *Costing the Earth*, Boston, Mass.: Harvard Business School Press.

Kahn, Alfred (1991), *The Economics of Regulation*, Cambridge., Mass.: MIT Press.

Munasinghe, Mohan (1991), 'Electricity and the Environment in Developing Countries with Special Reference to Asia', in *Energy and the Environment in the 21st Century*, ed. by Jefferson Tester, David Wood and Nancy Ferrari, Cambridge, Mass.: MIT Press.

National Power Corporation, Office of the President (1993), 'Power Development programme (1993–2005)', Diliman, Quezon City.

Nuqui, Wilfrido (1992), 'Study of Government Regulations in the Philippines: Power Generation and Distribution', PIDS Working Paper, Makati.

Price Waterhouse (1992), 'Study on the Privatization Options for the Philippine Sector', Report prepared for the Office of Energy Affairs, Manila.

Quintos, Paul and Ponciano Intal, Jr. (1994), 'Environmental Regulations and the Philippine Economy', A UNDP-funded Study for UNCTAD, Manila.

RCG/Hagler, Bailly, Inc. (1990), 'Philippine Power Sector Studies', A Report to the ECC, Manila.

RMI (Resource Management International, Inc.) and CRC (Centre for Research and Communication) (1994), 'Electric Utility Pricing', Paper prepared for the Energy Regulatory Board (ERB), Pasig.

Siddayao, Corazon (ed.) (1993), *Energy Investments and the Environment*, Washington, DC: Economic Development Institute, World Bank.

Viray, Francisco (1993), 'Technical and Operating Aspects of the Philippine Power Marketplace', Paper delivered at the POWERTECH Conference, Mandaluyong.

Winje, Dietmar (1991), 'Electric Power and the Developing Economies', in *Energy and the Environment in the 21st Century*, ed. by Jefferson Tester, David Wood and Nancy Ferrari, Cambridge, Mass.: MIT Press.

Index

Guidelines on State Policies 1973 235

Hadad, I. 229–49
Hammond, K. 138
Hansen, J.M. 188
Harmon, P. 124
Hawken, P. 117–18
hazardous waste 150–1, 233, 234–5
Heidenheimer, A. 123
Henderson, J.C. 124
high-level nuclear waste (HLNW) 147, 148, 153–5
Hong Kong 84, 89
households 254–5
Hsiao, H.H. 179
Hsieh, C.T. 123, 125
Hu, C.P. 122–40
Hueting, R. 111
Hungary 36, 159
hydroelectricity 15–16

ICs *see* industrialized countries
income transfer and economic impact 54–5, 63, 64
India 5, 11, 16, 19, 35, 84, 85, 93
  Bhopal 222
  economy–energy–environment equation 86
  global environment initiatives 75
  sustainable energy development 8
  trading in greenhouse gas emissions 51, 53, 56
Indonesia 5, 31, 35, 84, 87, 100
  AMDAL 244, 247
  Bank of Indonesia 247
  Basic Provisions for the Management of Living Environment Act 236
  Blue Sky Programme (LANGIT BIRU) 237
  Bureaux of Population and the Environment 235
  Business Performance Rating programme 247, 248–9
  Clean Cities Programme (ADIPURA) 237, 247
  Clean Rivers Programme (PROKASIH) 237, 238, 239, 240, 247, 249
  Environment and Development Supervision 235

  environmental audits 247
  Environmental Impact Management Agency (BAPEDAL) 236–7, 238, 239, 240, 247, 248, 249
  Environmental Management Centre 240
  Government Regulation No. 20 (1990) (Water Pollution Control) 236, 238
  Government Regulation No. 29 (1986) 236
  Government Regulation No. 51 (1993) 237
  gross domestic product 231
  JAGATIRTA 247
  Minister of the Environment 238
  Ministerial Decree (1988) 239
  Ministerial Decree (1991) 238
  Ministry of Communications 240
  Ministry of the Environment 237
  Ministry of Industry 240
  Ministry for Population and the Environment 236, 237
  National Cleaner Production Centre 237
  natural gas 88
  pollution-abatement equipment programme 247
  Second Long-Term Development Plan (1994–2019) 229, 245
  State Ministry for the Environment 247
  State Ministry for Population 240
  see also pollution control and industrial efficiency
industrial ecology 116–18
industrial efficiency *see* pollution control
industrial effluent standards 238–9
industrialized countries 3, 5, 6, 8, 13, 20
  see also newly
information dissemination 205
inner-directed development 113–14
inspection 255–6
insurance utilization 223–7
Intal, P. Jr 266, 273
Inter-governmental Panel on Climate Change 18, 43, 49
International Energy Agency 5